THINKING
IN TRANSIT

THINKING IN TRANSIT

EXPLORATIONS OF LIFE IN MOTION

MEGAN CRAIG AND EDWARD S. CASEY

Columbia University Press *New York*

Columbia University Press
Publishers Since 1893
New York   Chichester, West Sussex

Copyright © 2025 Columbia University Press
All rights reserved

Library of Congress Cataloging-in-Publication Data
Names: Craig, Megan, author. | Casey, Edward S., 1939– author.
Title: Thinking in transit : explorations of life in motion / Megan Craig and Edward S. Casey.
Description: New York : Columbia University Press, [2025] | Includes bibliographical references and index.
Identifiers: LCCN 2025004023 (print) | LCCN 2025004024 (ebook) | ISBN 9780231221344 (hardback) | ISBN 9780231221351 (trade paperback) | ISBN 9780231563680 (ebook)
Subjects: LCSH: Thought and thinking. | Movement (Philosophy)
Classification: LCC B105.T54 C73 2025 (print) | LCC B105.T54 (ebook) | DDC 121—dc23/eng/20250328

GPSR Authorized Representative: Easy Access System Europe, Mustamäe tee 50, 10621 Tallinn, Estonia, gpsr.requests@easproject.com

Cover design: Milenda Nan Ok Lee
Cover photo: Megan Craig

In loving memory of Richard J. Bernstein, who inspired us both at critical moments on the journey to thinking anew.

Tell me which infinity attracts you, and I will know the meaning of your world. Is it the infinity of the sea, or the sky, or the depths of the earth, or the one found in the pyre?

—Gaston Bachelard, *Air and Dreams: An Essay on the Imagination of Movement*

CONTENTS

Preface xi

1 Water 1
Interlude 1: Journeys to Nowhere 27

2 Air 43
Interlude 2: Earth/Garden/Sky 70

3 Earth 81
Interlude 3: Thinking in Painting 125

4 Fire 141

Postface 167

Acknowledgments 183
Notes 185
Bibliography 203
Index 209

PREFACE

The present work began several years ago when we (Ed Casey and Megan Craig) were asked to contribute a paper to a volume entitled *Philosophy, Travel, and Place: Being in Transit*.[1] We decided to write together about thinking in transit, based on our shared experience of commuting for many years between our homes in Connecticut and our work in the Philosophy Department at Stony Brook University, on Long Island. For Ed, that meant driving the nearly three-hour trip between places. For Megan, it entailed travel across the Long Island Sound on the Bridgeport–Port Jefferson ferry. Beyond this, for both of us, it also included travel by train, plane, and car as we made our way to conferences and professional meetings and to teach classes in Manhattan or Brooklyn.

When we first discussed our travel routines, it became clear that we had devised our own ways of thinking in transit, using the long commute (sometimes more than six hours in transit on a given day) to think, write, and reflect. This was a practical necessity (publish or perish!), but it was also a way of exploring alternative modes of expression. Of course, neither of us used all of the time in transit, but we each found that our methods of writing and research changed under the pressures of travel.

In our coauthored paper, we explored the ways that our specific modes of travel by car and by boat affected the shape, texture, and style of our thinking. Our joint thesis at the time was that thinking changes under conditions of travel. Thought takes on some of the environmental and material aspects of modes of transportation (the rock of the boat, the sound of an engine), and the body being carried between places finds itself suspended in a way that can give rise to creative, unbounded thinking. Our itinerant lives have played a significant part in the quality and content of our thinking—even as travel has disrupted these lives in various ways. We are testament to the fact that serious thinking need not be confined to the oft-cited ideal of a solitary, sedentary individual toiling away in a quiet study. Picture Descartes in his nightdress, alone by his fire. Now picture Ed whizzing down I-95 in the blur of the night, talking aloud into his tape recorder.

Part of the changing model of thinking relates to changing technologies of thinking, writing, and transportation. These throw us into highly varied situations replete with screens, wheels, and hulls, all of which affect bodily modes of experiencing, inhabiting, and traversing space. Our bodies undergo and in many respects merge with the vehicles devised to carry us. We are modern creatures, and our habits differ widely from those of Descartes in many ways. But somehow the picture of the philosopher has not changed as rapidly or as emphatically as the world all around. Philosophy remains a stubbornly individualistic discipline tethered to the prestige of single-authored books and the traditional apparatus of an ivory tower: office, desk, chair, task light—all this—as supporting sequestration.

In writing this book together, we have embarked on a strange journey. We felt there was more to say after we finished our article, and we spent several years talking together about how we might go on. This involved finding a joint writing practice that we could sustain from different shores (Ed mostly on the West Coast of the United

States and Megan on the East) and being honest with each other about the scope and limits of our own thinking. It has also involved reflecting on personal experiences more than we had anticipated, for the story is neither neat nor easily contained. Thinking about thinking raises a host of problems; thinking about thinking in transit only adds to the pile. We have had to devise ways of merging and differentiating our voices in this text, structuring our chapters as one might direct a film comprising close-ups and long-range shots. Sometimes one of us took the lead. Other times we groped our way forward together. As we wrote, the text opened out into directions neither of us could have anticipated beforehand—sometimes convergent, sometimes divergent.

One aspect of writing this book about thinking in transit is the different ways commuting and travel have affected our lives. Our initial article celebrated the ways that thinking in transit instills habits of experimentation and open-ended research. But the picture has not always been rosy, and the commute has not always been smooth. For both of us, our immediate families have borne the brunt of our ceaseless movement back and forth, which has taken us away from our homes. It seems important to confess that travel has opened new possibilities while impinging on or closing others. Part of writing this book has been an exploration of how we each got to this point in our creative/professional lives and what we have sacrificed or lost along the way.

Our text aims to celebrate forms of thinking and movement that recalibrate readymade academic models. This recalibration begins by our writing together. It's not unprecedented, but it remains an anomaly in the humanities to coauthor a book. Next, we think about thinking and writing as rooted in movement, whether the subtle movements of the mind, the pen, or the fingers moving across a keyboard or the more visibly apparent movement of a physical body across space on foot or carried by a vehicle. One thinks differently when in motion, and the differences compound when one is carried along by a car, a train, a wheelchair, a boat. . . .[2] We are coextensive with our environments and our modes of transportation. They lend something to us, and our minds can be bent to fit their shapes. This is not to disparage stillness, the quiet oasis of a serious library or a room of one's own. We only hope to expand the repertoire of possible postures and locations for thinking, which in turn invites us to think about thinking, embodiment, and movement in more expansive terms.

Thinking together is not simple. Writing together is even more of a challenge. But the guiding principle of collaboration is "yes . . . and." We have proceeded in this way, not always knowing where we were headed. Yet the project unfurled between us, making this text another site of transit in which you can find the back-and-forth movement of words that have gone from shore to shore. Things change as they change hands. Thoughts change as they change minds. Writing together forces more movement of thinking than writing alone—almost like merging from a single-lane road to a multilane highway. You pick up speed; you sense the danger.

Compounding the complexity of cowriting is the fact that we come from different geographical, temporal, and cultural backgrounds—Ed from Topeka, Kansas, where he was born in 1939, and Megan from Potsdam, New York, where she was born in 1975. You will learn more about each of us in this text, as we did by writing it. In many ways, the intersection of our lives on the north shore of Long Island amid the 1960s brutalist buildings of a public university and the routine of getting there and away provides a striking point of overlap in otherwise divergent existences. Often, we have met in between, on the road, in an odd café or hotel lobby. But we also meet on the page, in this book. We have found what Deleuze and Guattari discovered upon drafting *A Thousand Plateaus*: "The two of us wrote *Anti-Oedipus* together. Since each of us is several, there was already quite a crowd.

Here we have made use of everything that came within range, what was closest as well as farthest away."[3] Likewise, we have drawn on things near and far: memories, faces, landscapes, animals, skies, machines.

As we struggled with ordering our joint—and at times disjointed—writings, we landed on an elemental structure for our text. Ed had always wanted to write something relating to Bachelard's psychoanalysis of water, dreams, air, and fire. We both took inspiration from the clarity (and audacity) of Bachelard's writing in those volumes. Our book proceeds according to the four elements: Water, Air, Earth, and Fire—basic elements as recognized in ancient Greek, Tibetan, and Indian thought.[4] We were spurred to this scheme by the question of how it is that human beings move differently with respect to the different elements. How are we carried, buoyed, transported, or submerged in relation to them? What different experiences do they engage? What do we need to survive when exposed to, suspended in, or immersed in the different elements? How do these elements inspire different kinds of thinking and imagining? What are the vehicles human beings have devised to move across the earth, over the water, and through the air? How are the elements themselves sources of or invitations to travel?

As the Earth heats and storms increasingly force, complicate, or interrupt travel, we also found ourselves thinking about the fate of human beings and other animals who have lost their native habitats and homes. More creatures than ever are on the move. The air is changing. Waters rise. Fires rage. It is wrong to call the forced migration of humans and nonhuman animals "travel." Something more dangerous and urgent is underway. Something unchosen and often deadly. We mean "transit" (the act of passing through, across, or between different places) in an inclusive and open register. Our work, rooted in first-person phenomenological reflection, centers on our own mundane, privileged routes to and from work, but we hope that it also has implications for the harrowing journeys of those crossing vast expanses of land and sea in search of habitable ground—stories we may not be fit to tell but that we must collectively be primed to hear.

Our text invites thinking about thinking in a time of great upheaval. As we drafted chapters in the summer of 2023, fires and storms ravaged diverse habitats and took countless lives. In one week alone, an earthquake in Morocco left thousands dead, and flash floods in Libya killed 5,500. Transition is—and has been—irrevocably underway as beings across the globe confront the accelerating effects of climate change coupled with the ongoing effects of poverty, racism, colonialism, and violence. The future seems certain to include more mass movements of peoples across the earth in search of water, air, land, and freedom from political oppression. They will be moving by any means possible, suffering as they go, and thinking in duress. The elemental nature of being in transit and of being transitory beings deserves attention at this moment of danger, fragility, and planetary emergency.

Note on reading: You will find passages throughout this text where we have chosen to identify ourselves by our first names. Specific memories and experiences (we call them "travelogues") are set off with subheadings.

THINKING
IN TRANSIT

1

WATER

The sea is the original home of the mind, or at least of its first faint forms.
—Peter Godfrey-Smith, *Other Minds*

In every culture I know of water is a major part of thinking about life.
—Kay WalkingStick, artist, Cherokee nation

Every human animal begins life in water. This is sometimes easy to forget, especially for those whose lives are later landlocked, who are aquaphobic, or who never learn to swim. Yet each of us started out with a nascent ability to swim in the womb, developing from egg and sperm in a perfectly calibrated, aqueous habitat until becoming the already elaborate creature who emerges into the bright and dry world. Babies younger than six months retain a certain body memory of their life underwater, and so new parents can (with enough courage, forethought, and access to a body of water) put their infants back into the water and watch how they swim. Megan observed this once at the edge of a swimming pool where a mother let her tiny infant drop like a stone into the water, after which the baby wriggled and squirmed like a tadpole below the surface before popping up to catch its breath.

If water is the habitat in which human creatures first develop, then it is likely also the first habitat of human thought. By the time most babies are born, they have complex brains. They are responsive to light and to touch. Most babies—though of course not all—hear, see, cry, coo, squirm, and suck. They are pliant and soft, unable to hold their heads up without support. Everything about them is a bit slippery and blurred—not unlike the water from which they came. Why not attribute aqueous thinking to infants who know how to swim—knowing with perfect fluency something so many of us will have to learn all over again later in life?

The word "infant" derives from the Latin *infans*, meaning "unable to speak." The fact that human babies are born without speech has led to a persistent and pernicious characterization of them as lacking knowledge or rationality—indeed, as lacking thought. Some have even argued that because infants cannot speak, they don't feel pain.[1]

William James, however, wrote, "To the infant, sounds, sights, touches, and pains, form probably one unanalyzed bloom of confusion."[2] James's point is that sensation for an infant remains undifferentiated in a way that is unique and marks a special era of human intelligence. In the developmental story James tells, speech acquisition happens together with other psychic and motor capacities that allow a child to carve up and differentiate the world and to begin to find its way there. Experience goes from being a "bloom of confusion" to something more ordered, discrete, and predictable (though this doesn't happen for everyone in the same way or at the same rate). Another way of thinking about this is that the aqueous, preverbal world of the infant gives way to the more articulated and responsive world of the child: a world that includes increasing awareness of the earthly and social situation into which the child enters.

Water to earth, lying down to sitting up, sitting to standing, preverbal to verbal. This is a course many follow in the first years of life.[3] The infant's thinking changes in stride with all of its rapid developments in movement and speech. We will never know the thoughts of an infant—for they cannot tell us about them. That is a part of what is so mysterious and mind-bending about spending time with infants—especially for new parents but also for caregivers, family members, and anyone else trying to enter into relation with one of these new arrivals. They are participating in our world yet have one foot in another realm where we, as adults, cannot tread. We imagine their thinking along the lines of James's "bloom of confusion"—something vivid, wild, alive, and without edges, something not yet disciplined into the shapes of words and the grammar of sentences. Their thinking must be watery, open, boundless—and smooth.

In *A Thousand Plateaus*, Deleuze and Guattari use the adjective "smooth" to describe space that has not been carved up, mapped, or otherwise delineated. In their account, spaces can be "smooth" or "striated"—or some combination of the two—depending on different rhythms, forces, potentialities, and the degree to which human beings have inhabited and demarcated a given space as their own. We will return several times to Deleuze and Guattari's analyses of the smooth and the striated in this book, as they, like us, were concerned with different forms of space, voyage, and thinking. They associate smoothness with multiplicity, openness, nomadism, and indeterminacy; striation implies linearity, cultivation, politics, and war. The paradigmatic smooth space in their account is the ocean (though they also reference the air, deserts, certain parts of cities, and outer space).[4] As an element, water resists striation by frustrating or disallowing efforts of stasis. Plant your flag in the sea, and it shifts with the tide. The important point for considering the possibilities for infant thought is that thinking, like space, can be smooth or striated (or something in between).

If infants excel in smooth thinking, then one wonders what happens to thought under the pressures of linguistic striation. What is gained and what is lost? Are we destined to more earth-sensitive thinking the more we speak? Does writing add an additional layer of striation, further distancing us from our aquatic beginnings? Could we reclaim or remember the aqueous thinking of our own prelinguistic selves? Could we learn it (as we may have relearned to swim) again?

Of course, it is as easy to romanticize infancy as it is the sea. Lest we forget, both are prone to storms. Smooth thought is not equivalent to placid thought. Instead, it references a kind of thinking untethered from the norms and regularized patterns of written and spoken language. It seems related to what Julia Kristeva called "the semiotic," an early, prelinguistic stage of making meaning, akin to the ambiguous speech of depressed women whom Kristeva considers in *Black Sun*, or to what Emmanuel Levinas named "*le dire*" (saying) to signify the inarticulate, emotional core of expression.[5] Thinking might be smooth and violent or smooth and calm. It is likely unpredictable in its scope and its movements. Like water, smooth thinking can pool, seep, or surge into places where a more rigid kind of thinking cannot enter.

Once we have crossed a threshold into language, there is no going back, just as once we have crossed a threshold into earthbound existence, we no longer recall how to swim.[6] That is one reason why we will have to consider aqueous thinking in conjunction with the vessels that return us to or buoy us in the water. Watery thinking takes infinite forms, all of them related in one way or another to infancy and the original, elemental openness of being human. We are thrust into the air, put down onto the earth. In the water, we return.[7] We go back to a being we once were, to a place that was once but is no longer inhabitable. It's a devolution, one with powerful lessons and its own risks. Water marks the beginning of human life and thought, an aboriginal well. Thereafter, being in or near the water bears a special relation to a kind of thinking that brings us close to the intensities, confusion, and wisdom of infancy. "So I am here with my ear to the water / Listening for the secrets of the sea again."[8]

A part of what we will consider in this initial chapter is how different vehicles in which thinking occurs not only entail various bodily experiences but also inform the quality, pace, and scope of thinking. There are many modes of human transit in or across the water dating back hundreds of thousands of years.[9] Some of them involve being submerged below the surface (submarines, scuba gear, etc.); some involve being carried on the water's surface (boats, kayaks, surfboards). Yet others involve some combination of water and air (parasails, hovercrafts). We cannot and will not attempt to make a full inventory here or in any subsequent chapter. Instead, we will consider a handful of different experiences of aquatic submersion or buoyancy of which at least one of us has some intimate knowledge. In cases where vessels or equipment are involved, the vehicles and tools contribute to and augment the relationship between thinking and water we describe, transforming the body by extending or transforming its basic comportment. Overall, we can attribute smoothness to thinking in relation to water considered as nonstriated and taking on its own protean shapes. This is thinking that is involved in a reactivation of nascently embodied wisdom. But as we consider the specificities of the human body as it is carried into or across the water in various ways, thinking takes on continuously new forms.

SWIMMING

Before anything else, there is the simplicity of sliding into the water all by yourself. Swimming is the human body's first unintentionally choreographed movement. Before birth, a fetus can be seen in an ultrasound waving its nascent limbs. Perhaps, though, the movement in the womb is better described as floating: a suspension in amniotic fluid, the body either still or with arms and legs (when they emerge) moving and kicking.

Floating is in fact often the first step in relearning how to swim later in life. Lie on your back, take a deep breath to fill your belly with air, and float. This will be easier in the sea, where salt adds density to the water, increasing the likelihood that a body will be less dense and rise to the surface. Floating is surprisingly hard for many, but it is a crucial skill. Without knowing how to float, you don't know how to rest in the water. And without being able to rest, you can easily drown no matter how strong of a swimmer you happen to be. Once mastered, floating is also a favored form of being relaxed in the water. Lying on your back in the middle of a lake or calm sea, staring at the clouds above, letting yourself drift with the current. Bachelard associates daydreaming with the tight interior spaces of a child's first apartment or a house—the nook under a table or the hidden spot in a closet or beneath the stairs.[10] Such imaginative reverie might also be connected, however, with floating, with being held away from the shore in the hands of the water, the world's sound muted by your own submerged ears and nothing but infinite sky above. To think in such circumstances is to feel simultaneously cradled and conjoined with the pulse of a hidden world.

Travelogue: Megan on Learning to Swim

I recall learning how to swim in a public swimming pool in Belgium when I was four or five years old. My older sister had already mastered the basics, but I was petrified of the deep end. "Jump in!" my dad called, treading water near the edge where I stood. "I'll catch you." So I jumped. Only to discover that he was moving backward away from me on and on across the pool until we had traveled far enough that I could touch the bottom with my own feet. "See. You can swim," he said. And that was the end of the first lesson.

As with anything else, there is swimming, and then there is swimming. I would not learn this difference for many years, despite a childhood spent happily splashing in any body of water I could find and body surfing the big salty waves in the summer at Nauset Light Beach on Cape Cod. My dad, always intent on adventure, taught me early on how to swim in rapids (feet downstream in case of rocks, slow sidestroke in a diagonal line toward the shore, not fighting the current too much); how to deal with a riptide (don't struggle, relax, float, start swimming once you're free of it); and what to do if you fall through the ice (get a piece of clothing out of the hole and onto the ice, which will stick and serve as an anchor to help you pull yourself out). In addition to all the survival training, I took swimming lessons when I was a teenager at a frigid lake in Connecticut in hopes of becoming a lifeguard. The course ended with a deep dive to retrieve a red bucket at the bottom of the lake. But I had neglected to tell the instructor that I was essentially blind without my glasses. I was the only one in my group who couldn't find the bucket in the murky water. Needless to say, I had no future as a lifeguard.

Swimming is something other than the haphazard flapping of arms and legs in the water or splashing around in the shallows. At a certain point, one learns to swim in a way that feels natural and relaxed. This can take a lifetime, though sometimes it comes naturally to someone, and they look as effortless as a fish from the very beginning—as if reclaiming the gift of infant wisdom brought forward into the present. For most of us though, there is a limited repertoire of strokes and practice. Megan started to swim regularly as an adult when training for a triathlon. It was then that she discovered she could build endurance and change speeds in the water. This struck her, at the time, as a miracle; up until then, she had thought of swimming as a utilitarian way of getting from point A to point B or as what you did when you were trying not to drown. She had no idea one could go faster or slower. That one could breathe and think. Suddenly swimming became its own form of thinking.

It's not surprising to find that something improves with practice—you get better and then you don't have to think so much about what it is that you're doing. At that point, you can sometimes begin to think about something else. The occupation of the body in a nearly mindless, repetitive set of movements opens a special, creative space for thought. Here is an early form of thinking in transit. Megan glimpsed this possibility while swimming in a pool during rigorous training sessions, but we imagine others have experienced it more profoundly while swimming long distances in open water.

Megan's older sister routinely swims laps in the ocean. We have also heard the philosopher Alia Al-Saji describe her love of open-water swimming, her routine of going out far into the sea with nothing but a wetsuit and a safety float tied to her body. But the main person we associate with open-water swimming is Oliver Sacks. In his 2015 autobiography, *On the Move*, Sacks describes his lifelong love of swimming. Physically large and a bit clumsy, Sacks found a certain relief of his own gravity while in the water. "Swimming timelessly, without fear or fret," he wrote, "relaxed me and got my brain going. Thoughts and images, sometimes whole paragraphs, would start to swim through my mind."[11] Sacks captures the liquid quality of thinking while swimming, where thoughts can become silvery, slippery fish darting through the dark currents of consciousness.

Given his lifelong love of water, the element most tied to infant wisdom and ancient modes of embodiment, perhaps it is not surprising that Sacks was also a champion of so many groups of marginalized and forsaken human beings, beginning with his work with patients suffering from encephalitis lethargica who were housed in a psychiatric ward at Beth Abraham hospital in the Bronx and continuing into his work with autistic individuals and those with debilitating migraines, brain injuries, and blindness. Sacks was drawn to alternative wisdoms. He could see life, creativity, and connection in places where other able-bodied people only saw inaction, inertness, and blanks. Sacks was attuned to vivacity in many forms and understood consciousness in an expansive, fluid way—almost as if he was immersed in a living world that others could only observe (and thereby *misinterpret*) from the shore.

Sacks seems emblematic of aquatic thinking that knows the value of immersive sympathy. He credited swimming with allowing him to relax and to refocus his mind—not just a form of physical exercise but also a meditative practice and a way of setting thinking free, as if releasing a turtle to the sea. He had an unusual intelligence, just as he had an unusual fixation with the water. Swimming was a crucial part of Sacks's thinking and writing, but it also seems emblematic of his openness to a greater variety of life-forms than ordinary people tend to be. His swimming coincided with (and perhaps even helped develop) a heightened sensitivity to patients who were nonverbal, sedentary, blind, deaf, or otherwise outside the narrow parameters of normativity, suggesting that water might be crucial to efforts to see and to think beyond entrenched paradigms. Submerged in the water, thinking seems to loosen and elongate, while the borders of the predictable, visible universe soften and bleed.

Travelogue: Ed on Being Landlocked

My Kansas childhood left me far from any but artificial bodies of water—and even these I rarely ventured into. My parents were entirely city folk (where "city" meant Topeka, population 100,000, a place with no natural bodies of water, only a river that occasionally flooded). I swam, fitfully, at the local country club and the YMCA. But I never "took to" water and am now even more averse—even being very uneasy about taking a shower. Unlike Megan, I was launched into a life of aversion to water—a literal "land lubber." Only on land was I at home. I remember going far outside town to Lake Shawnee—constructed in the 1930s as a WPA project and named for an Algonquian-speaking Native American tribe—only to stare at the water of this entirely artificial lake and wonder "what am I doing here?" (Indeed, what was *it* doing there, on the barren prairie that contained only a handful of lakes?) A few years earlier, I was taunted by friends to jump into a local swimming pool from a high platform. I stood and trembled for what seemed like an eternity before finally letting my body move over the edge of the platform and finding the water into which I fell something of a foreign substance: What am I supposed to do down here? A long time later, I was living in Santa Barbara, where everyone seemed to swim. I bought a "wet suit," but I never got wet in the Pacific Ocean—preferring to read and sketch on the upper beach, where I could settle in without having to navigate the incoming waves that enticed so many others who preferred being lower down on the same beach, closer to the incoming/outgoing ocean. Like my Swiss ancestors, I felt at home only on dry land. These same ancestors had settled in Kansas, a prototypical "dry state" (in several senses of this last phrase)—only to discover that, as millers by trade, they needed to seek out rivers with enough force to move the revolving wheels of the mills they built.

FERRY

Swimming puts the body directly into the water. Sometimes the entry is tenuous and slow, as when one inches into the cold ocean from the shore—starting with just a dip of the toe. And sometimes the entry is abrupt and all at once—as when one jumps from a cliff into a lake below, tumbles into a swimming pool, or dives into a pond. Sometimes the water chills the bones, and sometimes it feels like a warm bath. Whatever the conditions or locale, swimming puts you into another world. It is a wet world where you (as a human being) are no longer in your element, and it tempts you to remember something about a former life, a former shape, a forgotten knowhow.

Between the body submerged and the body firmly on dry land lies another realm of possibilities offered by boats. A boat can be anything that sits on the water and is propelled by paddles, oars, sails, or a motor. The earliest boats were hollowed out of tree trunks or made by strapping pieces of wood, bamboo, or grass together. Boats in endless shapes and sizes are used for recreation, physical workouts, travel, exploration, commerce, conquest. As Christina Sharpe reminds us, ships facilitated the transatlantic slave trade. "The ships set out one in the wake of another. Five hundred years of voyages of theft, pillage, and bondage."[12] Her work highlights the hold that ships, water, weather, and slavery continue to exert on contemporary Black life in the diaspora. Today, migrants cling to rafts or crowd inside vessels too small to hold them. Meanwhile, cruise ships the size of small cities lumber into ports. When we move from swimming to a boat, we move from submergence in the element to a perch just above. Now what is embodied is held in a vessel that moves across the surface of the water and protects the voyager (to some degree) from the wetness, even when such "protection" exists in a larger frame of violent displacement and subjugation. Now the body can be shuttled farther from shore—by choice or by force—thrusting one's thoughts into new directions and depths.

On a ferry, everything depends upon the weather. On a fine day, the sky is clear, and the water is flat. The flags near the terminal lie limp against the poles. As the ferry churns out of the harbor, it swings around to face the open sea, leaving a frothy swath of white behind.

Travelogue: Megan on the Bridgeport–Port Jefferson Ferry

Several components collide to make a passenger ferry an exquisite place for thinking. On the ferry I know the best, the Bridgeport–Port Jefferson ferry between Connecticut and Long Island, the sailing time is one hour and fifteen minutes—an ideal amount of time to focus on one thing. I have spent years writing on the ferry, sitting down to begin as the boat pulls out and scribbling the last notes in a yellow legal pad as we pull into the docks at Port Jefferson, a recorded voice alerting passengers to return to their vehicles and prepare for disembarking. Thinking within the confines of a prescribed time gives me the sense that I am under a bit of pressure. I don't have all day. This makes each crossing feel exciting and slightly daunting, like the start of a race. I ready my pen and try to work in one burst of effort to the end.

Added to the sense of time being delimited definitively between two shores, the boat itself, while crossing, is removed from the pace and scenery of ordinary life. As soon as the dock, elevated train tracks, and parking lots of Bridgeport recede, there is only water and sky. Sometimes other boats or small vessels appear. At dusk, buoys light up with single flashing green or white lights, and the horizon begins to glisten. But mostly there is the feeling of being held on all sides by water—a suspension in the giant blue. Thinking here feels different than thinking that transpires in less suspended space. Surrounded and supported by water, thoughts can become fluid, open. Water lends itself to thinking new thoughts because thinking, when it goes well, flows.

Then there are the sounds of the boat. A steady hum of engines and moving water, a chugging machinery that practically begs you to think along. Most powered water vehicles can have this effect—synchronizing thinking with the turning of actual gears and wheels.

On the ferry (on calm seas), the boat moves forward with just the slightest backward lag, as if thrusting itself through the waves. It makes a difference where you are sitting—whether outside on the open deck near the front or the back of the boat or inside at a small table next to a window. It's nearly impossible to write anything in the open air once the boat reaches full speed and the wind whips everything in circles. The deck is for daydreaming and thinking up future plans, for watching people drape over railings and corral their dogs, smoke, or stare at their phones. The inside is for more focused activity—such as spreading out at a table (if it's not too crowded) and seeing the waves ripple by through a pane of glass. The chug of the boat provides a soundtrack for thinking anew—a mix of low grumbling engines and the din of people talking and moving about. These sounds possess their own rhythm and seem to encourage or even create momentum.

Other sensory factors contribute to the quality of thinking on the ferry. There is the visual palette of the boat—drab grays and beiges with sudden dots of bright orange for various safety signs. The white rails and tall smokestack, the green lower deck. Down below, cars line up in the dim belly of the ferry in lines of black, white, gray, and the occasional red. The workers wear dark blue as if to embody the fact that outside the ferry and all around it, various blues ricochet against one another—sky, water, clouds. Blue must be the shade of thinking on a ferry. Depending on the weather, it could be a bright, crystal cerulean blue or a muted Payne's grey. Once, in an early morning fog, we pushed through opaque layers of white, with only an ultramarine line where the fog refused to touch the water.

Outside the ferry, the air snaps and smells like salt. Inside, the cabin retains the odor of bleach mixed with hot dogs and pretzels. In the very back of the cabin, a small red lounge reeks of alcohol and cleaning supplies. These reminders of human life and the ordinary efforts of eating, washing, and drinking keep thinking grounded. The boat is working; the people are going to or returning from work. Thinking works too.

Sounds, sights, and smells all contribute to the specificity of thinking in transit on a ferry boat. It must differ with each vessel and according to each crossing ("*Every voyage is a journey*").[13] But added to all of this is the feeling of being carried—something common to almost any vessel. On a car ferry, the carriage has the peculiar quality of being nested within multiple machines, like a Russian doll. The ferry carries cars and trucks, which in turn carry people who sometimes carry other people (children and babies) in their arms. Sometimes when seeing a truck with a large trailer, one can imagine smaller cars inside, which might carry yet smaller vehicles (strollers, bicycles, skateboards). The various compartments of the ferry boat convey the sense of inhabiting nesting space—space that Gaston Bachelard associated with a feeling of "intimate immensity."[14] Thinking in such a space has not only the aqueous, blue quality of the sea but also the pregnant quality of the boat. Thoughts sit within other thoughts like the cars in the boat. A bigger thought carries a smaller one curled within it.

Of course, the weather is not always fine. On stormy days, the boat pitches from one side to another, and most of the people stay below deck or confine themselves to their cars. In turbulent seas, the horizon dips below the window, and waves reach up over the top of the boat and come crashing through the oval windows in the open lower deck, leaving cars streaked in salt. Then it is not possible to think. Or at least, it is not possible to think of anything except dry land. The body wants a smooth place for thinking, and the sea, which seems clear and flat in good weather, turns into a churning place of disruption. Forget about the sounds and smells—they all collide into an ill green. Forget about the aqueous quality of thinking and the generous feeling of being carried along. Instead, you grip the rail or your steering wheel and wait for it all to end. The feeling of the pitch and heave of a boat in a storm can stay with you long after disembarking, as if part of you remains still present on the tumultuous ride.

The same could be said of the ferry boat in the dead of winter, when the air feels like a knife and no amount of heat can blunt the cold on open water. Stars shine unbelievably bright in the winter sky. Thinking of almost nothing but warmth, the crossing seems to take forever, though the time from port to port always remains exactly the same on a clock. Whatever the weather, the decisive departure and arrival time of the ferry as it adheres to clock time creates a suspended middle zone of the crossing itself, in which time flies or stalls according to rhythms entirely their own and at the mercy of the seas. Here we feel the difference between striated and smooth time, the latter moving at its own rhythm, the former according to the dictates of the clock.

All of this suggests that a ferry boat, like any vehicle, has optimal conditions of operation and more or less ideal possibilities for traveling and for thinking. When things are just right, when one has the freedom to board and disembark at will and is not plagued by illness, fear, or the long wake of violent histories, the boat contributes its heft and rugged frame to thoughts that can carry one another from shore to shore. The sea, a sheet of blue, lends its materiality to thinking that flows and ideas that seem to crest with the waves. This is different from the kind of thinking that transpires on land or in the safe and usual enclosure of one's home or office. The water plays a crucial role in reactivating an expansiveness first present in infancy. The ferry provides just enough of a reliable remove from the elements to facilitate diligent and fresh thinking and just enough pitch and roll to keep thought from solidifying into something stodgy, repetitive, or predictable.

CANOE

Travelogue: Megan on Canoeing

Growing up, I learned how to canoe from my dad. When I was age three and living in Belgium, he and my mom (both teachers) paddled me and my sister across Europe in a six-week trek in a canoe one summer. We camped in a tent each night and spent the days wedged in the middle of the boat, watching the world drift by like a scroll unfurling with each paddle stroke. Years later, on a small beaver pond behind our house in a tiny town in rural Connecticut, we'd haul the green boat into the water and practice steering around the dam. Later, we would hoist the canoe onto the car and take it several miles up the road to the Housatonic River in Cornwall and practice in the rapids, my dad in the stern while I knelt in the waves crashing over the bow. We took first place in the family division of the Housatonic River Race ("The Covered Bridge Slalom") in 1994, earning a shimmering blue ribbon emblazoned with a golden canoe.

As with any boat, it's hard to think of anything except survival when the weather or the water (or both) are rough. The variable conditions and sudden shifts make things unpredictable. A part of your mind is always trained on the practicalities of staying afloat. But on a glassy lake or stretch of calm river, a canoe provides a unique vehicle for thinking. It's a simple object—just a hollow cradle with two seats. Not much happens beyond the slight rock of the boat and the sound of your own paddle dipping in and out of the water. It is possible to stop paddling altogether and just drift. Push off from the shore, and you're held just above the water, as if suspended in a liminal gap between water and sky.

Thinking in a canoe can yield simple, expansive thoughts. Unlike on a ferry boat, where one can relax into the role of being a passenger, some agency is required for steering and moving a canoe along, and so the rhythm of physical action becomes tied to the rhythm of thinking. This is typically a slower, less precise rhythm than anything one encounters in a vessel with an engine. You might speed up your paddling or slow it down. You switch sides when your arm gets tired. You hold the paddle in the water as a rudder to steer or reach out and skim the water back and forth to slow or stop the boat. All of these actions can happen almost automatically if you've had some experience in a canoe, which means that mostly you don't need to think about them. The body performs as an extension of the paddle, while the mind is free to roam. The repetitive choreography of paddling produces a certain condition for meditative reflection, not unlike the basic tasks Stanislavsky recommended his actors practice—stacking blocks, putting cards in numerical order, etc.—while reciting their lines.[15] The canoe holds the body and gives it a prescribed repertoire of actions, often coordinated with the body of a fellow paddler with whom you learn to calibrate weight and motion in a duet. The body, taken care of or busily occupied, recedes into the background as a part of the landscape that makes up canoe, water, and the surrounding environment—at which point thinking moves into the foreground.

You're close to the water in a canoe—directly exposed to it—and so the sensory experience of thinking in a canoe is quite different from that of a larger boat. The water has a smell—murky or clear, briny or not. It drips from the paddle down your arms and sometimes into your lap. On bright days, the sky reflects off the water in a nearly blinding glare. Wind, sun, rain—the canoe remains exposed to all of it, with no space for retreat or protection. Everything feels tactile and close—the water, the weather, the paddle, the thin rails of the boat. Thinking in this minimal space of separation has an almost immersive quality in relation to the more-than-human world of larger landscapes.

Thinking in a canoe shares a similar aquatic quality with thinking on any boat, but the style of movement through the water is distinctive, and therefore thinking too takes on a special momentum. The canoe can slice silently through flat water without any lag or backward tug. It's graceful and elegant, the lines through the water seeming fluid, like the swoop of de Kooning's strokes in many of his later paintings. It's unlikely you're in a hurry to get anywhere in a canoe (if you're not in a race), and so things unfurl in a temporality that is divorced from urgency. Thinking follows suit—thoughts meandering in a slightly suspended state. If thinking on a ferry boat adopts some of the mechanical labor and time-bound forward thrust of the machine (a good motor for the act of writing), thinking in a canoe borrows the simplified arc of the boat and the relative hush of human motion. In the canoe, your hands are occupied, and so it's not a very good place for writing. But this means it allows for a form of thinking untethered to ink, type, or script. Nor is it limited by the syntactical structures of complete sentences.

This is meditative, meandering, and open thought. It doesn't need to coalesce into full sentences or be spelled out in any detail. One might call it elemental thinking that is attuned to a prelinguistic world, one older than human language.[16] One might call it poetic thinking. One would never set out in a canoe under the pressure of a deadline (unless it was tied to hunting and survival). The boat and the water and the manual labor converge in a scenario where the mind can wander. One can have a similar kind of experience of thinking while exercising (as we discuss later in sections on walking and running on the earth), and these bouts of unscripted, free-floating thought are often crucial (as prelude or corrective) to other exercises of thinking. Often the tight space of a desk or table, the very *effort* to think clearly in the Western academic mode, can produce a posture and a mindset that are stunting. Then one needs to *move* in order to think, as one needs to open a valve for water to flow.

Integral to what we are considering in these reflections on different modes of transportation and different registers of thinking is that both the moving vehicle and the element(s) through which one moves contribute *materially* to thinking. Thinking on the water adopts some of the aqueous nature of the water, a fact William James learned when navigating the tributaries of the Amazon River with his teacher and guide Louis Agassiz.[17] As James discovered, a canoe on flat water is an ideal boat for experimenting with aqueous thought: letting ideas flow and pool, thinking according to the rhythm of the tide or the slow glide of a wide river, keeping cool and balanced, letting thoughts come and go. The river would in fact become James's early model for neural pathways forged in the brain and the complex tributaries of the human mind.[18]

KAYAK

A canoe and a kayak both bring the body into close proximity with the water below. Both require skill and action to maneuver, making the person inhabiting the boat a critical part of a delicate choreography. Any sudden movement tips the balance of the whole. A kayak, however, sinks the body lower and holds it in place with a skirt or a strap, merging vessel and body into a more hybrid creature. The deeper seat and intensified stricture allow for more powerful and precise movement in the water—sharp turns, quick acceleration—while raising the stakes for the paddler, who cannot abandon ship. One sits in a canoe, but one *wears* a kayak as a fin or an appendage.

As Megan learned to canoe from her dad, she also learned to kayak at a young age. This was coupled with training in what was then, problematically, called the "Eskimo roll," the technique of being able to go from an upside-down, fully submerged position in the boat to a fully upright position by leaning back, drawing a flat paddle backward in an arc from the bow, and flipping your hip toward the surface to jettison yourself into the air, with your torso emerging before your head. To practice this, her dad would flip over the boat and then (measuring time with his stopwatch) wait for her to right herself. She was told this is crucial and life-saving training for anyone who hopes to paddle their own kayak in fast water, though she only ever used the technique in the beaver pond behind her house. The maneuver comes from Inuit and Aleut peoples who first developed the kayak as a hunting boat and who also practiced rolling techniques without a paddle, using only one hand, and sometimes without any hands at all.[19]

Unlike a canoe, a kayak is often (though not always) a solo vessel. The body sits low with legs and feet straight out ahead, and the paddle, rather than having one end intended for the water, has two symmetrically sculpted ends. You hold the paddle in the middle and alternate sides as you dip one blade and then the other into the water. In rough or fast water there is sometimes a skirt that stretches around your body in the boat, creating a seal and making the whole contraption (boat, torso, paddle) into a centaur-like creature (all the more reason to know how to roll, as now you are clinched in the boat and will stay there if you capsize). This is the boat Megan most associates with her dad (a big guy), who often raced whitewater when she was young. The kayak forgives all weight. The heavier you happen to be, the lower you sit in the water—giving a certain advantage to larger bodies (like that, for instance, of Oliver Sacks). Once you are in the boat, you are as graceful as a swallow. Heavy bodies transform on the water into feathers—a magical transmutation of weight into weightlessness. There is no lumbering footfall or (as sometimes in a canoe) jerky thrust of the paddle into the water. Instead, one finds a rhythm of dipping side to side, letting the paddle roll slightly between the hands. On the water in a kayak, you glide, and your thinking glides with you.

Canoers and kayakers move through waters internationally classed I through VI (class I is "moving water with a few riffles and small waves"; class VI includes "extremely long, difficult, and very violent rapids, nearly impossible and very dangerous, involves the risk of life"). At the upper end of whitewater, sport kayakers wear helmets and attempt life-threatening drops over falls, where they often submerge entirely and pop out of the water like a blast from a cannon. These Western categorizations of water types attempt to quantify what Indigenous communities know by other names and through other means—the "big water through a rock garden" and "heavy water through a rock garden" that Shelbi Nahwilet Meissner describes, along with the warning that not all waters are open and that we need to "work together to retool dominant canoes."[20]

Lower in the water, solo, the body more conjoined with the boat, kayaks produce their own quality of thinking. It is probably more individualized than the thinking that happens in a more communal kind of vessel. It is likely that thought in a kayak also borrows something from the double-edged paddle. It would be thinking in a more ordered, symmetrical style than one could do in a canoe. Thinking that feels itself immersed in the river or ocean and can feel the slap of the waves. Thinking mixed with the water dripping into the boat and the bow cutting through the waves. This (again) only holds in class I or class II waters. Anything more adventurous demands a level of concentration that eradicates the possibility for any thought save survival and the task at hand. Yet the power of a kayak, the feeling of slicing through the water and gaining speed, seems related to forms of thinking that are less dreamlike and more propulsive than in a canoe. Kayaks enable a sense of progress. Even if one feels disempowered on land, in a kayak one can feel emboldened or enabled in a new way. Nothing but water and the force of your own arms, nothing but speed and the rush of the wind. It would be flight if it were in the air, but here, on the water, you become an ambiguous creature poised between sea and sky. Shark, hawk, dragon—something ancient or mythical, something fast and momentarily free.

ICE-SKATING

We started this elemental section on water with the body fully submersed in swimming. The swimming body is suspended in the water, touched on all sides. The body carried along in a boat lives at a greater remove from earthly elements, even as the boat is subject to waves and wind, to more or less impact from the water in its calm or violent modes. Boats and ships cut through the water. Boats with sails capture the wind in the project of gliding swiftly. Flat vessels provide space for sprawling out on a deck, while narrow ships keep the body tucked in a tighter posture, and submarines convey the body far below the surface in a pressurized cabin—into a world as foreign as outer space. All of these differences in the expansive or more limited splay of a body affect the kind of thinking that might occur. As Iris Marion Young famously argued in her essay "Throwing Like a Girl," when the body is constricted, either by physical, cultural, or psychic obstacles, so is the mind.[21] Thinking in transit in or on the water reactivates the natal core of our being at the same time that the vessels of transit lend their own heft and shape to thought.

It seems fitting to conclude this chapter with something that lies halfway between fluid and solid, halfway between water and earth: ice. As on the water, on the ice a body can glide in fluid movement not possible when on land. In the same beaver pond where Megan practiced rolling a kayak in the summer, in the winter she spent most weekends and afternoons after school ice-skating. The quality of the ice depended on the beavers' activities during the season before: whether the pond was deep or shallow, whether water was present or absent, whether sticks poked through the surface. It also depended on long stretches of freezing temperatures (something that was common in the years when she was growing up but much less common now in northwestern Connecticut) and on rain (which could leave the entire surface pockmarked and bumpy) and snow (which had to be shoveled and swept away).

As with swimming, one learns by doing. Put on ice skates and set off. Fall often. Get back up. Ed has never tried skating on actual ice even if during turbulent periods of his personal life he has found himself all too often on thin ice.

Travelogue: Megan on Skating

I would carry an old boombox with a cassette deck down to the pond and practice figure skating "routines" to the soundtrack of *Les Misérables*. The cold air, the gaunt trees, the flat ice. I could stay outside for hours. My dad eventually hooked up a floodlight in a tree so that I could continue to skate after dark. I was in my own world ice-skating on the pond in the frigid night. Hours evaporated in the thrill of gliding and turning and even attempting some leaps. By the end, my feet and hands frozen, I would trudge up the hill to our house in the pitch dark, where, over the next hour or so, my bare feet painfully thawed in the warm air.

It is special—almost magical—to be on the ice. Ice reminds us of transience. There is a small but critical window in which water becomes ice. As temperatures drop, water molecules move slower, until, at around zero degrees Celsius, the molecules stick together and form ice—though they continue moving at a rate imperceptible to the human eye. On a frozen pond or lake, you sometimes hear the crack of the ice—a loud, reverberating thwack—that reminds you to be careful and not get carried away. It's crucial to go down to the pond with a drill and put a small hole in the ice to see how thick it is before skating (a minimum of four inches of dense, milky ice). Sometimes the edges of the pond closest to the muddy shore are just thin rivulets of lacey ice that you could poke a finger through. So the rule is always to stay away from the edge (and of course, remember the survival lessons about what to do if you fall through).

There are lots of ways to be on the ice: dragging a sled around is great fun, walking in snow boots, lying flat on your back, shooting a hockey puck, cutting a hole for ice fishing, or scooting around in snow pants. But with ice skates, as in a canoe or a kayak, you can transform into another kind of creature altogether. Suddenly the ice makes sense as a place of movement, a place to dance. Ice reflects the fluidity of water back into you, making a temporary stage upon which you can skim if not swim. Like a world suddenly turned upside-down, you, a land animal, can spin and glide in fishtails above while the aquatic creatures below hang motionless in the cold.

Of course, ice is also brutal: A fall can result in lots of bruises and serious injury. Megan learned this lesson much later in life when she sustained a major concussion falling on the ice. Water offers a forgiving surface to dive into. Ice reminds you that, though brilliant and bright, the world is hard and harsh.

What does it mean to be in transit on the ice? You aren't really going anywhere. Often, on a public skating rink, you go around and around in circles (counterclockwise) in a herd. On a pond or lake, although you can skate in any direction you choose, the circuit is determined by the shape of the water or the extent of the frozen area. It is only in really cold climates (in Canada and northern parts of the European continent) that people commute by ice. Ribbons of frozen rivers and canals form icy highways where people zip to work on their skates. They must arrive someplace with flushed cheeks and bearing the scent of frozen air. Breughel's winter paintings like the 1556 *Winter Landscape with Skaters and a Bird Trap* or *The Hunters in the Snow* show whole communities of humans socializing on ice: playing hockey, holding hands, ice-fishing, racing, twirling, and more.

Ice-skating is not really a form of transit in the way that swimming and boating are. Perhaps that is because you could (with effort and great care) pick your way across a frozen surface without skates, whereas you'll have to swim in the water, and you'll need a watercraft for any significant stretch of travel. Nonetheless, ice-skating seems worthy of consideration as another example of the human body transported out of its habitual form of embodied movement and into another, different form. When you board a boat or ship, you become subject to the rocking motion that can stay with you for hours (and sometimes days). When you ice-skate, your body takes on the rhythm of side-to-side gliding—a different but related form of rocking reminiscent of movement in the womb, the cradle, the sling. The skates make you taller, and the added few inches (like high heels) change your posture and standing. You are suddenly a bit elevated—held a bit aloft. Additionally, the cold of the ice seeps up through the skates and imbues the whole environment with a distinctive snap. One is alert on the ice, not lazing about as you might on a dock or floating in a lake.

So far we have associated water with aqueous thinking that meanders and pools, thinking that is tied in some mysterious way to a forgotten infant life. Water activates a form of creative thinking and open-ended curiosity. It is a site of mixture—not a place of isolation or definition. On the ice, all of this is changed. We meet water in hardened form. It is not static (often you can rub the ice with a glove or mitten and see the moving surface—perhaps even a suspended frog or fish—just below). It isn't impervious (just a kick of the boot or a hard enough fall might make a crack). Ice, despite its hardness of surface, reveals water in its resilient but still vulnerable becoming. It can't last. We see that now in a particularly glaring way as glaciers melt into the seas under the accelerations of climate change. We see it every winter as the trees stand frozen like glass sculptures after an ice storm, only to lose their shine the next day.

Ice on our planet is becoming more and more rare. We wonder if there will be ice for our future grandchildren and great-grandchildren.

We wonder if they will learn to skate. We wonder what kind of thinking and embodiment will be lost if the planet continues to heat—in addition to the loss of all of the creatures and places and environments being displaced even as we write. Megan tried once to carry a snowball in her pocket to school, only to end up with a wet pocket (akin to Peter in Ezra Jack Keats's *The Snowy Day*). We would like to keep some piece of ice just in case. A remnant of a time when things could freeze and when what was fluid could become solid enough to glide across.

It's true that "ice" is sometimes used in a pejorative sense to describe something or someone who is uncaring or indifferent. The Ice Queen. An icy stare. A cold heart. Death's icy fingers. But we will forever associate ice with abandon. A slice of glassy, smooth surface. Reckless stunts. Spinning until you fall over. The feeling of laying your cheek on the ice to see how long you can stand it. The sound of snapping icicles from the edge of the roof to use as lollipops or spears. The sound of the skates on the ice, and the lines etched in the surface or shaved in a splatter of ice dust after a hard stop. The push and glide of each foot as you skate mimics the push and pull of thinking itself, which sometimes requires concerted effort and sometimes seems to slide. On the ice you might be reminded of the syncopation inherent in thinking as well as the trust required to let yourself go. As with swimming, you might return to a memory of childhood and the feeling of being immersed and at home in a world that was originally suffused with water.

Those are our icy thoughts. Thinking tied to the cold and to water forced into another form. Imagine the feeling of the water as the temperatures plunge in the moment just before it turns to ice. Is there panic? Is there excitement? Sometimes there is a strange gelatinous quality to water that has only partially frozen. Stare long enough, and you can see the ice taking shape. It grips the surface in long fingers. The process begins there and (with enough cold) continues layer by layer, cementing itself into shape.

Thoughts too can crystallize. What was amorphous takes on a form. Ice reminds you of that possibility, reminding you that things harden and become traversable, even if only momentarily and with a certain fragility. Aqueous thoughts cede to more structured ideas. Freeze and melt: It is the logic of holding and letting go, winning and losing, rising and falling.

INTERLUDE 1: JOURNEYS TO NOWHERE

Water flows and freezes, pools and eddies. It is tempting to associate water with the rushing movement of a current sweeping everything downstream, but water also reminds us that things move in circles or sometimes barely at all. The pull of a tide is akin to the pull of memory, calling us back to a former life, a long-forgotten past. Staring out to sea, you can find yourself traveling terrific distances in time and space without leaving any shore.

For the most part, we think of travel as getting us from one place to another—as a moving scene that unrolls from a beginning point toward a distinctively different destination. Why else would we travel except to get somewhere other than where we were when we started? Exceptions to this implicit rule are just that—exceptional. But what if we think in accordance with a different model, one in which travel consists in *staying in place*? This means going nowhere in geographical space. Staying put, the journey consists entirely in *thinking and feeling in place*: thinking and feeling from here, just here and nowhere else. These are the journeys of what Deleuze and Guattari called "the true nomad."[22] This is the person who doesn't need to board any vessel or move any distance to travel. In *A Thousand Plateaus*, Deleuze and Guattari emphasize the advantages of such stationary travel, juxtaposing a gallivanting, reckless style of travel (one they associate with Goethe's flamboyant trips to Italy) with an intense, inner focus (a form of "traveling in place" they connect with Heinrich von Kleist).

Their point is not unlike Baudelaire's in *The True Travelers* or María Lugones's insight in "Playfulness, 'World'-Traveling, and Loving Perception": just because one sets off (bags packed!) for distant lands does not mean that one will arrive anywhere new. True travel entails focus and an openness to being moved and changed. This is one of the reasons Emerson was also skeptical of voyages to far-flung places, entreating us instead to "stay at home in thy own heaven."[23]

Meditation is one form of such a nondestinarian journey: witnessing whatever crosses our minds, whether this is replete with vivid detail or radically empty. This is still a journey—but in meditation, one travels with the content of what one is thinking (imagining, remembering, feeling) rather than between different geographical locales. "Having thoughts," visiting them, suffices no matter how seemingly barren or obvious these thoughts may be. It is a matter of traveling *with them*, *in them*, and *through them*—and when one returns to the breath, they return after having truly been somewhere. Meditation entails a trip—just not a trip from one determinate place in geographical space to another: from here to there, or there to here. Now *the there is here*, just here and nowhere else. We do not *return home* in the manner of Thoreau coming back from the westward walks he describes in *On Walking*. We are already home, in each moment, in a place that has no determinate destination in mappable space. The only destination consists in continuing to think. This thinking-feeling-sensing-breathing is itself the journey.

We can get there in ways other than meditation. It is no coincidence that we describe using psychedelic drugs as going on a "trip," during which a person may find themselves somewhere else, somewhere they have never been before. Any sheer rumination in which we engage counts as a journey of the sort to which we are here pointing: daydreaming, reminiscing, contemplating, feeling, even losing oneself in an emotion such as grief or rage, and the list goes on. Reading books, watching movies, writing, gardening, knitting—these are also forms of travel in which we remain in physical place while roaming far and wide in thought. In fact, we are taking such trips all the time—often without valorizing them as such. Indeed, this is so often the case that we take these flights of thought or feeling for granted, only rarely pausing and attending to them, much less naming them. But they are no less journeys for not being designated as such, however much they differ from the more quantifiable trips to which we tend to restrict the very meaning of the word "travel." But we can travel otherwise; indeed, we are continually doing so, whether we recognize it or not.

One name for such trips is "mindfulness." As described by Thich Nhat Hanh, in being mindful, "the elements of body, mind, and breath become one."[24] This radically counter-Cartesian way of thinking indicates that the kind of journey to which we are here pointing can be far more comprehensive than we might imagine on first consideration. What we tend to designate as "just thinking" can be much more inclusive than if "thinking" means merely cogitating, as in the Cartesian conception of pure mind (*res cogitans*). For one thing, such thinking is an active *doing* and not a mere contemplating of what is already formed and then presented to us as a fait accompli. The doing can take many forms, including imagining what is radically other than what we ordinarily expect—something literally extra-ordinary, bizarre, and sur-real. But it can also concern what is altogether banal and predictable. Both ends of the spectrum that stretches from the expected to the unexpected are fair game for the psychical journey to which we are here alluding, along with all that lies in between. Any attempt to devise a typology of the precise kinds of journeys at stake in psychic traveling reduces their spontaneity, as with any concerted nomenclature. The acts here in question are always beyond, or short of, determination in definitely definable concepts or words.

It is for this very reason that such peri-phenomena have only rarely been valorized by philosophers, given philosophers' obsession with defining and distinguishing what is determinate—with "presence" in the way this word has been employed by Heidegger and especially by Derrida. Heidegger and Derrida see determinate presence as the legacy of an obsession with certain and definite things, whether designated as "Forms" in Plato's sense, *cogitatione* as Descartes construes this term, or "categories of the understanding" as posited by Kant. Hegel and Bergson attempted to dynamize these static designators, but the area of experience to which we are here pointing is still more volatile—so much so that it defies any attempt at reification. No wonder, then, that it has only rarely been recognized by philosophers, who tend to dismiss unstructured or unnamable forms of psychic activity as "mere thinking." Thinking it is, yet it is not an empty act—such traveling in place demarcates a rich arena of human experience.

We are here talking about what is traditionally called an "inner journey"—a trip within our minds rather than on our feet or in transportational vehicles. Such vehicles have become paradigmatic of journeys regarded as "outer" for an entire complex of reasons that include, at the mechanical level, the invention of the steam engine, the carburetor, jet engines, and much more. But at another level, the driving forces for favoring transportational movement over land or sea have included colonialism and capitalism, with their ever-expanding ambition to claim new territories, encouraging movement into spaces unknown but deemed promising for occupation or the extraction of wealth and resources. Alongside colonialist/capitalist expansiveness is the "ontological expansiveness" that Shannon Sullivan attributes to any socially privileged person who feels they have a right to comfortably inhabit any and every space.[25] Bodies display "ontological expansiveness" by mindlessly spreading out, relaxing, and excessively occupying psychic and physical space. Though Sullivan frames her discussion in terms of the habits of white, male, and hetero human bodies, her analysis has implications for the ways cargo ships and planes, stadiums and warehouses, gated communities and luxury houses, dams and reservoirs also take up and transform geological space—often at the expense of marginalized populations and at the whim of corporations intent on monetizing every square inch of sea, sky, and earth. Habits of "ontological expansiveness" go together with an increasing obsession with *speed* and *acceleration* in many areas of human life, exceeding what is organically or evolutionarily necessary. Together, colonialism, capitalism, and speed have led to a privileged position for outer journeying—at least for those seen as the active agents of history: *getting somewhere* and getting there as expeditiously and as fast as possible. Ever more expedited vehicles—ranging from steamboats to submarines, automobiles, trucks, trains, and flying from one location to another in a jet—have proven virtually irresistible in the mania for acceleration in getting from one place to another. Predictably, even as travel in the twenty-first century has been smoothed for the wealthiest people across the globe, it has become more difficult for those who cannot afford it or whose homelands have been cut off (physically or politically) from favored metropolitan nodes of mass transit.

All this stands in contrast with journeys that get us—literally—*no-where*: nowhere geographically, nowhere on the land or sea. Such journeys take place *just here*: wherever I am now engaging in a series of thoughts or feelings. In this case, my exact location does not matter, nor does the speed of my psychic action, nor my physical mobility or lack thereof. We can undertake such an inner journey virtually anywhere we happen to be: even in the midst of violence or when stymied by colonialist expansion, when we might be driven to take this kind of journey into our very fears or to escape these fears altogether. Less has been said by philosophers about such inner journeys, even as such journeys have long been a cornerstone of philosophical method. Not surprisingly, we cited Thich Nhat Hanh, whose focus on mindfulness, especially that inculcated in meditation, provides rich examples of inner journeys. His guidance is as rare as it is necessary, for it reinstates the value of traveling *within*—within the compass of our own minds, a very different compass than that which has oriented us all too efficiently in the late modern period.

Beyond the solitary and meditative inward turn, many feminist thinkers have paid special attention to forms of travel that do not rely on traditional modes of transportation. This is, in part, because women have historically been kept in place: Penelope methodically weaving and unweaving her work while Odysseus gallivants far and wide. Sometimes women have emphasized the possibilities afforded by inner travel, but other times they have explored possibilities for traveling together, traveling through storytelling, sewing, cooking, or friendship. María Lugones, for example, writes about "'world'-traveling" as a form of psychic travel connected to capacities for playfulness and loving attention. In her analysis, we "'world'-travel" when we allow ourselves to be moved into the realm of another person's concerns and ways of life, a movement that requires openness, focus, and vulnerability. One of her own examples of world-traveling includes a description of trying to know and to love her own mother despite being raised to "arrogantly perceive" her mother as a servant. Lugones attends to the various creative ways that women can forge loving relationships with one another and cross into one another's disparate worlds, even, and perhaps especially, when those "worlds" are geographically proximate yet existentially foreign. The point is that merely traveling from one *place* to another (however geographically far or near) does little to bring us into meaningful relationships with others (or with other cultures or environments). For that, we need to travel beyond ourselves in ways that require emotional engagement, personal transformation, and full-bodied presence.[26]

bell hooks has also written extensively about traveling from her childhood home in Kentucky to other parts of the United States, trips that left her feeling depleted and depressed as she encountered new forms of racism and misogyny everywhere she went. This led hooks to return home to Kentucky, a journey that she describes as both physical and psychological: "I would return to Kentucky and feel again a sense of belonging that I never felt elsewhere, experiencing unbroken ties to the land, to homefolk, to our vernacular speech."[27] hooks's homecoming might seem, at first glance, to share the shape of the classic *Odyssey*: travel to far-flung places that ends up leading back to the point of departure. But hooks describes her own return to Kentucky as coinciding with a realization that she had never really left in the first place. With hooks, we are invited to think about the ways we carry our homes with us, no matter how far away we go. This may include carrying painful things we might rather put down or leave behind. hooks tells the story of traveling as a form of coming home to the reality of one's life, debts, and history. Both Lugones and hooks stress forms of travel through memory and love, foregrounding the difficult work of going back to our childhoods (seeing our child self and taking her by the hand) in a journey of reclamation, forgiveness, and reconciliation.

For the most part, our own examples in this book are outer journeys: All too temptingly, we have subscribed to the priority of traveling somewhere in space—from Stony Brook to New Haven or back—as opening paradigms for both of us. This is symptomatic of how most of us usually think about traveling as involving an individual physically moving from one more or less determinate place to another. This is to subscribe to the primacy of *interplaciality*: traveling as going between identifiable and usually nameable places. But we must also take seriously the real possibility of *intraplaciality*: traveling-in-place. This is a matter of taking a journey even as we stay in the same place: a mental or psychical journey that gets us nowhere in measurable, striated, space—nowhere at all as we ruminate meaningfully in the same place.

Much as we have just insisted on the sheer difference between inner and outer journeys, it is important to acknowledge that the two may be combined and frequently occur together. They do so *in the same place* and *at the same time*. Later in this book, we describe an episode in which Ed, on an airplane speeding across America, found himself struggling with abrasive thoughts as he sat sequestered in a middle seat. These thoughts not only distracted him from work he wished to do, but they occasioned a mental struggle within him that took the form of a lived paradox: Here he was flying fast, and yet he was stuck in place. The very thinking of this paradox of im-motion while in motion constituted an inner journey on his part: He was traveling among his thoughts, indeed obsessively focused there, even as the aircraft he was on kept moving rapidly through spacious skies.

Different as these two modes of traveling are—one measurable in miles per hour, the other having its own timing, its own TPM (thoughts per moment, where "moment," different from "minute," is not made up of the sixty seconds that clocks measure), the two occurred together, at the same time: They were literally *synchronic*. Yet each presented a world of its own. Different as these were, they could, and did, coexist.

Such commixtures happen all the time—not just on frustrating airplane journeys. Sometimes psychic travel comes to the rescue of physical stasis or transit—as when Matilda, of Roald Dahl's book of the same name, disappears into the worlds of her books to escape the neglect and abuse of her immediate family. She remains sequestered in her room, but—through reading—she takes herself away. A similar thing happens when one tries, in transit, to escape the demands of physical travel by sheer effort of imagination. On a turbulent flight or rocky boat ride, you might try to forget where you are by placing yourself elsewhere in memory, through music, books, a film, or by some other means. We sometimes find ourselves in the midst of two journeys at once, each with its own characteristic integrity. One is inner, the other outer.

At stake here are two senses of *embodiment*. Merleau-Ponty was the first to elaborate the intertwining nature of two images of the body. The first is the "objective body," which, like all physical objects, has a particular shape, size, and weight. The second is the "lived body," the body as it senses and feels and moves. Merleau-Ponty worried that philosophers had treated the human body as only an "objective body," failing to take account of how bodies impinge on one another and how they *feel* in a complex, textured world. Drawing on his language, we can say that my "lived body" serves as the common ground of both psychical and physical travel, making each possible in itself while also enabling their coexistence. The lived body, we might say, is the *common carrier* of inner and outer journeys alike.

How does the lived body perform the synchronous duet we have just described?

It does so by being several things at once:

1. The *subject* of the journey to nowhere; it, my lived body, undergoes the journey at every point; it is that to which what is happening happens: even if what is happening has little if anything to do with moving from place to place
2. The *witness* of the experience: taking it in, *being there* for it and in it
3. The *pivot* of this ordinary/extraordinary experience: its turning point
4. The *source* of whatever we may remember of the experience: a source that is a resource insofar as it is able to follow what is happening in detail and nuance
5. The basis of the *recognition* that a journey may involve *being* and *staying* in place even as one is also moving between places

We can say in sum that the body-subject who is the true subject of the kind of trip we are here discussing is (in T. S. Eliot's phrase) "the still point of the turning world. Neither flesh nor fleshless"—the immobility in the heart of mobility.[28] Motionless journey can occur while the body is in motion, but we do not have to be in literal movement for the journey to nowhere to be happening. It can happen all the same, whether our body is in literal motion from place to place or standing or sitting in one spot. The lived body (barring chronic conditions of schizophrenia or other dissociative disorders) feels itself as *one being* even as it moves between geographically determinate places on the earth; it is the source of *myself* as on a perpetual inner journey that may get us nowhere in objectively determinable, stratified space but that takes us to multiple locales we could not otherwise ever have come to know.

Our lived body moves among and between determinate things in the world and among and between "things" in memory, imagination, and all forms of thought. We are constantly negotiating the tensions inherent in these different forms of movement (along with the largely automatic and unreflective movements of air, blood, and syncopation happening within our own bodies all the time). Sometimes, when we are especially mindful of where we are in a given moment, our whole being can coalesce in one place, as sometimes happened for Megan when canoeing on flat water, lost in the syncopation of paddling with her dad.[29] We feel suddenly *present*. Other times (and most of the time), scattered thoughts pull us away from where we are, or external pressures (heat, noise, crowds) interrupt our internal voyages. We are part way wherever we happen to be and part way somewhere else entirely—a situation exacerbated in the age of digital technologies that further divide our attention and beckon us to constantly "travel" in place. For those with acute sensory sensitivity, as with many on the autism spectrum, the outside world itself can present as a constant barrage of violent interruptions.[30]

Another case in point is the immobility that being physically sick brings with it. Suddenly it is not just a matter of being still and traveling in thought. In illness, the lived body may lose its ability to move in ways it is used to. When confined to bed and not having the energy to move ourselves, we are acutely aware that *we are not going anywhere*—anywhere other than the room to which we are confined. Nevertheless, we are on a journey—a trip composed entirely of thoughts and memories of other times and of dashed hopes in the present. There is plenty of psychical activity going on; indeed, we are taking a trip in our minds, often one that is quite diverse and intense, with many chapters, some of which can be very disturbing. But these are altogether internal voyages that get us nowhere in the larger world of interaction with others. We are nowhere in that world—with the notable exception of being in the company of those who attend to us in our affliction.

This is one of the most poignant dimensions of being ill—being cut off from the ongoing world of which we were once an active part. Suddenly that world is alien, inaccessible. Virginia Woolf wrote: "The whole landscape of life lies remote and fair, like the shore seen from a ship far out at sea."[31] Otherwise put, in being ill and confined to bed, we are *marooned in place*—in the single location of our bed and bedroom: in that place alone and no other. We travel there and there alone in a distinctive version of a journey to nowhere. The bed might become a vehicle in our illness journey—lending a part of its materiality to the quality of thought. The sheets, the mattress, and the bed frame become one with your sensory landscape and the quality of your thinking (Megan is reminded of a blanket on her bed when she was sick as a child and of the hours she would spend looking at the world through the holes of the weave). Certain features of the sickbed or the sickroom linger with you even after you are well again (the smell of Vaseline, the taste of ginger ale, the feel of a certain T-shirt, etc.). Cancer patients report feeling nauseated by the sight or smell of anything they encountered during chemotherapy. Illness, particularly severe or prolonged illness, can hover in the body like a lingering shadow.

When ill, instead of focusing on a single basic truth as articulated in a mantra such as "I am here"—in which case we anchor ourselves in a given place—our thoughts and feelings tend to be dispersed. In our deeply distracted state, we are all over the place—but often a quite impoverished place, with few if any exits. If there is any single focus, it is likely to be a version of an obsessive thought such as "I want to get well" or "I have to get better" or "how can I improve?" We tend to get bogged down in such monothetic thoughts, which mirror our being confined to a single bed of convalescence. Gravity reigns in the sickbed. A related obsessive line of thought is "how did this happen to me?" or "where did I go wrong?" We know there may be no fully coherent answer to these questions, but we cannot help but ask them nonetheless, seduced as we are by what Eli Clare has described as an obsessive sense of "loss and mourning." Clare continues, "We wish. We mourn. We make deals. We desire to return to the days before immobilizing exhaustion or impending death, to the nights thirty years ago when we spun across the dance floor. We dream about the body-minds we once had before depression descended, before we gained twenty, fifty, one hundred pounds, before our hair turned grey."[32] Our journey to nowhere when sick is often a trip in the Land of the Hopeless.

Travelogue: Ed on Pneumonia

I recently came down with pneumonia, which brought me quickly to extreme physical exhaustion. I slept a great deal—not having much of a choice to do otherwise—but when awake I found myself in a markedly obsessive state of mind, preoccupied with being suddenly so sick and so weak. Equally preoccupying was the medical knowledge that pneumonia may take a long time to heal, especially for someone of my own advanced age. When overcome with such repetitive thoughts, I experienced a sense of hopelessness that was little short of despair. Will I ever emerge from such stasis, such confinement, such a setback? Everything took on an inescapable "spirit of gravity" (in Kierkegaard's phrase) as depression began to set in—which only began to lift on the day when, six weeks later, I suddenly felt better energy, which seemed to come from nowhere. Welcome as this was, it was also confusing. How did this upswing happen? Would it last? Was it a sign of genuine healing or just a momentary and thus misleading blip in my physical state? (Thankfully, the upswing proved to be the first sign of real improvement, which continued apace.) Throughout this ordeal I was thinking: thinking how I would get to the other side of this affliction but also thinking—as remembering— how it was when I was more energetic.

Travelogue: Megan on Brain Rest

Something else transpires for those with ongoing mental illness, brain injuries, or dementia—those who have lost the capacity to organize their own thoughts or to travel in place. This was something I discovered after sustaining a major concussion in the winter of 2018, when a young child in my daughter's class lost control on his ice skates and toppled me from behind.[33] Physically I was well enough (bruised, whiplashed, and sore, but able to move about). Anyone who saw me would have thought I was perfectly well. Except that I had lost the capacity to remember basic things (the names of my daughters, my birthday, my home address), read, and focus my eyes on a page. I lost the connective threads of my thinking, so that as soon as I had a thought, it was cut short. Was it even thinking anymore or something else? Any attempt to concentrate only seemed to make things worse, leading to debilitating headaches and fatigue. Rather than thought leading from one idea to another or accumulating into a narrative thread, thinking itself was cut up into dissociated bits, among which I seemed to stand like someone stranded in a desert. Where am I? I wondered. Who am I? I couldn't recall, though I sensed the loss of myself and everything I thought held me together. Sitting next to my daughter on the couch soon after the accident, she pressed her hand into mine. I knew it was hers and I knew it was mine, though I couldn't conjure what to call any of it.

My brain needed to heal—a journey that would take several years and that would entail recalibrating my entire notion of "recovery." For me, there was a way back (or rather, a way forward) to memory and language, but there was also the necessary adaptation to a new way of being and an altered reality. Survival rather than recovery. In the acute part of the injured phase, I lost not only my own ability to think coherently and to travel in place but my very sense of identity and connection to those around me. This was an odd and terribly sad experience of being able to physically travel as easily as I had before but of being psychically stranded—which meant that I was always going nowhere, no matter where I was. As with Ed's description of pneumonia, this led to depression and a sense of the crisis of having lost my mind and lost my way.

―――――

Being temporarily ill—and all the more so becoming chronically ill—brings with it a sense of severe *curtailment*: curtailment not just of one's normal everyday activities, including most personal relationships (with the exception of immediate caretakers) and almost all concrete commitments (e.g., teaching, being part of an office staff, driving, making dinner, putting a child to bed). All these things are *cut short* in the literal meaning of "curtailment." But beyond these praxiological stoppages, there are darker shadows. One of these shadows is that of opaqueness: Things that were obvious before are now not making any sense. As Virginia Woolf writes: "Incomprehensibility has an enormous power over us in illness."[34]

Another emergent shadow is the darkest of all. At the pitch of an illness such as pneumonia, a severe case of COVID, cancer, or a major accident, one can all too easily imagine the curtailment of one's ongoing life—indeed, of life itself. Havi Carel describes how illness is not just a falling apart or out of phase of some biological aspect of one's own body but a "systematic shift in the way the body experiences, acts, and reacts as a whole. The change in illness is not local but global, not external but strikes at the heart of subjectivity."[35] When illness becomes prolonged or severe, when the prognosis is poor, one can find oneself looking into the face of death, into the end of one's life—the end of consciousness as one has come to know it, of being awake and alive. At this extreme point, one faces the vanishing even of the difficult thoughts and imaginings that arose from being very sick. No wonder that in response to the prospect of death, one clings to all one's ruminations, unpleasant and unwelcome as they are. They at least betoken being conscious—indeed, being alive, however unsatisfying and frustrating such a liminal state may be. At least this much is not curtailed but serves as evidence that one is still living. It is a journey even if its outcome is far from clear—an ongoing journey to nowhere determinate, which nevertheless counts as evidence that one remains in the land of the living.

Journeys to nowhere show themselves to be more frequent in number and in type than we might at first imagine. They proliferate in our conscious lives and are no less significant than classical journeys to somewhere in particular. For the most part, we tend to ignore them or to repress them—especially if they belong to challenging or unhappy periods of our life such as illness might bring. But they are not just divagations from some imagined norm of journeys with a definite destination. Even if they are often not remembered as such, they have their own place in our ongoing lives—a place we cannot afford to ignore if we are to do justice to the density and complexity of the convoluted life of human beings who move between diverse locales and situations. Each of us has a densely layered mental life even when—perhaps *especially* when—forced to be stationary, whether this be in a seat in a classroom, in bedridden illness, or in some form of solitary confinement (including the type enforced in many modern prisons). The mind is often the cutting edge of adaptation into new forms of being, incubating the possibilities for going on when, from the outside, it might appear one has stalled. Hannah Arendt wrote of thinking in *The Life of the Mind* that "the everywhere of the thinking ego—summoning into its presence whatever it pleases from any distance in time or space, which thought traverses with a velocity greater than light's—is a *nowhere*."[36] Nowhere in the physical world around us tied to things and creatures within arm's reach or farther away, but somewhere in thought, in a place with its own unmappable realities. Journeys are still being taken even if they take us nowhere—that is, to no determinate location.

2

AIR

> We came crying hither;
> thou know'st, the first time that we smell the air
> we waul and cry.
> —*King Lear*

The first trip every human being takes is from the watery habitat of the womb into the air. For human animals (as well as for many other mammals), water is the first element and air the second. Once born, we will never again breathe underwater. Now our sustaining element is the air—and breathing is the most basic and fundamental activity of our lives. Before the modern determinations of death by the measurement of brain activity, which accompanied the invention of ventilators and other life-sustaining machines, humans associated life with breath and breath with the soul. Early physicians held a mirror above the mouth of a patient to discern the telltale fog left by even the slightest exhalation.

What does it mean to arrive in the air? We don't yet have our feet on the ground. We are suspended in the air in what John William Miller called "the midworld"—halfway between ground and sky.[1] Often this means being cradled or carried in someone else's arms. It might include being swaddled, strapped to a board, nestled in a sling, perched in a high chair, or buckled in a car seat. Even when (if) one begins to crawl and to walk, the human body remains suspended most of the time between earth (at our feet) and air (around our heads).

As an element, air is associated with ethereal things: dreams, fog, gauze. Though we tend to associate air with the sky, it is all around us, above and below. It even emanates sometimes from the depths of the ground, in volcanic eruptions or other explosions of gases from Earth's mantle. Francis Bacon associated air with the winds, calling them the "the wings of mankind" and "the sweepers of man's habitation, the earth."[2] Air fills our lungs. It inflates, transports, pressurizes, sweeps, roils, cools, heats, and (sometimes) destroys. People use the pejorative expression "airhead" for someone lacking substantial ideas. Of a perpetual daydreamer, one might say, "her head is in the clouds." As the story goes, people did say this about Thales of Miletus when, lost in thought and gazing up at the night sky, he stumbled into a well. Philosophers since then have been plagued with a characterization as having their heads in the clouds—as flighty, distant, or detached from practical reality.

"Airhead" and "head in the clouds" are phrases that convey a sense of a thinker and thinking that are untethered and undisciplined, or of ideas so remote that they fly away into the upper atmosphere, where oxygen becomes thin and scarce. We refer to subtle ideas as "high level." Yet one also might say that an idea is "above my head" if it seems too difficult to grasp. We seem to associate air with both vacuous and profound forms of thinking, as well as coming to overly hasty conclusions, making air itself a site of confusion and ambivalence.

Contrary to the tendency to link the air with an *absence* of substance, Gaston Bachelard associated the "aerial psyche" with a state of "open imagination."[3] A person whose thinking is most captured by the air is one who is also drawn to height and flight in various forms. Bachelard thought that this implied a particularly poetic nature, and he crowned Nietzsche as the consummate *"vertical poet, the poet of the summits, the ascensional poet."*[4] Contrast this with thinkers like Aristotle, Heidegger, and Wittgenstein, who claim to have kept their gaze on the ground.

Air is perhaps the most protean of all the elements, changing shape at every turn. Scientifically regarded, it is simply the invisible mixture of gases that surrounds Earth: 99 percent nitrogen and oxygen. Humans and other animals inhale this mixture and exhale carbon dioxide—which plants then use to produce additional oxygen through photosynthesis, in a beautifully choreographed rhythm of intake and return. In and out, over and over. The air feeds and fuels the cycle of life, for which it forms the essential circumambience. About air, the poet Howard Moss wrote, "It is a cage of sight and sound."[5] Thinking of air this way reminds us that our vision and hearing are caught in the intricacies of air. We who can see can see across and through the air when things are clear. When they aren't, we see only the air itself, thick with fog or ash or whatever lends it opacity. Similarly, we who can hear can hear according to sound waves that travel through the air as medium, first hitting the outer ear, which sends vibrations to the inner ear and, from there, onward to the brain. Husserl associated hearing with a unique form of consciousness characterized by simultaneous impression, retention, and protention—a mix of the sound itself, a sense of what came just before, and a futural sense of what might come next. Images and sounds are carried forward through the air on invisible currents according to which we experience the world as loud or soft, bright or dark, dense or ethereal. In addition to filling our lungs, air facilitates or frustrates vision and hearing, serving as a conduit of sense impressions that wraps bodies in invisible layers.

While air alerts us to the syncopated inhalation and exhalation of living creatures, it invites us also to think about height and the upper vaults of the heavens. Air pushes down upon everything with equal and undifferentiated force (about 14.7 pounds per square inch at sea level). It is strange to think about the weight of the air—a bit like thinking about the weight of grief or some other invisible baggage. Some days feel heavier than others. Sometimes the air (especially when hot and humid) feels like it must weigh more than it did at another time, in another place. "Get some air," one might tell a friend who is upset. Those with respiratory ailments were often sent to the seashore to breathe in the salty air (as Beth was in *Little Women*, as the boy with scarlet fever was in *The Velveteen Rabbit*, or like the protagonist of Thomas Mann's "Death in Venice," who finds the air that once seemed "damp, thick and filled with rottenness" yields to air that feels "thinner and cleaner, the beach with its huts and boats more colorful, though the sky was still gray").[6]

Sometimes a person or an event "sucks the air right out of the room." The room is suddenly heavy, inert, or empty of any basis for empathy. Air is often sensed when lacking more than it is noticed when in abundance. Indeed, this lack can cause panic, because one senses the scarcity of what is necessary to life.

Air, a bit like water, asks us to reimagine ourselves. We aren't built for prolonged suspension in these elements, and, thrust into them, we find ourselves in need of accessories: masks, bathing suits, flippers, oxygen tanks, apnea machines, wings, parachutes. Water and air are basic requirements of survival and of life, yet we (human beings) can only take so much of either element. We risk drowning in water and being blown off a cliff in a strong enough wind. Ascend to the highest points on the globe, and air no longer supports breath (and even moderately steep altitudes can cause a host of problems, from dehydration to delirium). We seem to be creatures predestined to the middle ground and the midrange. Perhaps that was one of the insights of Aristotle's description of the ethical *mean*. Being human entails ongoing calibration of where the middle is. Aristotle described this in terms of the pursuit of virtue (just enough courage of the right kind in the right conditions for the right reasons), but it works just as well as a directive for elemental stability (just enough air of the right kind in the right conditions).

Unlike the other elements, air is essentially invisible, though it circulates around us all the time. We live in the air and of the air. The sky is built of air, and we see the coming storm in the darkening clouds and damp feel of air that suddenly seems heavy (as Ed will describe in his experience of sitting on the porch and sensing the sky bearing down in "Interlude 2").

We sense seasonal shifts in air that is cool and bright, leaves cascading down its invisible veins to the ground. Sometimes the air is flecked with white crystals or ragged flakes, and sometimes the air gives way to water in a heavy rain, as if someone has opened a valve in the sky. Sometimes the air is utterly still and seems to hold everything in a jar. Other times the winds whip around, and the air seems furious and unrelenting—and sometimes, in a tornado, this is literally the case. In *Mary Poppins*, when the wind picks up in the east, the cherry trees begin to swirl, and all the nannies get carried off into the sky. In *The Wizard of Oz*, Dorothy runs for cover from the "twister," only to feel the house lift and spin and see all of her family members, neighbors, and assorted farm objects flying by outside the window. Those living in Topeka, Kansas, used to claim that this very tornado happened just outside town.

Travelogue: Ed Remembering Tornadoes in Topeka

In 1967, I experienced a tornado in Topeka that destroyed much of the local college campus as well as many buildings downtown. It had been thought—according to Shawnee Indian lore—that Topeka was protected from tornadoes so long as a high wind never came over and down "Shawnee Mound," a hill southwest of the town. The storm of 1967 came straight over the mound and directly into the city, thereby confirming the Native American myth. My father and I hid out in the basement of our house in the southwest corner, as that was where the storm was coming from: the idea being that the tornado would somehow leap over our heads if we were stationed there. Fortunately, our house was spared, but we were only blocks away from where the tornado first touched down. The sound of the storm was frightening; it seemed to be everywhere above the city even as the funnel set down in specific places—but which ones were not known in advance. Some friends of my father attributed the storm to the wrath of God over the American presence in Viet Nam.

Travelogue: Megan Remembering Tornadoes in Connecticut

Hurricanes are a more common source of destruction in Connecticut, but I recall a tornado in 1989, when I was fourteen. The tornado touched down on Mohawk Mountain, clearing all the trees, leveling the ski lifts, and scattering the red lift chairs miles away.[7] For years afterward, we would look at the bare mountain in disbelief at the wreckage and destruction. More recently, in 2018, a tornado touched down just behind our house in Bethany, Connecticut. We were not home when it hit, but we returned the next day to closed roads, downed power lines, and acres of debris. Picking our way toward the house, we could see several trees leaning against the roof. Behind the house, the tornado had cleared a path as wide as an airplane, leaving every tree splayed, shattered, or in a heap of limbs on the ground. The wreckage was unimaginable. Neighbors' houses up and down the road were either ruined or spared in a hopscotch pattern without logic.

Sleeping Giant, the mountain closest to us, was, like Mohawk Mountain years before, sheared of its trees and completely remade in the wake of the tornado.

———

Strong winds of any kind can cause significant damage and pose their own risks. The air, when moving fast enough, sends things in circles or carries them away. High winds can sometimes be scarier than torrential rain, thunder, or other assaults from the sky. In hurricanes we see trees bend, sense the power of the wind to break solid things in half, to pick things up and hurl them through space, to blow without stopping. Each element has its menacing side, but air seems especially duplicitous because of how little one senses its presence when the sky is calm. How could something so invisible be so destructive? How could the day turn so suddenly from light blue to dark gray? How can air be both the invisible atmosphere all around us and the black funnel barreling down a nearby street, hopping over one house and leaving the next in ruins, in a form of arbitrary violence whose logic is impossible to discern?

Most of us learn to be careful with water from a very young age. "You could drown in a teaspoon of water." (*That's what my grandmother used to tell us, and my siblings and I laughed but couldn't stop thinking about it in the bath.*) No one tells you to be careful with the air. And even if they told you, what would you do? In tornado zones, one is taught to rush to the "storm shelter" in a school or one's own basement—or just to sit in the bathtub. When air betrays us, we have no recourse but to seek refuge in solidity: concrete, metal, earth.

In June 2023, the air in the northeastern part of the United States turned gray, the sun a pulsing amber sphere that seemed pinned behind a mesh curtain. Smoke from wildfires in Canada had traveled south and remained stuck over New York, creating the worst air quality conditions ever recorded. Megan happened to be in New York

City on those days. Walking south on Fifth Avenue, she could no longer see *through* the air, which seemed a silty wash. News reports warned people to stay indoors, and the streets were surreally empty. Oddly, it was also the inverse of what we had collectively practiced through two or more years of the COVID pandemic. Rather than mask indoors and go outside to avoid contagion, everyone was suddenly forced indoors to escape the toxic air and wearing N-95 masks outside to protect themselves from inhaling particulate ash.

It is likely we all take air for granted. People living in areas prone to wildfires and those with asthma or other respiratory ailments know something more about air and its absence. Miners, sherpas, and others who labor in places with scant air must also have special aerial wisdoms. Air circulates around us all the time, yet access to fresh, clean air is increasingly a matter of wealth and privilege across the globe. Yet without it, none of us can live. Unlike water and earth, air circulates freely. Human beings have not yet invented dams or dikes or other funneling devices in the skies that would control the air. As of now, the pollution generated in one place is carried, unrestricted, on planetary winds to other places—like the smoky air blowing south from Canada. The air also carries dust and debris, mixing elements in the sky to be deposited far and wide. Recently, the *New York Times* reported that Saharan dust blowing into southern Florida would increase heat, affect rainfall, and diminish the air quality there.[8] In Cabo Verde, hundreds of miles west of Africa, Saharan dust has to be swept weekly out of one's home. In such cases, earth and air commingle, the air transporting dirt and transforming—*abstracting*— geography as we know it.

In the 1930s, severe dust storms (caused by the intersection of prolonged drought and industrialized farming practices that obliterated native grasses across the American and Canadian prairies) left the land stripped of topsoil and the skies blackened with dirt. In 1933, dust storms from South Dakota blew over twelve million pounds of dust into Chicago and cities stretching farther east.[9] During the nearly decade-long Dust Bowl, millions of impoverished people fled the American prairies and went westward in search of work, water, and fertile soil. Even today, momentary local dust storms emerge suddenly in Kansas, as Ed discovered when driving west on I-70 and getting entangled in a multiple-car crash, drivers blinded by thick swirls of dust blowing in from nearby farms.

As climate change intensifies the disparities between livable and unlivable places, more and more people are in transit across the globe. More air carries more dust and debris. Cities tend to sit in their own smog and pollution-induced heat domes, but the air respects no boundaries. It rises above us and falls all around—and sometimes far away. At the outer limits of Earth's atmosphere, it gets thinner and thinner until it dissipates into something else, which we have little choice but to call *space*. Anaximenes argued that air is the neutral stuff out of which everything else is made, and he attributed to the air divine powers. Just as doctors used to associate air with life, ancient philosophers associated air and breath with the soul—the self-moving, divine principle of life. Air lifts. Air circulates. Air is inspiration as well as expiration.

In the first chapter, we considered water as the native element of human life and travel in and on water as indicative of an immersive return to primal knowhow. Humans have moved into and over the water for thousands of years. Comparatively, mechanical air travel is quite new. Just as air represents an elemental developmental step from the earliest forms of life to later forms, human transit in and through the air represents a shift in tools and technologies that coincide with the mechanical advancements of the early modern and modern period. The movement of human beings across the globe seems to be at first lateral across the waters and into or forcibly away from native lands and only later aerial—up into the air and (just in the last decades) beyond Earth's atmosphere into outer space. If transit and thinking relative to water are paradigmatically rhythmic and smooth, reflecting back the aqueous substance, transit and thinking relative to the air are paradigmatically diaphanous, nebulous, and scattered, reflecting back the dispersive qualities of air. Here, as in chapter 1, we consider some means of transit through the air alongside corresponding modes of thinking.

FALLING

Apples fall from a tree. Leaves fall, as does night. A shadow can fall across a page or a face. Depending on the weight and density of a body, the fall is fast or slow. These lessons in gravity and the variations of falling inscribe themselves into bodies as a part of their initial experiences of size and movement. What is possible? How far and how fast can one go? Will the landing be soft? Will you catch me?

Travelogue: Megan on Falling Through the Air

Strangely, perhaps, my first memory of air is of being in midair. Sometime between the ages of one and two, I crawled to the top of a makeshift staircase in an old schoolhouse in upstate New York, which my dad was renovating for us to live in. The stairs were made of plywood, with large gaps between the risers. I got all the way to the top before slipping through the gap and falling from the second story to the first—luckily onto a floor of packed dirt. I am told I did not cry when I landed, which my parents took as a sign that I was either mortally wounded or completely fine.

The latter was true, though I retained a vivid memory of that fall well into my childhood. For years afterward, I could—with enough concerted effort—conjure the feeling of being in midair. It was a bit like flying, and I loved (especially at bedtime) to put myself back into the slow-motion arc of moving through the air. I never remembered the impact; I only remembered the flight. It is my earliest memory. I could return to it at will until I was nine or ten years old, at which point it faded and became something I knew had happened but could no longer relive.

Travelogue: Ed on Falling and Bouncing Down the Basement Stairs

My family was preparing to drive to Abilene for Thanksgiving. We had packed the car, and everyone was ready to go—when I managed to fall down the stairs to the basement of our house, bumping against each successive step and finally reaching the basement floor. My parents were consternated, being convinced that I must have broken a bone or, worse, sustained a concussion. But I assured them that it was an innocent fall occasioned by my playing on the top step of the stairs. I recall my seven-year-old body hitting one hardwood step after another in what seemed more like a game than an accident. I had taken a "free fall" in which I felt that I was rolling downward through the thick air of the basement. At the bottom stair, however, I was breathing very heavily, as if to belatedly acknowledge the danger in which I had just been engaged. Not surprisingly, after this incident my mother installed a wooden gate at the top of the stairs.

For many of us, the first experience of the air as a place of movement is probably tied to early childhood experiences of falling. Being thrown into the air and caught again (hopefully) in familiar arms. Almost as soon as a baby stands, they topple. Rough ground, scattered toys, rocks, stairs, rugs, snow—all of them invite a fall. When you are small, the distance from an upright position to the ground is not so great and therefore not usually dangerous, but a tumble down a long staircase, a hill, or from a high surface produces a rush of air and the momentary sensation of weightless flight. Terrifying and exhilarating, the heart leaps into the throat, the sense of embodied solidity vanishes, and distance transfigures in a flash. For the briefest moment, airborne, everything changes. If there is time to think in the suspended space of falling, the thoughts are as dispersed and open as the air itself. The interlude between leaving the ground and hitting it again (an inevitable and often painful trajectory that might include skinned knees and having the wind knocked out of you) can feel unnaturally expansive, as if transpiring in slow motion. Here you are in the air, in midair, like Alice falling down the rabbit hole. The air is rushing past you and into you and all around, blurring the boundedness of the body, which has condensed in the back of your mouth. Later, those who crave the feeling of falling might seek trees or rocks to climb, trampolines, roller coasters, and other devices built to raise a body high into the air only to let it plunge in a wild free fall.

SWINGS

Whether a simple rope with a knot tied to a tree, a plank of wood balanced between two lengths of rope, a tire, or a rubber seat suspended by creaking metal chains, a swing is likely a child's first taste of controlled flight, more conducive to thinking than the unexpected experience of falling is. Some like to sit and let their feet dangle just above the ground, maybe twisting the chains or ropes and letting them unfurl in a dizzying spiral. Others like to pump their legs and travel up into the sky, feeling the lines go slack when the swing reaches a pitch almost too high. From there one can come down again in a whoosh of speed, or (if brave enough) cast off into the air at the swing's highest point and try to land on two feet without falling over or breaking anything.

Swings provide rhythmic movement back and forth, a potentially soothing rocking motion. They are easy to find in both rural and urban areas. Swing sets often serve as sites for impromptu gatherings among young parents or as a low-pressure form of socialization for kids who, while swinging, don't have to face or talk to one another. Shy kids go to swings to play alone (or, as Toni Morrison described in *Sula*, to meet one another: "facing each other through the ropes of the one vacant swing ('Go on. No. You go.')").[10] Rambunctious kids flock to the swings to test their speed. Side by side, they all set off on their swings, finding themselves suddenly (momentarily) in sync with the stranger on the adjacent swing. The swing itself provides levity to a body and lends its own free motion to a person who may or may not feel graceful, coordinated, or light. Once on the swing, none of it matters. All kinds of bodies lift off into the air in an equalizing release.

Not all children love to swing, but those who do can spend hours going back and forth, up and down (as Robert Louis Stevenson wrote, "Up in the air and over the wall / Till I can see so wide").[11] The swing is a first vessel of freedom and abandon. You can test the limits on a swing—going higher than feels comfortable or letting go of the chains for a moment. This makes swings perfect vehicles for experimentation and exploration. Tethered to the tree or the swing set, you are not going to get very far. But the *feeling* of swinging is one of expansive roaming. The height feels dangerous, the speed exhilarating. Swings are therefore crucial first sites of independence and imagination. They are where the youngest children (even infants and babies) learn that things come and go, that the sky is also a place, and that they are not defined by gravity alone. Swinging high into the air, the mind goes further than it has before—into imaginative thoughts of birds and rockets, dragons and distant planets. The swing can be (all at once) a comfort, a vehicle of escape, and an invitation to adventure.

Is it possible to imagine at all without first flying into the unknown on a swing?[12] Perhaps. But a swing activates thinking by releasing the whole being into the air. Ever after, one can recall the sensation of giddy weightlessness and endless possibility just before the ropes or chains snap back—and the swing and you begin the downward descent toward the ground, back from the possible to the real.

WINGS

The dream of wings begins with falling—if only you had wings to fly—and swinging—if only you could soar beyond the tethered seat. Birds overhead beckon in a spatter of gray. A dragonfly hovers, its transparent wings buzzing. Wings would take you higher and farther into the air, aligning you with mystical creatures like angels and dragons, storybook figures of grace and ferocity.

Perhaps the most ancient cautionary tale about air comes in the form of young Icarus, the son of the great inventor Dedalus. As the story goes, after being imprisoned together by King Minos, Dedalus planned their escape by building himself and his son wings made of blankets, feathers, thread, clothes, and beeswax. He implored his son to stay above the water so as not to get the fabric wet and to stay away from the sun so as not to melt the wax. But Icarus didn't listen. He soared into the sky, climbing higher and higher until the wax melted and he fell to his death.

Icarus is associated with hubris and the brash courage of youth. But it is also a story about getting carried away. Flight, and dreams of flight, often include both the thrill of newfound freedom or escape and the terror of going too far or spinning out of control: fears that must afflict those who entrust themselves today to hang gliders.

What was Icarus thinking? We'll never know. He was caught in the adventure of his own flight, spurred on by the beauty of the open skies and the heat of the sun drawing him upward. He seems emblematic of an adolescent urge to get away, to disobey, to be heroic, to not fear death. Thinking when you are a teenager is often tied to the feeling of heat and urgency, a sense of being intensely alert and alive (or sometimes ricocheting between that sense and equally powerful feelings of exhaustion, malaise, or despair). Adolescent thinking can lead to rash actions, but it is not only impulsive or juvenile. Dedalus could only see the wings he made as the mechanism of escape and safe landing—an expedient way down. Icarus put them on and realized the possibility of going up, climbing the vault of the sky, testing the limits. His "far-out" thinking ranged free from the practicalities of escape and safety as he took off on an adventure to see how fast and how far he could go. We need such thinking, risky as it might be, to expand the horizons of the possible and to urge us toward distant goals. Icarus is an original Rebel Without a Cause, and his story reminds us that the sky beckons with a promise of another form of life, one that is as tempting as it is dangerous.

Such danger is also felt with aerial gymnastics, such as is sometimes seen in circus shows. The audience is invited to actively imagine the fall of the daring performer—a risk comparable to that of a tightrope walker, like Philippe Petit, who walked a thin cable stretched between the two Word Trade Towers in New York City on August 7, 1974.[13] Petit did it without wings or any other safety devices. His miniature scale and bodily vulnerability stood in stark opposition to the massive rigidity of the two towers, which only years later, in 2001, would display their own precarity as they melted, buckled, and fell. We often look upon aerial feats as death defying, wanting to cover our eyes even as we can't stop watching. Even now, it is hard to imagine Petit striding out into the void above lower Manhattan, smiling easily and lounging on his taut line as people gaped from below. Equally unnerving are the aerial feats of free climbers or base jumpers—those with the courage to hang in midair from the highest heights with little or no sense of gravity or doom.

All of them recall Icarus. Fearless. In love with the sky. No wonder human beings are so fascinated with the flight of birds, who lift themselves from the ground by the subtle flutter of their wings—wings whose structures are explored by Marjolein Oele in her 2020 book *E-Co-Affectivity: Exploring Pathos and Life's Material Interfaces*. As Oele writes, "Between the plumes, the downy feathers, and the contour feathers, an intricate layering network of seemingly empty spaces provides sensitivity, insulation, and movement."[14] The complex structures of birds' wings match the subtlety of the many movements of air. Humans aspire to such intricacy and freedom of movement, even though the wings we build tend to be large, heavy, and prone to rip or fail. Still, one yearns for a metaphorical if not actual takeoff from the gravity of human affairs. This is, in part, what Simone Weil articulated in *Gravity and Grace*, writing, "I have not the principle of rising in me. I cannot climb to heaven through the air."[15] We need some other means of being carried skyward. Weil called it "grace." Emily Dickinson called it "Hope": "the thing with feathers— / That perches in the soul—."[16] Short of the wings of a bird or an angel, we need a soul like that of the young Phaedrus: one pricked all over with budding feathers and ready to take flight in the trail of its beloved or its god. These are the dreams of those who long for flight: to soar like a bird, to be young again, to kiss the sky.

BALLOONS

A less tragic story of flight than that of Icarus comes in the form of the 1956 French film *The Red Balloon* (*Le ballon rouge*), in which a young boy named Pascal befriends a strangely animate and empathetic red balloon. Pascal attempts to hide the balloon in his room, but it follows him through Paris to school, where the principal tries to take it away. Later a group of boys steals the balloon, surrounding Pascal and throwing rocks at him. The balloon is popped in the fight, leaving Pascal crying and holding the deflated red skin of his beloved balloon. At which point, all the other balloons in France fly to Pascal's rescue, descending toward him in a giant bouquet of candy-colored spheres. He grabs their strings and sails away into the sky over Paris.

Pascal, like Icarus, is a young boy who longs to escape. We don't see what happens to Pascal or the balloons after he takes flight, but the story leaves one with the sense that he has been lifted to safety, lifted not only out of the dusty lot where bullies jeer and cast stones but out of the city and a life where mothers make you go to church, principals punish you, and first loves disappear as quickly as the air in Pascal's red balloon. As for Icarus, flight for Pascal is a means of escape from danger and a rebirth into another realm. But unlike Icarus, who donned his father's wings, Pascal takes to the skies with the help of a rubber balloon, a device first invented by Michael Faraday in 1824 in London, forty-one years after the first launch of hot-air balloons in France in 1783. Icarus's wings were modeled after bird wings, but the first hot-air balloons were inspired by observing rising sparks from a fire.[17] Why do flames rise? Why do sparks fly? It is as if they, too, long for the heavens and can't bear to touch the ground. Scientists, meditating by the light of a fire, wondered if heat could carry upward not only sparks but other things. They began to experiment with hot air as a mechanism of elevation for human beings.

Heat proved an effective but dangerous means of making air lighter than the atmosphere around it, and it soon gave way to hydrogen gas in lifting balloons off the ground. Gas balloons were the primary mode of air travel from the 1830s and 1840s until the fixed-wing aircraft went into commercial use in 1914. Balloons could carry one or two passengers quickly over terrain that would have taken weeks or months to cross on the ground. They allowed for bird's-eye views and stealthy aerial exploration undetected by those below. Balloon travel exaggerates the feeling one can have when holding a helium balloon—the slight upward tug on your hand as the balloon tries to rise. It's a subtle sensation of being lifted and drawn skyward, which lends the balloon holder an elongated posture. Hot-air balloons move upward in a spectacle of billowing fabric stretching taut, the lift graceful and silent. Airborne, they float on the wind, where passengers perched in a basket are carried like eggs in a nest. The first humans to travel by balloon must have experienced the patchwork world below as a faraway place of noise and friction suddenly calmed and smoothed by flight. Balloons, large or small, capture air in a bag so that we can hold onto it. Clutching a balloon, running through a park, a child has a secret store of extra air. The balloon resembles a thought bubble filled with ideas hovering over their head—small ideas in a single balloon tied to a string versus big ideas in a hot-air balloon flying high above.

Once balloons became dirigibles, they were no longer as stealthy, as in the case of the massive *Hindenburg*, which was driven by motors even as it was suspended in the sky. No longer a balloon but an "airship," it replaced the dreamy, silent quality of flight with the steady hum of its machinery. Now passengers were not suspended in an open nest but sequestered, seated, in a rigid metal hull. This marked the beginning of a more rugged, noisy, industrial relationship with the sky and the air.[18]

Some of the complexity of humans' endeavors to fly is explored in the 1989 Hayao Miyazaki film *Kiki's Delivery Service*, a story about a thirteen-year-old witch named Kiki who, as the last stage of her training, must live for a year in a town away from her parents. At the start of the film, Kiki takes to the air on her broomstick, filled with a sense of adventure and optimism. Soon after finding a job at a local bakery delivering cakes and pies to customers, she discovers that her powers of flight are waning and that she can no longer incite her broomstick into flight. She befriends Tombo, a young boy in the town who is obsessed with aviation and has built himself a bicycle with wings. Near the end of the film, Tombo becomes endangered by the collision of an airship into a building in town. Kiki has to muster the courage and resolve to fly to save her friend.

As the story unfolds, one realizes that it is a parable about growing up and the difficult transition from a sense of unbounded possibility into a more somber, realistic sense of what one can accomplish.[19] Every child dreams of flight. Peter Pan, knocking at your window, sprinkling you with pixie dust and inviting you to fly. If you can do it, you remain a child forever, joining Peter, Tinkerbell, and the Lost Boys in Neverland. *Kiki's Delivery Service* dramatizes the hopes, dangers, and paradoxes of wanting to take to the air. Miyazaki noted, "To be able to fly through the air means to be liberated from the ground, but liberation can also create insecurity and loneliness."[20] Kiki has to negotiate a grounded world of strangers in a new city, figuring out how to support herself and how to make friends. Growing up happens to you, despite you—and nonetheless it is hard. Things come down—a universal law of gravity. Children grow up. Between the downward thrust of forces all around and the upward thrust of adolescence, we often find our first wings clipped. In the ancient myth invoked in Plato's *Phaedrus*, the feathered soul loses its wings and tumbles into an awkward human body. From that point on, the soul wants to fly, and it seeks out any bit of beauty, love, or truth that might remind it of its aerial life and spur the growth of fresh wings.

PLANES

Modern airplanes, like modern passenger ferries, carry considerable numbers of people together in a contained space. In a passenger airplane, one has less room to spread out or walk around, but there is at least a seat and a fold-down table—just enough space to read or write in transit. Barring turbulence, it is usually possible to write longhand or type without difficulty. The temporal transit frame (departure time to arrival time) provides a known start and finish line. You are virtually unreachable in the air and thus far removed from the urgencies of daily life. The plane is a vehicle for geographic travel from one place to another, but it is also a vehicle for intellectual and creative flight (ideas getting off the ground) and temporary release from practical demands. In some cases, the flight is an actual escape (as for those trying to board the last planes fleeing Afghanistan after the withdrawal of American forces in the summer of 2021). In other cases, the flight provides an opportunity for creative thinking that would not have arisen otherwise.

Thinking on a plane entails an effort of concentration and discipline somewhat different from thinking in a car or while riding on a train or ferry. Air pressure is lower the higher one goes into the atmosphere, and while airlines pressurize their cabins to ensure that passengers can breathe normally at altitude, there is less oxygen than one would have on the ground. This can make you sleepy, a situation exacerbated by flight attendants' requests to draw down window shades and the distribution of blankets, pillows, and headphones before takeoff. If there is any hope of concerted thinking/working on an airplane, one must resist the urge to settle into an aerial stupor.

Moreover, there's no chance to open a window or a door. As a result, one is sealed into an airplane to a different degree than in other kinds of vehicles. Being on a plane is something like being on a submarine of the sky, immersed in an element fully inhospitable. This can create desperate feelings of claustrophobia in some, but it can also create a sense of decisive departure from the norms of everyday life—a sort of permission slip for transformation. Airplanes seem to be excellent places for experimental thinking that departs from routine, however rarely this may be actually achieved.

In the air, the earth below spreads out like a neatly pinned quilt. Megan prefers the aerial view just a few hundred feet above the ground, when you can see the tops of roofs and rectangular cars inching along ribbons of black road. The world seems organized from above into coherent patches of color and texture. Cities glisten with lights and intersecting roads. Rivers, lakes, and seas fan out in wide patches of blue. Trees and forests merge into dense, stubby green shapes, with wide golden fields reasserting the human geometry of squares and circles. Ascending higher, the colors and shapes of the earth recede into a dim haze as clouds become the dominant scenery. Giant puffs of white envelop the plane as it climbs, until they too sit somewhere down below, cartoonish dabs or feathered wisps that seem like the froth of waves.

In contrast, Ed prefers the view from high up, being able to see "the lay of the land" in unique ways that are not possible when on land or flying low. He takes in larger configurations of the earth from a viewing point that is significantly more elevated than what any bird can attain. There is assurance that the earth—labeled *Erdeboden* by Husserl: "the ground or floor of the Earth"—underlies everything one does as one thinks high above it.

When viewed from high in the sky, the ground below loses all distinction. This is the bird's-eye view, the top-down, systematizing gaze that we often find and worry about in philosophy. It seems linked to the Ivory Tower and to thinkers who remove themselves from the fray of life in order to look down and analyze everything from a clean remove (*objectively*, they are likely to claim). It is good to be wary of the top-down view with its temptation to abstract everything on the ground.[21] But it is also good sometimes to let oneself be carried up and away. To be reminded that what appears a jumbled and incoherent mess from up close might rearrange into something else from a distance (as Bergson reminded us, there is no *disorder*, just multiple orders).[22] Thinking needs this back-and-forth movement (close up and long shot), just as painters need to work at various distances from their canvas and writers need to move between the digging work of interpretation and the soaring prose of an overview. Nothing seems right when your nose is to the page. Everything seems easy from way on high. Neither position tells the whole truth. Airplanes carry you up to impossible heights, reminding you that orderings are relative. One should be wary of the airplane's all-too-"top-ological" views of the earth below. Eventually you will land again, maybe even with a thud, wheels shrieking on the ground.

Another aspect of air travel is the sheer speed of planes. Time bends in the air. It is possible to leave one city in the morning and arrive in another city across the globe at nearly the same time you departed, thanks to the speed of the plane and the crossing of multiple time zones. Knowing this, one tends to strategize about air travel in relation to time. You might take an overnight flight with the hopes of tricking yourself into thinking you've had a full night's sleep (even though the flight is only six hours, two of which will be spent being served "dinner" just after takeoff and "breakfast" just before landing). You might travel during the day to arrive somewhere else with only a few hours before bedtime—hoping to stumble into sleep as soon as possible. Either way, air travel affects bodily rhythms more than other modes of travel (and more so for infants, young children, older adults, and those in poor health). It can take hours, days, or even weeks to recover from a given flight. One might have the persistent sense of having left a part of oneself behind, feeling that time has warped out of focus—or just feeling out of sorts. But an eager anticipation of one's destination can also be the case.

Airplanes exert a special effect on bodies and on Earth itself. They are among the primary contributors of polluting emissions causing climate change. For a brief time during the COVID pandemic, planes were grounded, and the skies were silent and clear. We remember hearing the strange silence of a sky left alone. People described seeing animals emerge in places they had never seen them before. The planet itself seemed on the cusp of taking a long-needed breath. But before long, the planes resumed, cutting their white trails, filling up the air with their high wails and throbbing jet engines while dispersing people around the globe. Animals retreated anew. The sky, which for a moment was a pristine vault of blue, became again a much-traveled and often over-traveled road.

Travelogue: Ed on Being Bound in Place on a Plane

Waiting for the plane in Dallas to take off, I had the sense of being stalled in space, suspended there. Partly this was attributable to exhaustion after a demanding sorting of books and memorabilia in my New York apartment over the last few days, but it was also because of the plane's being delayed for a long time because of high winds in Santa Barbara. Finally, the plane took off. Before long, I could see the earth being traversed below: so I knew the plane was moving. After we reached cruising altitude and the plane was droning forward at the same pace, I began to feel bound to my stationary seat. The striking fact was that I knew we were moving even if it was not perceptible as such. We were moving in place—where the place itself, the immediate scene on the plane, was rigidified. Same for all that was around me: Mary napping on my left, the man on my right watching the same endless football match on television, and me caught in the middle. I had become an unmoving mass in the midst of a highly static scene. It was a strange situation of experienced immobility in the very midst of rapid mobility in space and in the passing of time.

As Michael Marder would insist, I was a passenger, passing from one place to another.[23] My own body was going along for the ride—not to enjoy it as such (which in fact I didn't at all, given my exhaustion) but as a passenger paralyzed in place even as the airplane I was on was undeniably moving from Dallas to Santa Barbara, however much delayed it was.

In all this we confront a paradox of movement. The plane I was on was doubtless a moving object in space, but I felt immobilized in the midst of this very movement. The football game televised on my right was filled with players running at high speeds and in all directions. But their frenetic kinesis—itself also fixed on an unmoving screen!—only made me feel more stuck in place: a hapless passenger who was forced to be a sheer spectator, emphasizing my own immobility all the more.

I was getting desperate to land—finally. I'd been in the air too long, and my journey seemed endless. I found myself wanting to move—minimally, to move out of my seat and into the aisle of the plane but, more desperately, to move onto the solid ground of the earth. There, at least and at last, I could move about freely. But as long as I was up in the air, this was not an option. I was not just being held stationary—thanks to my seatbelt and lack of movement in the aisle—I was immobilized, held in place. From this strongly felt stabilitas loci there was no escape.

Strong winds suddenly overtook our plane, which bounced about, throwing us around as well. Now we were trapped in a tempestuous place. This only made me—and presumably others—feel my immobility all the more poignantly. We—we who were on the plane—were certainly moving and being moved, but we were also not moving—not even in this storm. The tempest around the plane—in all its dynamic movement—found me feeling immobile and stuck in place, even as the storm raged outside our plane, which battled its high winds. The momentary tempest contributed to my sense of sheer stasis: Its uncontrolled action only made my marooned self feel itself to be all the more immobilized.

In contrast with the situation just described is that which obtained in Ojai, California, less than a week later. I had gone there because the fumigation of our house for termites had rendered it uninhabitable. In Ojai, a storm was brewing: a rainstorm that was sweeping in from the ocean and occupying the valley below the Ojai Retreat, where we were staying. Now I was able to move about: move around the room we had rented and between the room and the much larger space of the patio at the center of the retreat. This time, it was the storm and not me that seemed stuck in place: It had moved in and filled the valley with fog, clouds, winds, and rain. In contrast with this, I took special pleasure in being able to move between the two locations available to me. At least I had this much felt mobility, modest as it was.

ROCKETS

Although still beyond the experience of most of us, there are rockets and spaceships—only recently made available for commercial travel (space tourism) to passengers with enough financial resources to book a seat. In space one moves beyond the four elements that govern our thinking about travel—moving through the sky at speeds upward of 17,500 miles per hour and into a realm with no air.

Travelogue: Megan on Watching the Launch of the Space Shuttle *Challenger*

I was in fourth grade in 1986 when the space shuttle *Challenger* broke apart seventy-three seconds after takeoff on January 28. My teacher, like most every teacher in America, had wheeled a television set on a black cart into the classroom so that we could watch the historic moment when the first civilian teacher, Christa McAuliffe, would go into outer space (the first woman was Valentina Tereshkova in

1963). And like children across the country, we stared in disbelief at the smoke and flaming debris falling from the sky, certain and yet uncertain of what we had just witnessed. My teacher wept, and we could hear a collective cry of horror resound down the hallways and through the whole school. Thinning wisps of gray smoke continued to coil downward on the television screen. The newscasters were speechless. It was my first remembered experience of catastrophe.

Any travel in the air has its dangers. Part of the wonder inspired by birds in flight must be related to the ease with which they appear to fly. Turkey vultures silently gliding in looping circles on the wind, swallows taking off in a flurry, geese on a lake beating their wide wings over the water and levitating seamlessly into the air in perfect formation. Hummingbirds, like miniature helicopters, suspended in midair. Bees, butterflies, dragonflies, gnats, flies, mosquitoes . . . all of them buzzing with perfect calibration and skill.

Humans, by contrast, seem clumsy and ill at ease in the air—except, perhaps, in a hang glider that mimics the grace of a bird or when one is extended upward by flying swings and kites that silently slice the sky. Planes lumber on and around runways amid personnel racing about. The takeoff seems loud and cumbersome, the machine pitching forward as the wheels clank up into the body of the plane. Rockets balance on launch pads, blasting off in a commotion of fire and smoke, leaving a thick, gray smudge behind them, roaring into space. Nothing about modern air travel is quiet or calm. The sheer mass of the vehicles, a factor of gravitation, seems painfully at odds with the very idea of levitation. Levitation for humans belongs in the realm of magic; in sober reality, human beings will never fly unassisted: We shall not grow wings anytime soon.

And air crashes are not uncommon, though anyone will tell you that it is safer to ride in an airplane than it is to drive a car. One of the special features of air travel is the wager one makes in taking to the air. Annie Dillard, writing about flying with the stunt pilot Dave Rahm in a single-engine Cessna, wrote, "I gave up on everything, the way you do in airplanes; it was out of my hands."[24] Once air-bound, there is little or no recourse should something go wrong. Gravity reigns. What goes up must come down. On the earth, we usually retain various strategies for moving ourselves out of harm's way—walking, running, crawling, seeking cover. In the water, there is the chance to swim or to float. In the air, the vehicle itself is the only means of protection, and if we should find ourselves pitched into the air without such support, then all is lost. We become nothing but a flimsy body falling through the air, a body never intended for flight.[25]

The dream of flight is also a dream of relinquishing human weight (both the physical weight of one's own body and the psychic weight of being human). Flight is tied to inner trips that move beyond the bounds of the real: trips of imagination, dreams, lofty hopes and wishes. The pilot in *Le petit prince*, who crashes in the desert only to find the small boy from another planet asking him for a drawing of a sheep. The old man in the 2009 Pixar movie *Up*, who ties thousands of balloons to his house to carry it up and away to the remote wilderness of Paradise Falls. On a good day or in a moment of good luck, one might say "I was flying high." It's not unusual to have days that feel heavier than others, just as one finds oneself in air that is suddenly stifling or under a leaden sky. Why not then try to fly, or at least pretend to do so? As children, we played games of flight, jumping with our towels spread out behind us from the tops of sand dunes or, holding a rope, swinging from the top of the rocks over the lake. In grade school we played superheroes and donned capes as we ran around the playground or spun on the whirligig until we were sick. The smaller and slighter one's body, the more flight seems possible, and so the games and attempts seem to subside as one grows older and heavier. We stop trying to fly as we age, knowing that the ground is where we're ultimately headed.

But the air retains its mysterious allure. *Up there*, one thinks, on higher ground, the thinking might be clearer, the air more crystalline, the breathing a bit better. Nearby hills call out to be climbed so that we can see what might be on the other side. We stand on tiptoes, wear high-heeled shoes, we get a ladder—we rig up all kinds of contraptions to raise ourselves a bit higher off the ground. We tip our heads back and cast our eyes to the moon and the stars. It is the space of the unknown, the extraterrestrial. It is both something and nothing, there and not there, open to exploration and closed off from our aggressive, often violent, colonizing gestures. Try as one might, there is no way to own the air. Air circulates everywhere on our planet all the time. It is the most cosmopolitan element. It is in the jar on the kitchen table, in the envelope in the mail, in the sky, in the basement, on the shelf. It is pumping into someone's lungs in a hospital at this very moment to keep them alive. It is pressing down with equal weight on everything on earth. Radically democratic. Barely anything at all. Quasi-visible. The very medium of our every breath.

INTERLUDE 2: EARTH/GARDEN/ SKY

Travelogue: Ed in His Garden

I am sitting on my porch, dysphoric because of the gray sky that has persisted over Santa Barbara for almost a month: "June gloom" has set in and seems to have no end. This is the price one pays in California for living so close to the coast, to which fog banks cling tenaciously. I am literally de-pressed—pressed down by the unyielding sky gray above me. If I shift my gaze from the sky to the garden before me, however, I feel instantly relieved. The flowers are uplifted—and uplifting. Even as they open themselves toward the sky, they pull my gaze back down to earth.

It is as if the earth is asserting itself in the face of the monotony of the weather—asserting itself by its sheer variety, its multitude of forms of growth, its panorama of colors. It presents itself as if in a visual rebuke—a decisive rejection of the unendingly dreary emptiness of the sky. Not that the sky registers the revolt. Part of its very monotony is a refusal to reflect what is happening on the ground, much less to enter into active relationship with it. The sky acts as if unaffected by what is happening on the earth below it; it presents itself as a featureless world without color, without movement, without life. Whereas in the garden before me I witness endless color and curvature, growth and movement, location and grounding.

I suddenly think of the fact that I am breathing with the members of this floral display: We are together breathing in the same air and breathing it out into the shared air above us. We don't do this at the same pace, nor is the air we emit exactly the same chemically, but we are tacitly joining forces, as if to protest the heavy sky above us. It is a contest between the impersonality of the heavy air of fog and the distinctive aerations set forth by me in concert with the plants before me. Together, we form an ecocommunity of equal partners in a shared protest against the oppressive air above. Breathing in and out, we channel air upward, contesting the downward force of the fog. We are bonded in a moment of emancipation, a common assertion of élan vital.[26]

Even the individual places of the plants arrayed before me are diversely rooted in the ground, each being anchored there in a distinctive way. The result is a placial multiplicity as well as a mixture of forms and colors, curvatures and textures. Everywhere I look down and around—everywhere in the patch of earth underlying the garden—I see differentiation and difference. This is in dramatic contrast with the monotony of the sky hovering above in sheer indifferentiation—its Oneness contrasting with the Manyness of the vegetal world below it.

Yet this very same stark contrast I take in all together from a single perch on the porch. Instead of two separate domains—distinguished as they are in terms of variety of shapes and hues—I am presented with a single but bifurcated spectacle. It is a matter of taking in the different, all at once. I do so from a stationary porch on which I sit as the witness of this redoubled scene. The trip I am taking from sky to earth and back again can only emerge if I am myself immobilized or moving slowly enough to take it in all at once—stillness being requisite for this kind of attentive voyage, a voyage without any actual movement. This is a visual trip taken from the distinctive stability of a grounded architectural platform: grounded on the earth and in my body as the source of perception and mobility on earth itself. If there is something recessive about a sky that is nothing but gray, there is something brash about plant life that seems to defy it from below. Plants rise up; even those that grow close to the ground are nonetheless lifted up from it, literally defying gravity by entering into contest with it. But even the most audacious of these plants cannot touch the sky. Despite their welcome uplift, they remain earthbound; they are creatures of the finite garden to which they belong. This garden has the earth for its base. It is rooted there, plant by plant.[27]

But this same earth extends far beyond this home garden; it underlies the street just outside, all the houses on the block, all the trees in the neighborhood (there are none in my garden), the whole part of town spreading as a descending slope between the hills above and the sea below. The extensive massiveness of this underlying earth answers to the pervasiveness of the sky situated far above it. It goes as deep as the sky is high—or so it seems to an earthling such as me, situated as I am between earth and sky. The difference is that the earth seems to well up from below, while the gray sky seems to come down from above—the two meeting in a middle plane such as is provided by the garden scene I am now witnessing. There, the lower edge of the sky meets with the upper edge of the earth in a bi-elemental commixture. The sky acts here as firmament: as something that, though diaphanous, has a being of its own—that which, in its very difference from earth, has a certain substantiality that, even if not tangible, presents a visual presence above that is the counterpart of the earth below. "Firmament" originally meant the vault of the heavens, and this theological origin of the word fits well with the phenomenological account I am here pursuing. It is an integral part of the gigantomachia between earth and sky that is unfolding before me.

Given this larger perspective, we can regard the flora in the garden as something more than sheer decoration.[28] They act as a *fil conducteur* that brings the earth upward into the immediate circumambience of air. But they also bring air downward into the breathing of the very same plants that are so securely rooted in the soil. The upreach of the plants' blossoming is complemented by their downreach into the soil at their base. Oxygen in the air and the breathing of the plants converge in close collusion with each other; oxygen and breathing converge in plant life as a site of circulation between earth and sky. Taken together, the plants constitute a "third thing" that is no thing at all but a bedazzling array of delicately structured living tissue. The array is both a coherent collection of vibrant entities perceived en masse and a set of highly individuated living things: both at once, both together.

This photographic image flattens what presents itself in living perception as three-dimensional: receding in depth from my position on the porch, the garden moves out from my lived body, regarded as the pivot from which I am viewing this scene. This implicit horizontal dimensionality is joined by a vertical axis that goes from the ground under the plants to the sky above. The resulting biaxiality of the floral spectacle—in which one dimension is complemented by another,

FIGURE 2.1 Ed's garden, Santa Barbara, CA.

Source: Edward S. Casey.

each being of equal emphasis—induces in me as viewer a profound sense of calm. The equipoise of the garden scene presents a clear if modest paradigm of a balance of natural forces that presents itself to me as a single, unsolicited spectacle.

I am speaking here of a gift of the plant world to myself as someone who sees and thinks all at once. Even as I savor the floral display, I think its coherence: its fittingness as integral to what I observe as I look out from my seat on the porch. I cannot think of anything more suitable to the circumstance than what I take in before me: The flower garden is the exactly right mediation between me as witness and the larger natural world as it presents itself in a dialectic between earth and sky.

Of course, the scene I have been describing is not only visual but olfactory and auditory: I can smell the plants before me and seem to hear their configuration, especially if the plants are enlivened by birds and insects large enough to emit their own audible sounds. The spectacle is multisensory, and this serves to anchor the plants all the more tenaciously to the earth, finding their place there. Certainly, other such displays may be experienced as equally satisfactory, but all that counts for now is the scene emerging before me, and this gives me food for thought.

Such thought qualifies as thinking in transit. For my stay on the porch is a trip there, short-lived as it is. I am traveling in place, very much as Deleuze and Guattari posit: "Voyage in place; that is the name of all intensities, even if they also develop in extension."[29] In fact, in this episode I am recounting two closely related trips—first, a polysensory voyage among the denizens of the garden I behold, and second, a linguistic voyage that comes to me as I write about the first. Just as we have to expand the scope of what we recognize as "thinking" to include the thinking that emerges spontaneously in an experience such as that just recounted, so the very range of what counts as a trip has to be correspondingly extended. I do not need to be on a transportational vehicle—a bus or train or plane—to take a meaningful trip. In the case before us, I travel with my eyes, ears, and nose, following wherever they lead me: They constitute my (altogether organic) vehicle. And my thinking, far from being abstract and programmatic, occurs concretely and reflects at its own level the polymorphic character of what displays itself before me.

Notably uplifting on the same beclouded day are bird cries. These arise from a group of sparrows that are intent on extracting seeds from a feeder hanging in the garden. They appear to be a family, with younger birds following the lead of the more mature members of their species. Their shrill voices are somewhat muted thanks to their intent actions of scooping up seeds from the portals in the feeder. Higher up, I spot a small group of crows, who arrange themselves imperialistically on telephone wires across the street, as if establishing themselves as the dominant avian residents of the scene. They chase away any smaller birds who may try to land on the same wires, being quite unwilling to share any of their self-established regal territory. Emerging from unseen and unknown places is a chorus of other bird cries whose sources I cannot locate but that I know to be in the vicinity.

What is most striking in this extensive cast of cries is the way that every cry is felt to be rising up from the vegetal base of the plants in the garden before me. It is as if these cries are moving, collectively, toward the sky and taking the life of the garden upward into the atmosphere, animating the sky's otherwise drab presence. From my limited perspective, I do not know just how high these voices go, but I know that these same voices are not discrete projectiles comparable to kites or fireworks. Rather, they are auditory outbursts that trail off into the upper reaches of the garden, receding as they rise upward and ending in a massive silence that imbues the entire scene.

The bird cries rejoin the upward thrust of the flowers in the garden. With both, there is a distinctive and decisive uplift—an arising from the earth that is their common ground. Whether we are talking about the verticality of the stalks of plants or the rising voices of the birds that move in and among the plants, we are confronted with a decisively upward-moving scenario, a local drama of conjoined herbal and avian life. Each current in this verticalizing movement represents a defiance of gravity, a refusal to be tied down to the sedentary solidity of the earth that subtends everything in this scene, including me as a solitary seated observer on the porch.

Just as we spoke earlier of "aqueous thinking" in the case of immersion in water or the womb, we also can speak of "herbal thinking" or "avian thinking" or "earth thinking." Each of these calls for its own detailed description—a task beyond the purview of this book (lest the book give way to infinite "travelogues" in which we try to remember the specificity of every scene of our lives). For now, we merely want to underline that there are not just various modalities of thinking but that these modalities are often keyed to environmental givens, starting with the four elements. We don't think in empty space; we think in the midst of elemental circumstances that enter into the content and rhythm of our thought—just as we also think in quite different circumstances that involve various forms of human interaction, each inducing its own characteristic modality of thought.

For thinking to happen, there is no need to be on a vehicle of public or private transport—to be moving on a ferry over Long Island Sound or driving a car on Highway 80—or actively moving one's body, as when walking in the midst of the Flint Hills or around one's home in Bethany, Connecticut. For Ed's glancing look took him on a voyage into the local world of his garden as it was anchored in the ground before him and enlivened by numerous small birds and butterflies flitting from plant to plant. This was an entire realm of the living that consisted in closely knit layers situated between the inanimate bulk of the earth and a sky enlivened by circumambient air.

This was not just a spectacle; it was a complex, multilayered scene. It was also an occasion for thinking—thinking differently than if such a world was viewed when in a passing car or in a plane overhead. It had its own internal integrity, thanks to its unique configuration of the living (plants and birds and butterflies) and the nonliving (earth and air). And all of this gave rise to the thinking that has been at stake in the pages of this "interlude."

Banal as it is, an ordinary porch can provide the setting for multiple episodes of thinking in transit—all this happening while being in *one place*, that of a space that expands a house outward. Significantly, a porch is a form of open-air architecture that allows people to be inside and outside at the same time, neither fully protected from the elements nor fully exposed. In *Belonging: A Culture of Place*, bell hooks wrote about the importance of the porch as "free floating space, anchored only by the porch swing, and even that was a symbol of potential pleasure."[30] Later, hooks elaborates porch-sitting as "linked to humanization,"[31] as providing a site for relaxed looking at the world and taking part in a community of seeing and being seen. hooks focuses on the porch's humanizing implications for African American families, while Ed's porch relates more closely to the experiences of aging individuals who might have limited mobility or feel otherwise ill-equipped for the bustle of the world. The porch is a quasi-public space that allows one to sit *in public in private*. From the vantage point of the porch, a potentially chaotic or unjust world can be momentarily framed or held at bay. The porch is an integral feature of what hooks elsewhere calls "home-place as resistance."[32]

The porch, the Adirondack chair—these are also vehicles of travel, just as paintings, books, letters, songs, and prayers can be—much as the bed with a magic crystal knob in the 1971 film *Bedknobs and Broomsticks* becomes the vehicle for travel to London and beyond. In Julian Schnabel's 2007 film *The Diving Bell and the Butterfly*, Jean-Dominique Bauby (the leading character, who is hospitalized after a stroke with "locked-in syndrome") lies motionless in his bed, his mind swirling with images and memories that he is incapable of relaying through speech or gesture. Later, pushed out to the beach by his wife and children, he sits in his wheelchair like a statue watching them (through his one functioning eye) frolic in the surf, his mind ablaze. We have a tendency to associate lively thinking with mobility, forgetting that the "vehicles" of thinking can also be bodies with no perceptible movement at all and bodies that move at other registers than those measurable by the eye alone—registers that have more to do with feeling and thinking than moving from one place to another. So much life lives above or below the crude thresholds of ordinary human perception and movement. The garden at Ed's feet pulsating with life, the air above him, the birds on the wire.

The American artist Martin Puryear described gardens as "gratuitous places."[33] He meant this in a salutary manner, as gardens provide opportunities for life to overflow traditional boundaries, providing sites of respite and transformational growth. The excess of color, scent, texture, and life in the garden (when blooming) reminds us that we are immersed in a sensible world that cannot be easily delineated into four elements (just as our travelogues serve as reminders that our attempts at ordering thinking in transit are only provisional). Water runs into air, and air rushes toward the earth. Everything verges on everything else, a tangle of sounds and bodies, an overload of detail. From immersion in perception we reach for things with our bodies and our minds. We bring them close by touching. A violet or leaf of sage pulled from the garden, a *this* with a particular texture, smell, color, and weight. Barely anything. Barely more than the weight of a moth yet dense and laden with meaning.

Travelogue: Megan in the Garden

It is mid-November. We've had a first hard frost. Violet and I spent a morning cutting raspberry bushes down to the ground and pulling up sunflower and cucumber plants from their roots. I am pushing the blunt ends of garlic into a new bed, a little late I'm afraid. I have an old wooden board to help me mark the holes in straight lines. The air is tinged with ice. The leaves have piled in the corners and along the outer edges of the raised vegetable beds like rumpled quilts. I gather them up and toss them on the newly hoed dirt, raking them out edge to edge. Everything has quieted down except for the mint. I dig up the dahlia tubers and carefully separate them and lay them in a bucket with some potting soil to sleep in the garage through the winter. Birds chatter and dive for the red berries on a dogwood tree. The garden looks tidy and resolute. Garden beds: sites of so much commotion in one season and solemn as graves in another.

3

EARTH

Use your head, can't you, use your head, you're on earth, there's no cure for that.
— Samuel Beckett, *Endgame*

Of Empedocles's four classical elements (or roots: *rhizomata*), earth is seemingly the only sedentary one. Water, air, and fire all exhibit visible or sensible motion. Even when a lake is utterly flat, one sees movement on the surface. Even when the air is thick and still, a wave of the hand creates a breeze. Returning to the metaphor of smooth and striated from Deleuze and Guattari, we might say that earth is the most striatable of all the elements: Its very solidity solicits mapping into regular metric units.

Of course, earth is not as solid or motionless as it seems, and perhaps it only appears that way to a human consciousness ill-equipped to grasp motion in a slower, more ancient temporal register. In addition to the planet turning on its axis and orbiting its star, the earth beneath our feet is also moving all the time, as we are sometimes reminded in dramatic form by earthquakes, sinkholes, floods, or landslides. Now, in our time of climate change, earth seems accelerated in entirely new ways. Formerly inhabitable, solid, striated places are giving way to the destructive, homogenizing effects of drought and fire. Formerly uninhabitable, solid, smooth places like frozen tundra, ice shelves, and glaciers are melting and collapsing, sometimes disappearing into the sea. In all such cases, what was once solid transforms into something else, leaving the creatures who lived in those places suddenly without a home.

In many ways, earth is the most robust of the elements, and yet we are facing the reality that earth is also the most vulnerable to change. Centuries of pollution, industrialized farming, deforestation, exploitation of water resources, drilling for oil, and other human interventions have eroded soils and upset the balance of our ecosystems. This is a planetary problem that affects every aspect of life, but in recent years human beings and other animals are feeling the effects of climate change primarily in the shrinking of livable land mass across the globe (disproportionally for nonhuman animals and for impoverished nations whose peoples have few resources to deal with the effects or to move elsewhere). What was once livable terrain is now too hot, dry, melted, flooded, or depleted to sustain life as it had before. As earth changes, living creatures move—often desperately—in search of solid ground.

Humans have devised innumerable means of traversing the earth, including wheeled vehicles (bicycles, wheelbarrows, wagons, skateboards, roller skates, wheelchairs, cars, trucks, tanks, trains), ambulatory practices (crawling, walking, running, skipping), and overland carriages (stretchers, piggyback rides, and transportation by horse, mule, or other human or nonhuman animals). Wheels roll over the ground and expedite movement across distance. Animals carry each other on their backs, in pouches, high on shoulders, in their mouths, or in their arms. The earth is amenable to being crossed in these myriad modes, providing (usually) enough resistance and solidity to withstand the weight of whatever is pushing against it. Things can get tricky in unusually steep, sandy, muddy, rocky, hot, dense, cold, or wet terrain. But, as an element, earth seems fundamentally connected to the possibility for traversal, giving support from below to what moves over its surface.[1]

We human beings are essentially terrestrial. We all live on the planet Earth, but we are also *of* the earth—"earthlings"—inhabiting the sites where we make our homes and conduct most of our lives. True, some live at sea, and a very few (astronauts) temporarily make their home in space, but most of us live on some piece of (seemingly) solid ground. When early American pioneers sought to settle in the West, they were seeking terra firma on which they could live and farm, as surely was the case with those ancestors of Ed's who settled in Kansas when it was still considered a "territory": a landed place considered to be open to exploration and exploitation, without regard to Native American populations who had lived there for millennia.

Travelogue: Ed in Kansas

Growing up in Topeka, Kansas, I took several formative trips out into the local landscape while in my boyhood.[2] One of these consisted in driving outside the city limits of town into a countryside that I experienced as unruly or "wild" compared to the well-groomed lawns of most of the houses inside city limits, including that of my own family. At a certain age, I had been charged with keeping this family lawn free of foreign presences such as dandelions, the scourge of Topeka. The aim was to have one entirely regular, monochromatic sweep of bluegrass, undisturbed by anything that could be considered a weed.

Perhaps because of my father's concern with the careful cultivation of lawns—part of his aspiring to upper-middle-class status as a lawyer in Topeka—I found myself drawn to venture outside city limits, going out there alone on my bicycle in early adolescence. Once there, I felt I could find my freedom. Earlier still, an art class I had joined at age nine or ten visited the same area, seeking views of the surrounding countryside that were worthy subjects of painting. This was already a form of liberation, at once personal, cultural, and visual. The uncultivated fields with their distant vistas presented a landscape that had a powerful allure. I was fascinated with how this rural scene might be captured in watercolor painting—initiating a lifelong passion for painting in this medium (as described in interlude 3).

When I was old enough to drive a car out into this wild world some years later, I found myself entranced by the same countryside west of town that had drawn me there earlier. Out there, one could do things frowned upon in a middle-class, Midwestern city, such as making out with girlfriends, inspired by contraband liquor I had carefully stored in a box hidden in a hollow. Such behavior had its own component of wildness and seemed called for by the uncultivated land, on which there were not even farms in those days—just open acreage with a few dilapidated fences that served as property markers. Perhaps this land had been pastureland fifty years ago, and further back the Kaw people had settled out there. But I arrived too late for these earlier worlds. For myself, I confronted a place made for wildlife—as wild as life could be for a teenage boy who found middle-class practices and values unduly constraining. (My parents, alarmed at my rebellious behavior, feared I would become a "bohemian" and sent me away to a quasi-military private school in North Carolina for three closely supervised years of high school.)

In this early phase of my Kansas life, the earth outside city limits presented itself as a place for what I took to be "free" action and movement, whether this was in the form of painting or of adolescent acting-out. The rough surface of its uncultivated fields stood in stark contrast with the cultivated front lawn of my family home and was powerfully alluring, suggesting as it did a way of life that was liberated in comparison with life at home. No wonder I sought to go outside city limits whenever I could manage to do so—not unlike bell hooks, who prized the wild hills of Kentucky in contrast with city life, as she recounts in her autobiographical memoir. In the hills she found a hillbilly culture tied to the land and nature that was somehow inoculated against the racism and class distinctions she found elsewhere.[3]

How very different was another sense of earth that I experienced years later in the Flint Hills many miles west of Topeka! Now the attraction was not toward the uncultivated—the rough and ready allure of the raw earth. Rather, the allure was based on my knowing that two ancient worlds had occupied the Flint Hills many years ago. One was in the form of an inland sea that had covered the entire Middle West, including all of Kansas, hundreds of millions of years ago. Signs of the presence of this sea were evident in the fossils unearthed by the cutting through hills to make way for I-70 in the early 1950s. I remember begging my father to stop by the roadside as we were driving to a family event in Abilene, one hundred miles west of Topeka. I collected the exposed sea fossils, which formed a prized part of my burgeoning rock collection. Here a raw edge cut into the earth yielded otherwise invisible remnants of a much earlier era in the geohistory of the Middle West.

With the disappearance of the inland sea many centuries later, the same region became hills and valleys populated by grasslands that attracted many thousands of bison, who roamed there freely, making it their proper home, converting it into a very different kind of place. In the late 1990s, I took a hike in the Flint Hills near Manhattan, Kansas. I didn't spot any buffalos, but the ground was mostly smooth; there was little evidence of the kind of rough countryside I had known outside Topeka, and the overall effect was that of a mellow landscape—of a portion of earth that, once at the bottom of a vast inland sea, had become a world of smooth surfaces, suitable for the grazing of bison as well as cattle and for those humans who wished to live peacefully in their midst. It was deeply satisfying to me to walk calmly in the Flint Hills—long after my rather tempestuous early adolescent engagement in the rugged countryside near Topeka. Decades older, I was seeking something more serene.

Such contrastive experiences both happened in a single stretch of earth—central/eastern Kansas—that was picayune compared to the entire earth's surface. They demonstrated that the earth is not some monolithic solid block but features—at and as its very surface—considerable differences that literally undergird highly diverse forms of animal and human life spent in that vicinity of the Middle West. They also show that the earth itself can have more smooth and less smooth areas. "Smooth" here does not mean literally even or level but refers to a way of being spatial by containment. Such volumetric space resists striation or metric determination as introduced by humans. Life on earth manifests an intensive dialectic between these two ways of being spatial.

Each phase in my Kansas life was a phase in transit and brought with it very different patterns of thought—whether those of adolescent turbulence or of a comparative calmness in later years. Two stretches of the same portion of the earth's surface—no more than seventy miles apart—were very different as they figured in the content and tenor of the experiences I had when in their presence. In the one case, I was resonating with something I experienced as uncultivated—literally, outside of (middle-class) civilization—a lack of cultivation that answered to the existential uncertainty of my life at the time. In the other, I entered into a calm reflectiveness that befit my advancing age. Whereas there was no clear path in the fields just outside Topeka, in the Flint Hills I was guided by a trail that directed me gently through an open landscape. These were two very different places of transition—on the land and in my life.

Very much contributing to the difference to which I here point was the texture of the land in the two cases: The roughness in the former instance meant that one had to make one's own way through demanding terrain—in a geographic mimesis with what was a very demanding period in my own life in the midst of many conflicting challenges. In contrast, the comparative tranquility of the Flint Hills footpath quite literally showed a way to move without obstruction of any significant sort. Walking along it was like going with the flow—the flow of hills whose ancient origins had led to their present smoothness of shape and contour. Despite these manifest differences in experiential texture, in each case the land took the lead. I kept step with it, following its allure, however diversely challenging or welcoming this may have been.

Each of the settings I have just recounted brings with it its own pattern of thinking. In the first case, my thinking was animated with a sense of discovery that was always looking forward, anticipating what might be coming next: not just in synch with a continuously changing terrain but at the edge of itself, as if it were a step ahead of itself. It was a case of peri-thinking: thinking on the periphery, actively anticipating what was coming next. In the case of the hills in central Kansas, my thinking was reassured and kept pace with my walking. It did not need to move ahead of itself but was satisfied with where it was: relaxed and reassured, smooth. In both cases, it was as if my thinking was mimetic with the landscape; its contour reflected that of the place I was in. The profile of my thinking derived from the shape of the landscape I had entered. This thinking was not necessarily about the landscape, but it was configured with it, forming what Plato labeled an "indefinite dyad" of same and other.

We travel over Earth at various distances from its outer surface: high up in an airplane or air balloon; higher still in a vessel to the moon or beyond; lower and closer to earth when we're on a Ferris wheel; and finally right down on its surface, over its lands or across its waters, when we are walking or gliding on it. (Ultimately, we find ourselves six feet under, in the earth, or scattered as ashes with the earth's dust.) In all these cases, the perception of Earth varies significantly: It is seen as a single planet from the moon, but only a finite area is visible when we are closer to it. These differences in perceived areas of Earth are not trivial, not just because of differences in detailed content (including seen and felt texture) but with respect to how we regard the planet we inhabit in terms of mobility and inhabitability. Such differences give scale to the perceived size of Earth, as well as its comparative massiveness, and thus to its sheer presence in our experience.

Travelogue: Ed in New York City

In New York City, where I live during my teaching semesters, I rent an apartment on the twentieth floor. From the window in the room I use as my study, I look over much of Harlem all the way to the George Washington Bridge to the northwest and to the RFK bridge in the northeast. The extensive overlook contrasts sharply with what I see from my living space for the remainder of the year—a suburban house in Santa Barbara. Looking out from its windows, one sees the garden that surrounds the house at ground level. In California, most everything is at the level of the earth, including the houses located on it; one looks out onto the surrounding earth—an earth that subtends the garden and the house alike. In my New York home, one sees only the barest glimpses of the ground—for example, at the edges of the sidewalks and the streets just below the apartment building, as well as a corner of Central Park. I look out over the city seeing only a diminutive presence of the underlying earth, which is mostly inferred rather than directly perceived.

This difference is not trivial when it comes to thinking in transit. In the case of the New York apartment, I am riding high, as it were, as if floating over a vast cityscape. In the house in Santa Barbara, I am literally grounded, stationed directly on the earth's surface, positioned squarely there rather than floating twenty stories above it. In the West Coast case, I sustain a more intimate tie with the earth where I am directly situated. I am oriented toward what I can or cannot do in this local scene: attend to the flowers in the garden, get into the car to go to the grocery store, pick up the mail from my mailbox in the street. In New York, there is no tending of any garden; the grocery store is a remote space to which I must walk a considerable distance, and mail appears in a box amid hundreds of others in the lobby of the building where I live. It is as if I am a phantomic presence in a building that is itself something of a phantom: "unreal" in its immensity, especially in comparison with the modest single structure of my home in Santa Barbara, whose proportions are tailored to finite human heights and habits.

In New York, I derive a special pleasure in writing while taking in the cityscape spread out before me. It is as if this literal "over-view" adds a dimension to my thinking and writing: a certain depth and outreach not readily available when writing closer to the ground. I think of this as providing the scene for a voyage—a voyage in the realm of ideas, those that are relevant to the topic I am writing about. Key here is that I do not have my feet on the ground but am suspended somewhere high above it—literally deterritorialized.

To be clear: My claim is not that I necessarily have better ideas when writing twenty stories above ground. Rather, it is that the conditions for writing—and thus for thinking—are felt to be significantly facilitated. As a very visually oriented person, I take a special pleasure in being able to look out—far out onto a major part of a major city—with the result that writing when up there benefits from a form of mental expansiveness that is less often achieved when writing on the ground floor of my California house—where I am continually reminded of certain practicalities that inhere in that location: going to the gym or the bank, which are situated on the same stretch of earth as is the house and are reached by an easy car ride. From the house, I look straight onto the street where I will take a walk later in the day. In this setting, my links to the world of ongoing errands are manifold and overt, whereas from high up in the building in New York I can more easily undertake a journey of ideas and thoughts that are largely independent of the practicalities predominantly present in the Santa Barbara scene. Rather than being "removed" and "out of it," as one might expect being in such an elevated position might entail, I get more fully into whatever I am thinking and writing about.

The reader may notice the affinities and differences between the elevated situation just described and that which Megan has described about her writing when on the ferry from Bridgeport to Port Jefferson (in chapter 1). To be out on the water of Long Island Sound, detached from either shore, gives her the space and the time for concentrated composition in words. In the hull of the ferry, she finds herself just above sea level. There, she is released from practical tasks, as is Ed when high up in the building located at 110th Street and Central Park West. While Megan's writing routine is tied to lateral transit across water and Ed's to vertical, aerial views in the city, in both cases the release from the ground is momentary. Ed can take the elevator to the ground floor of his building when he needs to do errands in the neighborhood, and Megan will soon dock at Port Jefferson, near to where she will be teaching on the grounds of the Stony Brook University campus. It is as if the earth asserts or reasserts itself in moments of practical need, giving support and stability to activities that require a solid grounding. In contrast, being above or below ground level—in a tall building, on a boat—offers a basis for making a voyage into the realm of ideas. In both cases, different as they are, we witness thinking in transit.

Our point is not at all that creative thinking is precluded when writing at earth level: William James found railroads and John Dewey buses to be propitious places for their writing, in contrast with others who favor the high perch. But we here point to situations that share with such auspicious places, despite their manifest differences, an especially favorable basis for having ideas and pursuing them in writing. What matters is being in a place where thinking and writing are supported by the character of the place itself, whether this be above or below ground—or on the ground, as with much public transportation. "Place" is not here to be confused with mere *position*; it includes a full sense of *setting* that draws out new thinking. For Megan, the setting is often public and might include sipping tea or making a few sketches as she sets about writing; for Ed, it often means looking out over Harlem from his apartment with a cup of coffee in his hand.

No such settings guarantee that the ideas emerging from such propitious places will be innovative, but they do provide circumstances where they are more likely to occur. All of the settings singled out in this book—each with its distinctive relationship with the earth—serve as places-of-transition. Of course, every place is in some sense or another in transition. Everything is moving and changing all the time. But certain places more fully enable the thinking-in-transit we are exploring, the lived body being carried out of its habitual environment and suspended for a time somewhere else. Such transitional places provoke crafty, sometimes scrappy, methods of capturing thought, and they furnish promising circumstances for the emergence of innovative ideas; ideas that might not have occurred to us otherwise.[4] Such ideas qualify as what D. W. Winnicott terms "transitional objects" that favor creativity of thought or action.[5] These ideas can be said to emerge more favorably in *transitional places*— places where our thinking moves more freely. This does not mean that such ideas are un-grounded, sheerly "flighty"; they do have their own justification and logic. Yet these ideas emerge in circumstances where we are not bogged down by practical duties—beleaguered in practical settings—but find ourselves momentarily freed to think new thoughts.

Thinking in transit in the various ways just outlined allows us to *think otherwise*. Vessels or structures that hold or carry us facilitate thinking by removing us—if only temporarily—from domestic and practical demands that otherwise might burden the field of thought (housework, yard work). We are suspended momentarily from the routines of our lives when we think in transit, even as our commutes may be dictated and demanded by our lives and jobs. This is not to deny that being at home or at ground level may also offer unique opportunities of their own. We have seen two of these earlier: The rough countryside just outside Topeka brought with it an opportunity for Ed to try out an alternative form of life. Its unevenness mirrored, and solicited, his own draw to a lifestyle that was not dictated by middle-class values—to biodiversity instead of manicured lawns, giving way later to a buzzing garden. In contrast, the grasslands of the Flint Hills provided a comparatively untroubled experience when he was taking a walk along one of its established paths. In both cases, he was taken up by what the earth presented on its surface, indeed *as* its surface in two of its very different configurations.

The larger truth here is that the character of the place in which one is located is not indifferent to the kind of activity one is able to undertake in that place.[6] On the contrary, it has a great deal to do with it. By this we do not mean that there is any one-to-one correlation between a given place and what one chooses to do in that place (how one can act, who one can be). Nor do we assume a universalizing view of human nature. But there are strong proclivities that emerge in propitious settings such as writing in the eagle's nest of a high-rise apartment or skimming over the surface of Long Island Sound. One can very well do other things in such locations, including troubled rumination or serene meditation. But it remains that certain places favor creative thinking in transit, and it is these we seek to specify in this book even as we concede that writing in those places calls for the presence of supportive surfaces on which the writing occurs and a comparatively untroubled mind on the part of whoever writes.

Such placements as have been here invoked, whether on the land or at sea, have everything to do with the character and fate of thinking in transit—whose alternative formulation could well be *thinking in place*. For we transit *between places*: places-of-origin as well as places-as-destinations. These places have everything to do not just with literal physical activities, like walking or typing on a computer, but with the modality and materiality of our thought while in a given place: quietly expansive in the case of the rolling Flint Hills, feverishly intense in the uneven terrain outside the Topeka city limits, densely engaging in the hull of a ferry, endlessly expansive when looking far out over New York. John Dewey emphasizes the interaction of the "live creature" with its environment and the degree to which our thinking is shaped and permeated by the environments in which we develop.[7] Transit includes a change of environment and the coincident augmentation of habitual modes of embodiment and thought. Being in transit or in transitional situations does not guarantee the kind of thinking on which philosophical writing thrives, but it is conducive to it and to other kinds of adventuresome thinking that innovates rather than repeats. It is a matter of a specific *place-proclivity* laying the ground for thinking in transit, setting the stage for it, as it were.

Travelogue: Megan on First Steps

My first steps were taken in Canton, New York, but my childhood was spent first in the city of Brussels, Belgium, and then in Goshen, Connecticut (population 1,700)—the same small town where my dad grew up on a dairy farm. I have many memories of Canton and Brussels, but Goshen, where I lived from age six to eighteen, is what I think of as home. My dad took over his father's farm, converting it to organic vegetables. We lived in a house my dad built on a piece of land adjacent to the farm and next door to my uncle's house. A narrow path led from the backyard over the swampy banks of a beaver pond and through the woods to the fields and farmland and the old brick house where my grandma, grandpa, and their dogs, Simba and Pepper, lived.

"Earth," insofar as I thought about the term at all, must have been conjoined with that pathway, the fields, and the woods where my sister and brother and I played. Earth was green and fragrant in the summer, white and frigid in the winter. In between, we waded through swampy waters and climbed crabapple trees. We ran on dirt roads and rode bikes on Route 63 up and down hills that seemed too steep to climb. We used a sheet pan to look for gold in the stream and dug up old bottles from the banks. Earth was all this conjoined in a hyphenated, never-ending season of buttercups-beestings-nettles-mud-snow-ice-sap-buds-moles-mice-grass-sky.

Unlike Ed, I never ventured very far beyond my own house to discover what was on the other side of the hills or beyond the stream that divided my grandparents' property from something else (more stream, woods, rocks, and trees as far as the eye could see). There were a few neighbors along the main road, but none (except my uncle) that had kids our age or that we knew well enough to visit. I dreamed of a neighborhood with matching rows of neat houses, immaculate lawns, and gaggles of kids trick-or-treating or running a lemonade stand. But I also loved the solitude of the woods and the slightly creepy, wild feeling of being alone in the middle of nowhere. The ground went from rugged to smooth in the transition from the dirt path to my grandparents' open field, where you could roll down the hill in the tall grass or pretend to be Laura Ingalls Wilder running, as Melissa Gilbert did in the opening credits of the *Little House on the Prairie* TV show.

I do have some distinctive memories of earth in other guises. Mostly these are based in experiences of travel or exploration in other locales—yearly drives to Wisconsin to visit my maternal grandparents and the long, unbelievable stretches of flat land I'd see from the car window. A trip to North Dakota where I stood among acres of sunflowers with their heads dropped beneath a brewing storm and where I wandered on mud flats of caked, cracked, brown earth that looked like dinosaur skin. Jagged cliffs on the Isle of Skye. Reddish mountains and one sheer expanse of pristine ice in the Tetons of Wyoming, scrubby pines and loose shale in the White Mountains of New Hampshire. Pebbled beaches and wild thyme in Cadaqués.

The earth, it seems, has infinite faces. Blacktop, concrete, clay, dirt, pine-needled, mushroomed, parched, stony, sandy, mossy, wet, clear, cluttered. No wonder people put a bit of dirt in a jar when they are forced to leave their homes.[8] Or dig into the earth until, reaching a pocket of clay, they can taste it.[9] Earth is literally one's own ground. But try as you might, you can't take it with you. The smell, the feel, the texture, and color. No patch of it will ever match the first patch you came to know. The Earth as a planet is a blue and green sphere hanging in space, but, as it enters our lives, earth is the structured and structuring sedimentation that undergirds our every step. It contributes to a sense of belonging to a place in which you know your way around—a place in which the dirt is familiar.

As we consider modes of transit across the face of the earth, the dominant direction is lateral. Dig too deep and you eventually hit water. Rise too high, and you are in the air. Earth coincides with the relatively narrow band of inhabitable terrain between extremes.

Though walking is not an activity shared by all human beings, it is a widely acquired skill that allows many to move unencumbered over the face of the earth. Some additional expertise is required for running, jumping, and climbing—though many master these at a young age as well. The body can carry itself across the earth, or it can be carried. Life often consists of a combination of these possibilities, often with more carriage in infancy and old age, as well as during episodes of illness or injury. In later years, walking may become problematic, and recourse to a walker or a cane might become necessary or all but irresistible.[10]

The earth represents the place of our dominant movement and thinking as terrestrial beings, as well as our final resting place as mortal beings. We return to the earth, ashes to ashes, dust to dust. Earth, as an element, is tied to the material realities of being bipedal creatures who roam, farm, and build, as well as to the spiritual realities of being creatures who long for homeland, seek common ground, and need sure footing.

"Come back down to earth." Someone might say it to a child daydreaming or to someone expressing overly ambitious hopes or dreams. We call on people to return to earth as if calling them to return to reality. *Come back.* The earth reminds us of stability and solidity. The earth is where seeds are planted and crops emerge, where leaves gather in the fall to rot and decompose, where worms wriggle and rocks sleep. It's where kids dig with shovels or their bare hands, where we bury our loved ones, where we pitch a tent. Gritty, dirty, rough—the earth represents resistance as well as gravity. It's the site of prosaic, directly referential utterance that Wittgenstein associated with building and "primitive" language games: "'block.' 'pillar.' 'slab.' beam.' A calls them out; B brings the stone which he has learnt to bring at such-and-such a call."[11] Of all the elements, the earth is the one most likely to lend itself to basic, practical words and grounded forms of thinking that are rooted or heavy as a stone.

WALKING

As swimming is the most basic human movement relative to the water, walking is often the elemental movement coincident with the earth. Babies usually crawl or scoot before taking any steps, but most find their way to a standing position between the ages of one and two, remaining upright and beginning to learn to stride with greater balance and coordination. In the evolution of the human individual, the order of elemental hierarchy goes from water to air to earth, following the emergence of human life from its aquatic environment, its immediate need for breath, and then its later reliance—lying down, then perhaps scooting or crawling, and eventually walking—on the stability of the earth. Earth, thereby, represents a developmental milestone for human beings, who acclimate to the dry land and begin to roam.

The kind of movement most closely aligned with the earth is walking. One foot in front of the other. Most of us who walk have forgotten how we learned to do it—what it involved in terms of coordination and attention. Only in spending time with toddlers or those uncertain or unstable on their feet are we reminded of how precarious it is to move on two feet. The whole of your body balances on one point, weight shifting from side to side. Every step entails a leap of faith in the support of one leg and then the other. Sometimes this faith is betrayed, and we fall.

Consider what happens in ordinary walking. In taking a walk, we carry our own body weight forward, moving from point A to point B. But we do so even as the thinking happening while walking occurs in another dimension, at another level. As Gary Snyder has put it, "Walking is the exact balance of spirit and humility"—where the root of "humility" is *humus*, ground.[12] We find ourselves engaging both in walking on the earth and thinking on our own—participating in both at once, despite their manifest differences. For we think as we walk. This is so despite the manifest difference between the "spiritual" activity of thinking and the physicality of walking on earth with one's own lived body. It is a matter of thinking in transit, but not now as supported by any passenger vehicle such as a plane or boat. Happening here is a combination of a lived and moving body with the thinking that accompanies this body but that has its own momentary autonomy.

Walking elongates the body from a crouched or folded position relative to the ground. When you walk ably, you carry your head into the air like a balloon. You get up off the floor, freeing your palms and knees from contact, freeing your hands to carry things while you move. And you go faster, covering more ground in a single step than you could ever cover by slithering or crawling along. Now you can step over things (drastically expanding the possibilities for a clean escape). You can move laterally, forward, or backward, with a simple tap of your toe. Any of these movements engenders not just progress on the ground but new views of the earth you traverse.

Historically, walking is the preferred motion associated with philosophical thinking. Since ancient times, and certainly with Aristotle's peripatetic school, walking has been associated with serious thinking. Kant, Rousseau, Emerson, Thoreau, James—they all walked. But that has also led to a problematic identification of walking with thinking, just as Descartes's sedentary posture and sickly demeanor lent us an image—an archetype—of the philosopher as male, pale, and confined to a chair in which he thinks philosophical thoughts. For these reasons, even though we celebrate walking as a form of movement that can activate and breathe new life into thinking (especially in an age of increasingly sedentary, screen-based habits), we must challenge the association of normative self-motion and ambulatory bodies with thought. Walking includes being taken for a walk—carried as a small child might be in a sling or perched atop shoulders. It includes being wheeled or helped across terrain—or wheeling oneself.[13] The crucial thing about walking is not the act of two symmetrical legs moving in tandem but the pace, the intention, the forward momentum or back and forth rhythm of *going*. Such movement can happen in many guises and under a surprising array of conditions. As Frédéric Gros writes, "When you are walking nothing really moves: it is rather that presence is slowly established in the body."[14]

Sadly, modern stereotypes of education and scholarship have bred habits that, for many, are isolating and sedentary. Small children in developed countries sit confined to their desks in front of Chromebooks. Graduate students and professors sit for hours in seminars or in chilly hotel conference rooms for days at a time. Many of us too often sit in front of the television, the computer, or a phone. What if we revived the ancient model of indoor/outdoor schools built for collective walking and creative collaboration, akin to walking meditation? What if movement (considered pluralistically and not reduced to the Aristotelian romance of able-bodied walking) and thinking *are* tied? Ferris Jabr notes the psychophysical benefits of walking, writing: "Walking on a regular basis ... promotes new connections between brain cells, staves off the usual withering of brain tissue that comes with age, increases the volume of the hippocampus ... and elevates levels of molecules that both stimulate the growth of new neurons and transmit messages between them."[15] As Rebecca Solnit reminds us, "I sat down one spring day to write about walking and stood up again, because a desk is no place to think on the large scale."[16]

Lateral movement across the earth's surface facilitates a kind of thinking that is also laterally expansive. The rhythm of thought changes when one's body is in motion. When the motion is derived from your own power—and this might apply equally to walking and to using crutches or a manually powered wheelchair —something changes in the perceived balance between mind and body. This is not to suggest a stark dualism as Descartes described it (the body an extended, physical substance and the mind as a nonextensive, mental substance). But when sedentary (and not in a condition of pain), one's body can recede from freely conscious thought to a greater degree than it can when one is engaged in self-generated movement.[17] This means that walking and other forms of movement on the earth bring the body back to mind.

Moving forward many centuries after Aristotle, Thoreau's posthumously published "Walking" (which appeared in the *Atlantic Monthly* in June 1862, just after his death) is a telling case of moving forward with one's own body even as one also pursues what surely seems to be an independent course of thinking. Thoreau makes a case for "the art of Walking" and the "genius of *sauntering*," telling us at the beginning: "I think that I cannot preserve my health and spirits, unless I spend four hours a day at least—and it is commonly more than that—sauntering through the woods and over the hills and fields, absolutely free from all worldly engagements."[18] Thoreau, like his idol Emerson, envisions walking as something elemental, tied more to the spirit of exploration than to the physical act of traversing a given landscape. It was Emerson who (long before Deleuze and Guattari championed the intensity of traveling in place) called travel a "fool's paradise."[19] To walk is to leave civilization behind and to reconnect with something beyond, meandering like a stream. For Thoreau, sauntering is also an act of "civil disobedience," an active resistance to a government that would have its citizens reliably stationary and employed in some more economically useful pursuit. Thoreau implores people to break out of their staid habits, even as he insists that "it requires a direct dispensation from Heaven to become a walker. You must be born into the family of Walkers."[20]

Both admirable and infuriating in his self-certainty and contrived experiments, Thoreau walked to think, to learn, and to commune with the wild world. Walking was his religion, and he was its preacher. The sense of walking as a mystical practice of a chosen few coincides with medieval accounts of pilgrimages and wandering saints. Few have the leisure to saunter for hours a day at will (fewer women than men, fewer people in poverty, fewer who, because of race or other visible identities, are targeted for surveillance). Thoreau set up his own life to enable it, living spare and lean, though philosophy is rife with similar accounts from Rousseau, Nietzsche, and others who not only needed movement and fresh air to think but had the means to ramble aimlessly for hours or days on end. All of them testify to an action of thinking while being engaged in a form of transit not supported by public transport but carried out by one's own bodily movements. Thinking certainly moves, but it moves very differently from the way the body moves—even if it depends on the body's being *able to move itself.* Thoreau could saunter in any direction, but he relies on what his body tells him when it stops twirling—*west* toward Oregon and the Pacific Ocean, into what he considers "*the future.*" Though he was known for his opposition to slavery and the Mexican-American War, his own sense of exceptionalism, divinity, and freedom while walking ("all good things are wild and free") reflects the "Manifest Destiny" of a man a who feels at home in a new land he imperialistically describes as "so fertile and so rich and varied in its production, and at the same time, so inhabitable by the European."[21] What began as sauntering becomes striding, strident. In *Walking*, Thoreau presents ambulation as if his body knows where he should go on earth, picking up clues from its seemingly random movement, yet he remained entangled in a violent history of Manifest Destiny that saw the earth as land to be possessed and its native inhabitants as obstacles to be removed.

Travelogue: Megan on Walking in the Pandemic

When I think of walking, I think of all the long walks in the woods my husband and I took with our two daughters and our dog during the early days of the coronavirus pandemic. Like almost everyone else we knew with small children, walking became the dominant activity of our lives—a way to pass time, to be together, and to be safely outdoors. We must have walked every trail in the state, going at the pace of our younger daughter and stopping often to collect rocks. Often I would cajole my daughters onward or up a steep incline by telling them stories I made up about a naughty little sister. Sometimes we pretended to be other people entirely, role-playing the whole way up and down a mountain. The walks were not meditative retreats like those described by Rousseau in his *Reveries of the Solitary Walker*. They were functional, sometimes laborious, jaunts. But they were also a way of reminding ourselves that, despite the uncertainty and widespread fear around us, we could keep moving at our own initiative and our own pace.

Walk—go out. It seems so simple, yet it is such an amazing gift to be able to open a door and emerge into the wider world. You can leave your room. You can get up. William James reminds us of the real difficulty of that first step (the one that gets you out of bed). It's not always easy or possible. But if one can muster the energy to get up, if the body and spirit cooperate, then you're already on the way out, and your mind will follow your body as ducklings fall into line behind their mother—intrepid and gaining courage in their forward momentum.

Today, many people across the globe are walking to stay alive. They are fleeing war, famine, violence, fire, floods, and earthquakes. They have taken with them whatever they can carry. They don't know where they are going. They travel in the harshest conditions with little food or water, sometimes in the dead of night. In conditions of forced migration, walking takes on new urgency and a different valence. These are not walks of leisure—healthy-minded doses of fresh air and sunshine so easily prescribed by philosophical walkers of old. Such traditional walks are not arduous but chosen, as with climbs in the mountains in search of the sublime. Instead, walking can become a tortuous, unyielding ordeal. If only one could sit. If only there was a place to rest. Walking includes those in forced marches, those unable to stop, and the eclipse of thinking by the instinct to survive at any cost, so that all one can think about is food, water, shelter, sleep. Unlike those in military marches—where a regulated movement is required—those who walk under duress have to adapt themselves, often immediately, to the earth as it presents itself in open fields or dense jungles. Their way is a continual struggle with the rigors that earth presents, more often than not directly provoked by human warfare, neglect, or campaigns of displacement.

RUNNING

When we move from walking to running, we change several registers at once. Speed increases, but there is also an intensification of breath and movement, arms swinging, feet hitting the ground with force and sending a jolt through the knees and torso. Sometimes a person runs for sport or for fun, playing tag, chasing, or just to feel fast. Other times they run out of fear or panic, thrown into motion in an effort to flee. In those cases, running can overtake a body in which the entire nervous system seems suddenly sent into overdrive. The heart beats in your throat, and a rush of adrenaline sends you flying.

When toddlers discover they can run, they are often delighted in how fast they can escape the grasp of a grownup, darting here and there, giggling as they go. Running seems related to freedom and the possibility of running away, just as the dish ran away with the spoon. Eloping, starting over, setting off into uncharted territory—these are all related to the sense of running as a form of rebellion and earthbound flight. In many instances, the effort of running eclipses the ability to think with any order or clarity. Catching your breath becomes the dominant concern, and it's all you can do to keep going. But in some cases, running itself becomes a form of meditative journey in which the rhythm of repetitive movement facilitates a unique form of thinking. Haruki Murakami explains, "At thirty-six miles per week, I cover 156 miles every month, which is my standard for serious running." He continues, "I run in a void. Or maybe I should put the other way: I run in order to acquire a void."[22]

Not everyone is a runner—though it is only a matter of practice. Megan started to run at a young age, growing up in a household where running was the proposed solution to almost everything. Upset? Go for a run. In trouble? Go for a run. Celebrating something? Go for a run. Lonely, bored, depressed, antsy, tired, frustrated? Go for a run.

Travelogue: Megan on Running

Initially I did not like running. It made me hot and out of breath, and it felt terrible on hills. I set off in my sneakers and shorts and huffed my way along the road. I was nervous and afraid of encountering a wild dog or some other hostile creature. I worried about running too far out and being unable to make it home. But over time, running became a central part of my life. When I moved to New York City after college, I ran each evening the eight miles from my job in an art gallery on Fifty-Sixth Street in Manhattan to my apartment in Clinton Hill, Brooklyn—crossing the Brooklyn Bridge at sunset or in the dark. The motivation was functional—it saved me from spending hours in the subway, but it was also a way of getting to know the city and of being outdoors. Eventually, it became a way of being happy, a way of life.

Later I trained for and ran marathons, increasing distance and speed. I was never a competitive runner, but I loved the feeling expressed by Alan Sillitoe in his brilliant short story "The Loneliness of the Long-Distance Runner": "Every run like this is a life—a little life, I know—but a life as full of misery and happiness and things happening as you can ever get really around yourself."[23] This is especially true of long-distance runs. You set out not quite knowing how it will go, hoping for the best. Along the way, things loosen up a bit. Your breath evens out, your limbs relax. You stop thinking so much about the labor of running and your mind begins to unhinge. Thoughts rumble about in a weird cacophony, interrupted now and then by the urgencies of running (an untied shoelace, a steep hill, a dog barking). As you settle into a pace, your arms and legs swing in an opposite cadence as your feet hit the ground. When all of this works, you can sometimes completely forget that you are running at all.

That is a brilliant time for thinking. It's not the kind of thinking that is methodical and deliberative, as you might try on a walk or a long hike. For me, at least, it is a slightly chaotic kind of thinking that shakes ideas around and mixes them all up. I have taken runs where I thought, suddenly, that I had the entire plan for a book—all of it crystal clear in my mind. Whole sentences rolled out in front of me like the road I was running on, and I was chasing them, trying to keep up. I've run up hills lost so much in thought (or sometimes to the rhythm of a repeating thought) that I forgot how steep the hill was. I've passed hours in running not knowing what I thought about at all, but I remained interested, alert, watching ideas tumble about as I might acrobats in a circus. For this reason, I can never translate running-thoughts into written thoughts, no matter how hard I try. The kind of thinking that happens for me while running seems to be unstructured, almost akin to a dream. As soon as the run ends, the thinking ends too. And I'm left wondering how it all seemed so clear in the midst of the run.

What kind of thinking is this? Is there an optimal pace for thinking, as there seems to be an optimal pace for running different distances? Could I change the pace of thought just as I accelerate on flat road and slow down on a hill? Running seems connected to freedom and flight—to the abandon of heading out with nothing but your sneakers, hitting the road. But it is also related to fear and escape—to running for your life. When you choose to go for a run, perhaps it activates something between these two instinctive modes of human existence: flight and fight. Perhaps thinking while running borrows something of the speed of your body and its agile, slightly dangerous, tilt. Perhaps thinking likes being set free to go as fast and far as it can, much as a kid likes to sprint across an open field.

Often we talk about letting thought "run" or describe ideas as "running together." Running and thinking are metaphorically tied together in our everyday speech. We think this indicates the intimacy between physical and psychical momentum. Sometimes, especially under the pressure of a deadline, thinking can feel sticky and disjointed. It can be hard to follow a train of thought, hard to stitch our thoughts together. With momentum, however, thinking moves out ahead and acquires its own rhythm. When this happens, it can almost feel as if the thinking is running on its own and happening without you—that you are an audience to thinking rather than the conductor or creator of ideas. (This kind of thinking can feel as exhilarating as any run—even if you are entirely confined in place.) Maybe this is what it feels like to have an "open mind." Maybe running is another reminder that thinking need not be concerted and pinned in place. Maybe running activates a form of thinking that is less tied to any individual subject and more geared into the ambiguous rhythm, speed, and consciousness of the surrounding world.

This would mean that running is one way of receiving thinking, as one receives a gift or an invitation. Walking does this too—opening the body and the mind to the open air and the unknown influence of the environment. You give up control as soon as you step outside. Running makes that emphatic, and a large part of running entails surrendering to the realities of the run—which are always different no matter how many times you have set out on the same route.

Travelogue: Megan Still Running

Over time, my relationship with running has changed. It used to be a ritual, a form of discipline and mental/physical hygiene. Later—under the pressures of a demanding job and young children—it became a luxury. The idea of a long run, several hours alone on a road with nothing to hurry back to, seems as remote to me now as my childhood in Goshen. As a result, I can't run as far or as fast as I used to.

The run I take now goes out the long curve of my driveway and left up an immediately too-steep hill. I'm winded before I'm halfway up. Push on, I tell myself, and then I reach the stop sign and turn right along a long slow descent on Wooding Hill Road under a canopy of trees that provide crucial shade in the summer. Another left at the bottom of the hill leads to a series of reservoirs, where I sometimes see herons standing on one leg and always look for bobcats, bears, and snakes. I run past the expanse of open water and turn right into a gated trail that meanders along the edge of the lake. On adventurous days, I run out on the dirt path and head back when I feel I've had enough. On most days, though, I stop at the gate and make my way back up the hill. It's uphill nearly the whole way back—always too steep—and I always seem to forget about it until I'm on it again, cursing the hill.

But sometimes, in the midst of that seemingly endless ascent, I still forget that I'm running. I'm thinking about something else. About something that I'm writing or painting or composing. About my kids or our dog. About a memory or a book. And the hill evaporates in the thinking like a city in the fog. I arrive home confused by how I got there already. And each time it feels like a miracle or like magic. The transubstantiation of running into flight.

SKIS AND SLEDS

We concluded the first chapter with reference to ice skates, which allow a person to glide over the frozen surface of the water. On land, devices such as skis, sleds, snowshoes, and sleighs allow human beings to navigate over frozen and snowy land, creating opportunities for locomotion and portage that would otherwise be impossible. Like ice skates, skis transform the movement of the person who wears them, elongating their stride and distributing their weight over the length of the ski. On skis, the body adopts a rhythmic movement somewhere between walking and skating. As with swimming, heavy bodies can find themselves relieved of gravity on skis, gracefully arcing down a mountain or gliding across a field.

Travelogue: Megan on Skis

I learned to ski at about the same age that I learned to walk, strapping a pair of skis to my snow boots and heading out into the cold. My father had learned from his father, a veteran of the Tenth Mountain

Division Ski Troops in World War II. All of us, therefore, learned the same Telemark (free heel) ski technique that he had mastered while training in Colorado during the war. And all of us skied as if we were carrying a twenty-pound pack on our backs. On my grandfather's farm in northwestern Connecticut, we'd ski the back hills in the winter, trekking up and down. If we ever ventured to the local downhill ski mountain, the rule in our family was that you had to climb up to ski down. My grandfather continued skiing almost to the end of his life, earning a gold medal at age eighty in a Telemark slalom race at Mad River Glen, Vermont (with the ominous slogan "Ski It If You Can"). My father took me on various ski adventures throughout my teens and early twenties—all of them memorable, especially the one to Tuckerman's Ravine on the side of Mount Washington, where temperatures on our overnight stay dropped below -20° Fahrenheit.

Skis, especially Nordic skis, provide the opportunity to be outside in transit in subzero temperatures, creating your own heat. The steady shlush of the skis and tap of the poles into the snow provide a syncopated rhythm for thinking. In the cold, thinking feels bright and brisk. The trees stand at attention; the body moves because it must. The first person to have discovered skiing must have felt exhilarated and intensely alive, moving with grace and speed across a sea of white, cheeks flushed, the wind snapping, and all the world hushed and new in a blanket of snow.

Sleds, like skis, can carry us downhill on preexisting slopes, but in this case sitting up or lying flat on one's stomach or back rather than standing. Unlike skiing, rhythmic movement while sledding is reserved for the trudge up the hill—a time when thinking is likely to include wondering if the trek is worth it, getting hot, winded, and breathing and ruminating to the rhythm of your own footfalls. The thrill of sledding lies in the rush of wind and reckless abandon of careening down, feeling released from gravity as you do on a swing or a rollercoaster. Then thinking gives way to sheer speed, and you forget the climb just long enough to want to do it all over again.

While skiing, the body stands upright, but when sledding, you sit or lie flat, hugging your sled as it makes its way down the hill. The sledder also clings close to earth as she makes her way down, often following preestablished paths that become slicker and icier over repeated runs. But the sledder can guide herself to some degree—which becomes important when in the company of other sledders, all moving downward on the same route. Sledding involves finding a good hill covered in snow (fresh is best) and being able and willing to drag yourself and your sled up to the top. Old toboggans held multiple passengers in a row (Ethan Frome style) careening down hills on wooden runners. Modern versions include plastic and metal disks, foam pads, inflatable tubes, and any smooth, hard surface a kid can find to sit on, hold onto for dear life, and swoosh headlong toward a distant resting place.

Travelogue: Ed on a Sled

I sledded on one hill only in Topeka: the sizeable backyard of a mansion that housed the person who had laid out the part of town—"Westboro"—where I lived when growing up. I trudged up the hill with others, all of us determined to be the speediest to sled down to the bottom of the hill. Along the way were numerous shrubs that we tried—often unsuccessfully—to avoid. Even more important was the need to avoid crashing into fellow sledders. Here was a form of mild competition—no one kept count of anything—that suited me more than football in the just prior season. I strongly preferred moving downward on my own momentum to being thrown into a fierce combat between two groups of boys intent on winning the game, seemingly at any cost. Sledding downhill provided a form of momentary autonomy that I relished in those early years. My thinking in this circumstance was on the breathless side and occurred coherently only when gliding smoothly downward as if following a predetermined route. The sledding happened in a moment of relief that answered the question: What am I supposed to do when it snows heavily in Topeka?

BICYCLES

Continuing the trajectory of fast, forward, lateral momentum over the earth (swinging, running, skiing, sledding), bicycles sit at an intersection between physical effort and mechanical facility. As in running, the legs are active but, in this case, not self-sufficing. They collaborate with the wheels by way of the gears that mediate between the cyclist's body and the open road. The cyclist is both *on* the ground as traversing it but *above* it as seated. At the same time, he or she goes *over* the ground, thanks to the wheels that maintain contact with the bike path below. Bicycles are *third things* that create movement in their intimate relation to the dyad of the lived body and inert ground. Supported from below, the cyclist is set free to entertain thoughts that move forward with their own momentum. Bicycles can be considered translation machines, translating circles into lines, pressure into acceleration, metabolism into propulsion. Thanks to the bicycle, lumbering movement becomes fluid speed, static landscapes become ribboning cinematic panoramas, scattered thoughts smooth into sweeping ideas.

Travelogue: Ed on His Bike

I forged my own itinerary to elementary school as something different from what my parents had recommended. Along the way I noted things that told me how far I had come: a certain house, a tall tree, a yard with a dog who had an insistent bark. Thanks to these reminders, I could judge not only how far I had come but how much space remained before I would reach the schoolhouse. I was proud of the fact that I never got lost and was never late. Being on my bike in such a concerted way was a first taste of the autonomy that I craved as a young person. This lasted until age sixteen, when learning how to drive a car became primary: Its four wheels and powerful engine replaced the two wheels and two legs that sufficed for bicycling.

Travelogue: Megan with Her Bike

In Belgium, our apartment backed up to a dirt path that ran alongside a patch of trees separating us from the adjoining highway. My older sister and I often took our bicycles out the back door to a concrete patio and pedaled off. More often than not, a group of local boys perched in trees waited for our departure and shot at us with water guns filled with cheap perfume as we went by. We came home reeking of it and sometimes in tears if they happened to get us in the eyes. One day, a few of them approached me when I was alone on my red bike (with training wheels still attached to the back). I must have been four or five years old. They pulled the bike out from under me and started to run away with it. I dashed back to call for help, at which point my mother (wearing bellbottom jeans and clogs—it was 1979) flew out of the apartment, chased them down, and came striding down the path with my red bicycle in her arms. My freedom and dignity were restored; it was the most heroic thing I had ever seen.

Bikes facilitate trips of a definite duration and length—prolonging and diversifying the body's range across land in the same way that boats do for bodies on water. They can also be employed in open cycling that follows no prescribed path but takes one to new and unknown destinations: just "gettin' around," as suggested by the title of a classic 1965 Blue Note jazz album, whose cover features the tenor saxophonist Dexter Gordon astride a bicycle.[24] In addition to extending the geographical terrain one can cover, bicycles also allow one to look around in several directions while moving, without the feet having to stop pedaling along. This is another instance of the bipolar character of cycling: Since your head is free, you are able to look fully around you as you propel yourself onward on a machine that always moves forward.

Bicycles offer a middle way between walking or running on the one hand and fully motorized transit on the other. Motorized bikes (scooters, e-bikes, motorcycles) eliminate all or most of the bodily activity of pedaling a regular bike, even as they allow you to attain speeds you cannot otherwise reach. While a bicycle implies elementary freedom and wholesome self-reliance, motorcycles exacerbate speed while alleviating effort, making them symbols of wild and sometimes reckless abandon. Oliver Sacks, who loved swimming, also loved motorcycles. The cover of his autobiography features a black-and-white photo of him as a young man, wearing a leather jacket astride a BMW bike in Greenwich Village. He developed an obsession with motorcycles and motorcycle culture, first in England and later in the United States: driving cross country, taking amphetamines, and pushing every limit.[25] Yet his love of motorcycles could just as easily apply to the experience of pouring one's energy into the pedals of a bicycle; he wrote that riding on two wheels "is so geared to one's proprioception, one's movements and postures, that it responds almost like part of one's own body. Bike and rider become a single, indivisible entity."[26]

For children especially, bikes offer independence: getting you somewhere by your own effort yet not requiring as much energy as walking or running there. They are both *liberatory* and *economical* in this regard. With the widespread use of bicycles in the 1890s and beyond, working-class people became mobile, fanning out across cities and the countryside farther from their birthplaces than ever before. The bicycle was a catalyst for change, democratizing speed, eradicating distance, and upsetting rigid notions of class and gender.[27] Similarly, the child who first learns to balance on a bicycle is learning something more than the rote activities of pedaling and steering. They are learning about independence and what it means to coordinate their own body together with a machine, learning how to make small corrections in tempo and weight distribution, learning how to fall and how to get up. In all of this, the child experiments with failure and recovery and develops a sense of empowerment that can be rekindled in every future experience of riding a bike. Swings offer a first taste of freedom, but bikes offer more. The child with a bicycle and a stretch of open road feels released into the wide world. Now they can fly away on two wheels, feeling the wind whip their hair.

While learning to ride a bicycle, the only thought is of balance and the seemingly impossible choreography of holding onto the handlebars and pushing the pedals. It is only when you get the gist of it, when the feet move freely and the body relaxes into the posture of riding, that things change. In many ways, you must stop thinking about riding a bicycle in order to ride one, for as soon as the machine beneath you comes too much into focus, it feels unwieldy and begins to tip. This makes a bicycle a model vehicle for occupying the body in continuous movement while letting the mind coast or roam. Prescribed movement in one place (legs and feet rhythmically pumping up and down) or the subtle core strength required to keep the bicycle upright while speeding downhill facilitates unscripted movement in another (eyes scanning the horizon and thoughts running all over the place).

Bicycles provide utilitarian modes of transportation, recreation, and even entertainment—for oneself and for others (as the juggling clown on a unicycle attests). Balancing on one wheel is harder than two, and the larger the wheel, the more outlandish and astounding the feat. Wheels spinning beneath the cyclist seem to replicate the image of wheels spinning in their heads, as if the bicycle externalizes the mechanics of thinking and gives us cartoonish brains under our feet. Rubber tires on a metal frame, spokes, hubs, saddle, interlocking gears, a greasy chain—all of it visible and open to investigation. A bicycle has nothing to hide. The elegance and simplicity of the machine inspires a sense of confidence. If only the inner workings of the mind were so reliable and open to view—and the only tool you needed to repair a broken mind could be folded up and carried in your pocket. If only concerted thinking was as simple as pressing your weight down onto a pedal.

CARS

Cars, which are of relatively recent origin, offer a purely mechanical way to get somewhere on Earth and to do so in a comparatively short time. They are *facilitating* in every regard. The driver is relieved of any demanding physical exertion; she need only start the engine, follow the signs, and stay alert—and she will be at her destination in a more or less predictable stretch of time. "Auto-mobile" captures this dimension of cars: They *move themselves*. We do not move them as we must do with bikes or mobilize our own body as in running or walking.

Writing to a friend about a favorite three-mile trip from Twenty-Third Street and Broadway in Manhattan to Bowling Green, Walt Whitman, who died just before the invention of the first gasoline-powered automobile, said, "You know it is a never ending amusement and study and recreation for me to ride a couple of hours of a pleasant afternoon on a Broadway stage in this way. You see everything as you pass, a sort of living, endless panorama."[28] Whitman also rode the ferry and became representative of a figure who could delight in the vision of fellow human beings in crowds. The generous breadth and air of his poetry derives, in part, from riding in vehicles, like the horse-drawn stagecoach, which carried him at just the right remove to watch the world go by.

Unless we are automobile aficionados, we tend to think of cars as mainly convenient means of transport—ways to get to the post office or some other place without having to walk or take a bus. If we own a car, we park it at or near our house so that we can just step into it, turn on the motor, and take off quickly. Or else we take "rides," cruising through town or country for the sheer pleasure of moving freely through the landscape. Sometimes we combine business with pleasure, as when Willem de Kooning would be driven through the Long Island landscape by a painter friend, noting particular vistas that he would then pursue in abstract paintings when back in his studio. We can also "give rides" to others who need transportation, as when we drive a friend to a local clinic and pick them up after they have gone through a demanding medical procedure.

Cars are quintessentially American insofar as they represent a certain freedom of movement and sense of individual prestige. Those with enough money to own a car often take great pride in the kind of vehicle they drive. Americans typically spend many hours in traffic commuting to and from work and fantasizing about (and occasionally taking) long road trips across the country. Over time, larger and larger cars, trucks, and SUVs have become status symbols and a part of the gas-guzzling economy and climate-altering reality of the United States. Cars clog highways across the country, leading to traffic jams and intense areas of pollution and congestion in and around major metropolitan areas. At the same time, cars are sometimes the only safe, interior enclosure for those who have found themselves without a home. In those cases, the car becomes the primary shelter for an individual or a whole family. The seats become beds, desks, kitchens, and anything else they might need to be.[29]

The car can be all of this and more—a utilitarian vehicle of travel to get you from point A to point B, a beloved object one polishes and keeps perfectly tuned, a shelter, a barely functioning jalopy that might give out at any moment, a tool for making ends meet as a taxi or Uber driver, a rusting hulk in a field, a sleek racecar, an old Chevy. The nostalgia associated with cars in U.S. culture leads us to remember our first cars as conjoined with first jobs and first freedoms (for Megan, a beat-up red Ford Escort she bought for five hundred dollars the summer before senior year in college, along with the breakdown and rebuild manual; for Ed, a used Volkswagen given to him by his father so that he could drive to graduate school in Chicago). Cars are sometimes given names. They figure in our childhood imaginations as things relegated to the world of adults: shiny, fast, dangerous. They are sometimes places of respite, as when driving slowly along a road just for the sheer pleasure of it. But they can also be places of strife or fear: fights in the car with no way to get out, driving too fast, driving drunk, driving on an empty tank without enough money for gas, driving through a place you'd rather not be, or breaking down in the middle of nowhere, stranded.

Travelogue: Ed Driving from Stony Brook to Guilford

My car loomed large in the life of my mind when I would commute from a rented cottage in Stony Brook, Long Island, to my home in Guilford, Connecticut, after teaching all week at Stony Brook University. Especially at night, driving alone, I would record my thoughts on a given topic about which I was writing at the time. I owned a handheld recorder, into which I would talk directly. I was in effect talking to myself so that I could explore a given line of thought freely. It was as if I was inspired by the open road down which I was driving; as it opened before me, so my thinking unfurled at the wheel. As virtually everything I said out loud was recorded, I did not need to worry about new ideas being lost. In fact, knowing that a recording was being made, I was assured of being able to retrieve my thoughts the next day or at virtually any future moment. (In fact, I rarely listened to these recorded thoughts, despite retaining only a partial memory of where my thought of the night before had taken me.) What mattered was the comparatively uninhibited outpouring of thought, not its exact expression. The sobriety and self-censoring of daytime consciousness introduced a rigor that was suspended as I was speeding down the highway at night.

Here the car functioned as a makeshift recording studio, and we have an instance of the oral pursuit of thought with no assistance from writing or typing. Eventually, it would require one of these latter if the thoughts were deemed worthy of publication, being taught, or put forth in some other more or less formal setting. But short of these extensions of thought there was license to think out whatever came to my mind or lips at the time. It was like talking to the night—where the night was a mute but highly receptive listener to whatever I had to say. This was made possible not just by the action of recording—where the ongoing character of the driving induced a virtually uninhibited flow of ideas—but also by the sheer fact of driving an automobile in which I was the sole occupant. Just as I could steer fairly freely at the wheel (so long as I stayed away from a collision), so I could also steer freely among various lines of thought. Unlike the experience of thinking-while-running—when Megan experienced unexpected lines of thought that she could not retrieve later on—I was able to count on the recording of the thoughts, no matter how labile and seemingly incoherent they may have seemed at the time of their utterance.

In such an experience as here described, the car becomes a key component of an apparatus for thinking in several ways. The thinking driver is variously enabled: (1) by the strict privacy of the circumstance, encouraging thinking that is not being judged or even heard by others; (2) by the reliable recording of whatever thoughts one can articulate at the moment; (3) by being able to move along an open highway at one's leisure, without being distracted by a surrounding landscape visible during the day; and (4) by being in a form of transportation whose direction and speed are within one's immediate control, providing a paradigm for directed thinking. As we described with swimming, boating, walking, and running, thought can take on the momentum of bodily or vehicular movement. In the case of cars, thinking can intensify in speed, clarity, and power, just as the car itself (when running smoothly) epitomizes fast control. For all their downsides—pollution of the atmosphere, the risk of an accident, cost and the need for upkeep—automobiles do provide a special space and time for thinking through a given issue, philosophical or otherwise. For Ed, it was a matter of speaking and thinking freely in the comparative tranquility of the night. Just as one can accelerate or slow down the car one is driving, so the person who records her thoughts while driving has access to forms of mental acceleration and deceleration and can profit from a virtually mimetic relation with the actions of this same car. Ed thereby came to insights while driving at night that were not likely to have occurred in more demanding and distracting daytime circumstances.

Cars, though sometimes social vehicles for families or friends, are more often private spaces or quasi-intimate enclosures for the two people in the front seats. (Car rides with children in the back or an infant strapped into a car seat have a decisively different feel than car rides taken alone or with one or two other adults.) When the road is smooth and uncrowded, cars can provide a retreat from the commotion of the world—a gentler way to get to work than the throngs on the subway or the variabilities of a bus or a train. In optimal circumstances, they lend one a sense of control—at least within the snug interior, where one can decide what music to play, whether to keep the windows open or closed, whether to turn the heat up or down. In these supportive ways, cars invite forms of thinking that include reflection on past circumstances (almost like replaying a movie in one's head) and the somewhat linear invention of new ideas as thinking evolves apace with the smooth road ahead. Thinking while driving, like the car itself, can be held in place by signs of order or their cognitive equivalents: painted white or yellow lines on the road, guardrails, traffic lights, stop signs, speed signs, on-ramps and off-ramps.

TRAINS

It's hard for a philosopher in America to think about trains without thinking about William James. He lived and wrote during the historical time period when the Central Pacific and Union Pacific Railroad companies raced toward each other building the Transcontinental Railroad—laying of thousands of miles of track through the sweat of (often exploited) Chinese and other immigrant laborers, as well as veterans from the Civil War. James romanticized the labor as much as the trains themselves, and in letters he often wrote about being on a train and feeling witness to the distinctive innovation and grit of America. Writing to his brother Henry while on a train to Boston in September 1898, for example, James said, "The trip has done me a world of good, morally and intellectually, & made me see this world's affairs—I think also a bit of the next world's—in a simpler and broader light. These magnificent railroads and new settlements bring home to one the fact that all life rests so on the physical courage of common man."[30]

James probably also liked the way the railroads signaled interconnection and movement—two of the driving themes of his own psychology and philosophy (especially his radical empiricism, which he described as a plural philosophy of interrelated facts). Though he famously coined the term "stream of thought" in his 1890 *Principles of Psychology*, in later work it is not rivers and streams but trains and tracks that capture his imagination. Trains represented human innovation and the possibility of mass transit across previously unthinkable terrain. Commonly called "the iron horse," early trains also intersected and further displaced native populations (already depleted and on the move), inaugurating a new era of towns and cities built as transportation hubs across America. The iron horse could carry freight and supplies, people and animals, without needing to rest or recover. She could run all day and all night. This created a new, industrial sense of "railroad time" untethered to sunrise or sunset, one newly attuned to the timetables of locomotives, the sound of an engine, and the blare of the whistle.

Travelogue: Megan on MetroNorth Between New Haven and Grand Central Station

My own relationship to trains centers on the MetroNorth train line that runs between New Haven, Connecticut, and Grand Central Station in New York City, part of a commuter rail line that dates back to 1832. I started to take the train when I was an undergraduate at Yale University. My first rail trip into the city was to see a de Kooning retrospective, but I soon discovered that my intractable writer's block could be somewhat alleviated by boarding the train and writing my papers in transit. This worked especially well for my senior thesis (an exploration of patience in the work of Emmanuel Levinas, Cora Diamond, and Kierkegaard). I saved money for a few precious round-trip rides to and from New York, writing furiously the whole way there and back again. At Grand Central I would get off the train, sit for a bit in the terminal gazing up at the ethereal ceiling of depicted constellations, and then board the next train home.

Later, the train became a part of my usual back and forth from my apartment in New Haven to teaching jobs at the New School for Social Research and then at the Manhattan or Brooklyn campuses of Stony Brook University. With repetitive use, the train for me lost the luster of its former days, but I could still find a window seat, splay my books on my lap, and spend the next hour and fifty minutes writing or deep in thought. Rides home at rush hour proved more difficult, both because of my own exhaustion and the wagons packed with hot and vociferous bodies of strangers. Still, the steady lurch of the train along the track motivated a special kind of thinking that shared some of the urgency and reliability of the engine itself. As with the ferry, the train relieves you of the need to do any navigation. It allows you to be carried along for a precise interval from point A to point B. This creates a hiatus-like time and space in which one can think energetically about a given topic, dialing in like a wheel into a groove.

At the same time, on a train, there is the special experience of seeing the outside world pass by your window in a blur. On one of my earliest train trips into the city, I saw a woman leaning out her apartment window—just a smudge of color against the concrete block. I was fascinated by how instantly and fleetingly she had entered my life, without my having registered for her at all. It gave rise to a lifetime of thinking back on that minimal contact and the mysterious ways that we become significant to one another even in passing.

The landscape, meanwhile, rolls by in a steady stream of buildings, factories, shimmering inlets of water, and land. It unrolls, actually, just as one might unroll a Japanese scroll painting. I would glance up from my page and catch things just as they were being passed by: a bit of graffiti, a dog, an old truck. Sometimes workers dot the adjacent track in bright orange safety vests. Sometimes rain splatters the windows and makes everything look like an impressionist painting. More than anything else, the scene out the train window always looks to me like a painting. Maybe it is because the motion of the train makes everything seem a bit blurred, edges blending into each other. Maybe it is the framing of the window. Maybe it is that I have always wanted to bring my easel on the train and get out at every stop to paint the tangle of wires and tracks and stations with their distinctive, small-town feel.

Pictures and words. Trains are good places for thinking about how they go together. The things outside the train provide a moving screen of images, while inside, the slight jostle of the coach wagon and the steady chug of the engine creates a lulling, grounding sensation of connectedness. The train is fast (in the United States, not as fast as in Europe, of course), and so you feel you are moving along at a clip. This can help you feel that your thoughts are also fast, directed, on time. When words fail, a glance out the window provides a steady stream of new vocabulary. When writing on the train, I always think that my pen is a little engine, chugging its own inky tracks along the page. This gives me a sense of urgency and a helpful bit of levity, as if I'm laying down track for new ideas in an old-fashioned race across fresh terrain.

But then—abruptly—trains also make us think of the Holocaust and the millions of European Jews transported in train cars filled to the roof. European railways were an integral part of the deportation and mass murder of Jews (as well as Sinti and Roma) from 1941 to 1944. Freight and passenger trains were employed for the same purpose: the movement of people to concentration camps in what was euphemistically described as "resettlement in the East." Many did not survive the trip. Of his own train to Auschwitz, Primo Levi recalled:

> There were twelve goods wagons for six hundred and fifty men; in mine we were only forty-five, but it was a small wagon. Here then, before our very eyes, under our very feet, was one of those notorious transport trains, those which never return, and of which, shuddering and always a little incredulous, we had so often heard speak. Exactly like this detail for detail: goods wagons closed from the outside, with men, women and children pressed together without pity, like cheap merchandise, for a journey towards nothingness, a journey down there, towards the bottom.[31]

It is not possible for many of us to sit in a train without thinking about these horrors. The trains running smoothly, running on time. The people getting on and off. The trim station masters with their dark blue uniforms and the conductors with their specially shaped hole-punchers collecting tickets. The ways that human beings have collected their thoughts and turned land into track, gathered their cattle and baggage and people and sent them off down the line. Trains are sites for the intermingling of diaphanous painterly thoughts but also for something dark and unyielding. To be on a train with enough space to sit and to read. To know where you are going and to be able to get off at the right stop—or at any stop other than the end of the line. It seems almost impossible—too good, too generous.

Megan recently sat on a train from New York toward New Haven with three men just released from prison in the seats ahead of her talking loudly about their lives in captivity. "Where are you headed?" one of them asked another. "Anywhere but back," was the reply.

All that we have discussed in this longest chapter of our book concerns *earth*. It is earth that underlies the garden that led to Ed's musing on his porch, as well as the sidewalks and streets of New York City he glimpses from the height of his apartment. It is on the earth that Megan walks and runs—and the land masses at either end of the ride are what give purpose to the ferry that takes her to Long Island and back. All the modes of transportation we have considered—ranging from bicycles to trains and from cars to planes—move on the earth or in relation to it. Not only is there no escaping the gravity of the planet, but all journeys we undertake, including those that get us nowhere in metric terms, are earthbound. Try as we might to leave and go to outer space, we start from Earth and, unless something goes terribly wrong, eventually return there. Earth in all these and many other respects shows itself to be the indispensable basis for life and experience on this planet. Moving itself, it animates us as travelers in transit who think and write, dance and paint, on or near its ground.

INTERLUDE 3: THINKING IN PAINTING

Even though we have structured our text according to the four elements, taking them in developmental order from the most native habitat of human life (water) to the least hospitable (fire), everywhere we turn in the lifeworlds we inhabit we find combinations of the four ancient elements: water, earth, air, fire. No wonder Presocratic thinkers in the Eastern Mediterranean world of the seventh and eighth centuries BCE. were drawn to posit them as uniquely substantial and, in most circumstances, coessential. Only rarely do we experience a single element; most of the time we find ourselves in the midst of several. As these words are being drafted, Ed is on his front porch—from which he takes in earth in the guise of a garden, water glimpsed in the ocean nearby, and air above it all. Fire is present in the form of the bright sun overhead.

When one sets about painting such a scene, the elements foreground themselves in surprising ways, and a configuration of these same elements can emerge in the painting. The painting is a scene in transit inasmuch as it is a place—a pictorial place—where the same elements are reconfigured, brought together, in ways that may depart from the original perception yet that gives to them a newly configured *com-presence*, a being together at the level of imagery.

In this "interlude" we shall consider how landscape or seascape paintings are instances of thinking in transit—where "transit" refers not to various means of transportation but to experiences in which we can be said to travel otherwise.[32] In the case of land or seascape paintings, the travel consists both in the original act of creation of such works and in their perception by the artist and others as they take in the result. As both of us are painters, we have experience with what it means to travel through painting and to think in paint. This mode of transit involves deep emplacement in one spot—the site where you set your easel or arrange your surface and painting supplies. But as soon as you begin to sketch the surroundings, time and distance transform. Suddenly you are there where your gaze and attention goes, consumed by the elemental specificity of how anything (a rock, blades of grass, a hill, the sea) relates to its surroundings and looms with such insistence in its own being.

Earth and water appear together when we perceive a seascape that features both a portion of the ocean and the presence of a land mass. In fact, such a conjunction is often the case—as when we notice distant islands or other land masses at the perimeter of a view of a body of water onto which we are looking. One of us (Ed) has for many years painted seascapes in watercolor, acrylic, and pastel crayons. In depicting seascapes in these various media—which share water solubility as a common feature—he has come to notice the many ways that land and sea combine forces in suggestive visual duets. It is almost as if they sought each other out—as if they were *meant for each other.*

In figure 3.1, it is as if land and water not only fit together but are co-requisite as delimitative factors: the water in the center seeming to call for land to frame it at its upper and lower edges, thereby containing it from above as well as below. The various dark strokes and

FIGURE 3.1 Edward S. Casey, *Burnt Cove*, watercolor on paper.
Source: Edward S. Casey.

areas are layered in keeping with the complex concatenation of water, land, and rock in the scene itself.

Megan has painted seascapes in Provincetown, Massachusetts. Unlike Ed, Megan works in oil paint, the viscosity of the paint thicker than watercolor and more likely to heap than to pool. Oil paint, as a medium that is half dirt, half oil, sits at the intersection of solid and liquid. You can thin it out with turpentine (as Rothko did) to emphasize its aqueous transparency, or you can apply it straight from the tube (as Van Gogh did) to emphasize its thick substantiality. Although Megan mostly painted the sand dunes (and not the sea) while she worked in Provincetown, a few paintings include a view past the dunes out to the Atlantic Ocean.

As with Ed's description of his own work, the land and water in figure 3.2 meet as co-requisite factors—if in a more differentiated palette and set of strokes. A blunt brush of white demarcates the surf cresting on the beach from the dune's edge, while a few strokes of Payne's grey indicate waves cresting farther out. At the intersection of sky and water, the colors meet in a steel gray band that dissipates into the upper end of the dune, where grass and sky converge.

In seascapes, we are not limited to earth and sea alone. There may also be air in the form of clouds, which collect and consolidate air masses. We see the sky in Megan's painting as a soft haze of blues and purples, distinct from the blunt and squiggly gray, green, and yellow marks denoting water or plant life. Clouds, if there are any, seem scrubbed into the horizon just above the water. Things appear otherwise in this second sketch of Ed's.

Notice that in figure 3.3, there is no distinct representation of a land mass, which is left suggested rather than presented as such: *intimated*, as it were. The viewer of this sketch cannot help but notice the contrast between the comparative placidity of the ocean, conveyed by broad horizontal strokes of the brush in the lower part, and the

FIGURE 3.2 Megan Craig, *Dune Shack (Atlantic Ocean)*, oil on canvas.
Source: Megan Craig.

suggested turbulence of the clouds that gather above it along with a fading sunset. This contrast presents the lightness of air compared with the heaviness of water: air being free to form fantastic shapes that fit no recognizable object on land or sea. If air takes us *up* and out, water bears *down* and *in*: down into (and as) its own depth, across the swath of water we confront when looking out to sea in a literal seascape. Merleau-Ponty associated water with the experience of depth, comparing painting with swimming and the "the immemorial depth of the visible [in which] something has moved, caught fire, [and] engulfs [the painter's] body."[33] In Ed's sketch, the mass of water has its own shape, as determined by the invisible bottom of the sea and the configuration of the clouds above.

FIGURE 3.3 Edward S. Casey, *Sunset at Barbados*, watercolor on paper.
Source: Edward S. Casey.

There are many variations possible in the trifecta of water, land, and air. Painting reminds us that we never encounter these elements in isolation. We stand or sit on land (even if the "land" is a boat or a dock floating beyond the view of any shore), suspended in and inhaling the air, gazing out to sea. Occasionally the elements interfere with one another or with the painter, as when clouds suddenly open to a downpour (eroding the distinction between dry land and wet sea), when winds whip and send sand or dirt into the air and into the sticky paints, when the sun beats down and dries things to a hard crust, or when the tide comes in faster than anyone expected. Amid all of that, the light is constantly changing, especially in the rapid transitions at daybreak and dusk, those hours known to painters to be the most remarkable times of coloration and the most challenging to depict. The multiplicity of the possible configurations of water, land, and air signifies that there is no such thing as a "perfect seascape" or an "ideal landscape." There is only an unending set of variations—"free variations" in Husserl's term—for what thinking (including imaginative thinking) can deliver from within its own resources.[34] In this spirit, we can say that each particular artwork renders *its own* free variation.

A major part of this inherent variability is based on the interplay of the elements as they figure into seascapes or landscapes. For the elements are not physical *things* but basic ways that things present themselves in characteristic modalities: water as transparent or translucent, rocks as opaque, land as underlying, fire as flaring up. The seascape or landscape painter can be said to take us on a voyage into the elemental, a trip into ways that the natural world disposes itself in our viewing of it. The artist is not seeking the abstractive view that a science of nature aims to offer in its search for the invisible substructures of what we see and experience. For the painter, it is a matter of valorizing such basic things as "water," "air," "land," "rocks," or "fire"—where these are generic labels for naturally given units of spontaneous perception rather than designating discrete objects. Whatever recognizable objects do appear in a painting or sketch—such as trees or rocks or clouds—are concretizations of one or more of the four ancient elements.

Also at stake in landscape and seascape painting is the undeniable fact that *imagery* is an indispensable factor in such painting—both in its generation and its appreciation. If one is physically situated *in the very scene* that is being painted, then an experience of the elemental is direct in that it is not mediated by a third factor such as an image or a text: One takes it in face-on. But in painting such a scene, one is generating something that is at one remove from it: an image of it that is valorized as such. This gives us the pictorial presence of something that the painter qua spectator confronts in perception (or sometimes in memory) but now renders as an image: as a stretch of water, a piece of land, cloud formations in the air, flames ascending. An image of these elements and their configuration does not have to resemble them as they are directly perceived; we need only say that such an image is a transmutation of them in an artistic medium (watercolor, oil, pastel), whatever the recognizability of the outcome.

A part of what landscape paintings can deliver is the sense of *being-there* in the elemental specificity of a place. The textures and tones, the light and air. Paintings, particularly those completed on site where the painter is exposed to the elements while working, convey the immediacy and urgency of elemental existence. In some cases, this appears as a battle against or among elements that rage or burn. The strokes are wild and jagged, and one can sense the intensity of the painter's effort to get it all down in a flurry of marks. In other cases, the work might convey something more tranquil. There was no hurry. The weather was fine. Everything seemed arrayed for display and open to investigation. The strokes are smooth, the colors clear. The elements might then, momentarily, seem composed.

The first level of transit involved in land or seascape painting is the basic movement of the artist out into the landscape. The artist leaves the studio and goes outside, or, if working from memory, they set themselves back in the landscape by imaginative effort, sometimes with the aid of a photograph. The second level of transit entails the act of painting itself. The gesture of brush to paper or canvas conducts the landscape from out *there*, beyond the artist, to down *here*, on the surface or page. Painting is not unlike walking, except it takes place through the hand. Several things shift and change in the transmutation of things into paint, and often the landscape is abstracted or condensed in the process. It is no longer just any scene but the scene as experienced at this moment, on this day, by this painter. The painting becomes an invitation to travel into the elemental world of a human being who has highlighted a particular array of shapes, colors, and textures. The third level of transit is the travel undertaken by the viewer of the painting, whether it is the artist theirself or someone else. Now transit entails a repetition of the outgoing gesture of the artist into the landscape but facilitated by the painting alone. The painter needed vision and touch to travel into the landscape. The viewer, with vision alone, travels into the painting and, through the painting, out again into the wider world. Paintings are not simply windows onto the world; they are portals that can enable a double, triple, or even more elaborate transit into the painted world and out (by the unexpected pathways of a single dab of color) to worlds beyond (lost worlds, remembered worlds, future worlds).

Can we say more about the commixture of air, water, fire, and earth that is at stake in land or seascape painting? What does such painting convey concerning elemental compresence as such and not just *re-present* at the level of image or word? How do four such very different ancient elements as water, earth, fire, and air relate to one another in paintings in which they figure?

In the paintings reproduced above, *Earth* figures not only as *grounding* or *sustaining*—its usual connotations—but as *providing perimeter* to a body of water, as we see in the case of Ed's *Burnt Cove* (figure 3.1), which features a distant shoreline that provides the outer horizon of such a body of water as well as a closer-in shoreline that furnishes an inner horizon. Either way, it is *within such bounds* as these offer that a body of water—in this case that of an ocean—presents itself to us as *encompassed*, thus as a discrete aqueous presence.

Water presents itself as both outward-going and downward-coming—thus as a matter of lateral presence and of presence in depth. The water shown in Ed's sketch *Sunset in Barbados* (figure 3.3), goes *out* as well as *down* and is two dimensional in this regard even if it is three dimensional regarded as a literally material *body* of water. It is also notably translucent. In Megan's painting *Dune Shack (Atlantic Ocean)* (figure 3.2) the water appears both thick and deep, as indicated by fat strokes and a purple hue. The water expands laterally beyond the dune and the edges of the canvas and vertically in a mass that presses forcefully down upon the shore in whitecaps, while seeming to evaporate or merge with the horizon in the upper third of the painting.

Air is the most transparent of the four elements. We can so often see right through it, and sometimes for vast distances: We see the moon through the night-time air surrounding the earth as well as the sun scintillating high in the daytime sky. We can only rarely see through earth (for example, in mines), and if we can sometimes see through water it is never for far—a few meters at best, beyond which objects dissolve in indistinction. Air is also often experienced as the connective tissue of a given landscape, which, for a painter, might tinge the entire scene. In Ed's *Burnt Cove* (figure 3.1), open gaps of white paper and the trailing smudge of pastels read as wind or circulating air. In Megan's painting, a burnt sienna underlayer pokes through gaps in the painted surface, creating a subtle rhythm of reds that undergirds the picture and creates a sense of pervasive blush.

A land or seascape painter knows all this—it is literally a form of *elemental knowing*—and they paint in and from such basic knowledge. We are here far from any discrete representational demand or expectation; we are down, around, and through elemental presences, and thus at a level that cannot itself be depicted as such, only adumbrated or suggested. In this sense, such knowing underlies what is identifiable in a painting, a level of pre-presence that will never yield a coherently narratable account either in image or in word. We are here at a level that Peirce would designate as Firstness—a sheer qualitative matrix that notably lacks Secondness (resistance) as well as Thirdness (symbolic expression).[35]

Here we must ask: What is the status of *writing* about the experience of land/seascape? Writing constitutes a second form of indirection in addition to imagery, as is signified in the adverb "about" in the phrase "writing about." Our writing in this interlude is a process of reflection-in-words about something that is not verbal at all but perceptual and/or imagistic: something *experiential*, that is to say, something that the lived body of the painter or spectator takes in.

This line of analysis yields the following semiotic chain of increasing indirection:

Engagement (between the artist and the scene witnessed or between the viewer and the painting)

Imaginifying (putting the engagement into an imagistic format or actively imagining the act of painting or the specificity about the scene depicted)

Verbalizing (writing about the previous two levels, reflecting on them in words, describing, or writing about the completed painting)

What is being discussed in this "interlude" engages all three levels: the artist's stationing their self in a given seascape before beginning to paint it; the painting or sketch that emerges from this engagement; and the verbal discussion of the entire process, as offered in the last several pages.

In the act of painting, there is very little verbalization, except, perhaps, as the transcription of the inner train of thoughts that might attach itself to elements within one's view. Being a painter confronting a landscape is a bit like being stalled at Hegel's "sense-certainty" in *Phenomenology of Spirit*, practicing a form of knowing that is immediate and receptive and realizing that "it is just not possible for us ever to say, or express in words, a sensuous being that we *mean*."[36] While painting, you respond to your surroundings with a gesture of acknowledgment: a nod, a dab, a yes or a no. Thinking too much only interferes with things and can create a fatal delay between vision and act. Yet in writing about painting, we embark on another level of transit, translating the paintings into descriptions that can be carried visually across a page or (in yet another layer of transmutation), sonically if read aloud. For those engaged in a tactile reading of Braille, the paintings would be brought back to the original touch of the painter, and reading the text would recall the painter's tactile "read" of the landscape.

All of this signifies multiple levels of transit. The transit of the painter into the landscape. The transit of the landscape into the painting. The transit of the painting into a verbal description. At each juncture, various kinds of embodiment and thinking come to the fore. For the painter, a visual/tactile sense of place fuels the choice of color and mark. The landscape is translated in the process of being painted, a process that is only partly mimetic and remains to one degree or another the invention of an entirely new entity. In the process of painting, the landscape becomes something else, and (in a reciprocal translation) the painter changes as well. She *undergoes* the painting as she endures the elements. From the painted image to the verbal description, another transmutation brings colors and shapes to words and brings a particular speaker (or writer) to articulation. When we think of painting and speaking/writing as modes of transition or travel, we can appreciate how much they convey us (as artists and spectators and readers) into different forms of attunement.

The painter knows the elemental substrate of their work, even if with an intuitive grasp that at once informs their painting yet can only rarely be given adequate separate expression in words. It is *knowledge-in* rather than *knowledge-about*. It seems akin to the knowledge we attributed to infants in the first chapter—an immersive knowing. It is knowing one is there *in the elemental matrix* yet without being able to spell out, in so many words, just what is there at the primal level.

Even if words cannot capture all that is there in a given landscape or seascape, the gist can be *thought* and thought by a unique thinking in transit. Such transitional thinking goes from one element to another, and back again . . . in an increasingly intense spiral in which several elements are often interinvolved. We are *given* this interbraided nexus in the perception and in the painting of a given scene, but, at the same time, we are encouraged to *think* it.

Thinking here consists in *pondering* the elements that intertwine— pondering by image if not yet by word—and in considering, however briefly, their ramified significance:

- Pondering by image—the image of something recognizably aqueous or aerial or terrestrial, however fragmentary: a snatch of sea, a glance of cloud, a glimpse of land
- Pondering by word—for example, a title we might select such as *Sunset at Barbados* or *Clustered Clouds* (in the case of figure 3.3) or "*Burnt Cove*" or *The Rock-Strewn Coast* (in figure 3.1)

In the thinking that emerges in creating or contemplating a painting—a thinking that is often instantaneous—one considers each of these factors, pondering not just how they emerge in a given painting as separate presences but also how they are *presented together*. The original meaning of "ponder" is to weigh and, in particular, to weigh the comparative significance of something—as when Ed was struck by how the perceived sea at Barbados appeared as having a gravity of its own: It presented itself as a stable body of water in contrast with fugitive clouds gathered momentarily above it at sunset. He literally saw such a difference in the very co-presence of these basic elements, as well as how they *con-figured* when emerging together in the same perception and, at a later remove, in the painting inspired by this perception. In viewing such a painting as *Sunset in Barbados*, we cannot help but notice these differences in the elemental presence of water and air. Taking such a visual trip, we are encouraged to think *through* these differences—through each other, alongside each other. We take in their respective differences even as they conjoin among themselves.

At the same time as we note differences in imagistic-scenic presentations of water, air, fire, and earth, we also sense a profound affinity between these elemental presences. The sea of *Sunset at Barbados* (figure 3.3) is the sea *of that scene* and belongs to the scene as a whole—thus it is intimately related to the sky hovering above it, despite the differences in manifest image. *The sea belongs there*, is co-inherent with the clouds—the two being partners in the common presentation that is the painting. This is not substantially different from the way that, standing before the same scene (as Ed did shortly before making this painting in December 2022), he also sensed the elements of sea and clouds not merely as juxtaposed but as coeval members of this same scene: not just two ways of being together casually but of being *affine with each other*. Indeed, we should expect just this insofar as sea and clouds are two ways of being-on-earth—or better, two ways of *being earth*: being equally (even if differentially) expressive of what it is to be earth-bound. At the atomic level, they are composed of the same elements held together in different forms—liquid or gas. Their affinity is so profound that it constitutes an elemental sameness that is perfectly compatible with differences in literal perception or painted presentation.

Both the painter and the viewer of seascape paintings are taking a special trip that involves no transportational vehicle yet is an instance of thinking in transit. We can designate this trip as one of thinking-in-painting. The thinking occurs in reflecting on the scene at stake—the original scene in the case of the artist inspired by it, the painted scene by the person who views the painting (including the artist as spectator of her own work). Heidegger described works of art as transporting a person "somewhere else than we usually tend to be."[37] There is a special intensity of focus activated while painting a given scene that can remain contagious in the finished picture. A spectator thinks *through* the perceived and painted sea or landscape, considering how form and color co-inhere as they obtain in the perception or painterly presentation of basic elements. With rare exceptions, such thinking is spontaneous and unprogrammed, and it is specified by the medium chosen by the artist (oil, acrylic, watercolor). This is a thinking that does not occur in concepts or words but in and by engagement with the images as presented by this medium—an engagement that is a trip in its own right, even if little or no literal movement between places occurs.

The two of us, for much of our lives, have practiced thinking in painting as well as thinking in words. They are different kinds of activities and involve different kinds of trips. Painting outside in the din and confusion of a new landscape requires a stamina and spirit of adventure distinct from that required to draft a text (not that drafting a text is any less adventurous or demanding!). We are curious about these differences. We are curious about forms of travel in which one doesn't move at all—travel by means of paintings and texts as vehicles that can carry one far away. At the edge of different seas, we have dipped brushes into paint and tried to capture a scene. Strangely, it was all made of the same stuff: water, clouds, land, plants, air. Our bodies, the colors. Yet the elements were utterly distinct and incomparable, even from one moment to the next. We are trying to trace movement and thought through the elements despite the fact that everything is helplessly mixed up. Painters know to wash the brush before dipping into a new color. Clarity is an achievement, a discipline. We face the rugged shore and try to slow the mind to the pace of the hand, attempting to trace out the shapes of things that are diaphanous and shifting. Water, air, earth, fire: all of them sensed in one glance and doled out on a palette in puddles of blue, white, gray, and red.

4

FIRE

If all that changes slowly may be explained by life, all that changes quickly is explained by fire.
—Gaston Bachelard, *The Psychoanalysis of Fire*

As an element, fire is the last and likely the most daunting of the four we consider in this book. It is last not in importance but because we have so far proceeded developmentally, beginning with movement and thought relative to water (the first native element of human life), followed by air as the second and earth as the third. Human babies emerge from the water into the air and onto the earth. There is no comparable step into or onto fire. Yet fire is as basic to human life as the other elements. Our entire planet derives its warmth and heat from a burning star, the sun, around which we orbit (at just the right distance). We need heat and light to survive, yet fire itself is not something we inhabit or willfully move through. If anything, we avoid getting too close to fire. Water, air, and earth each have dangerous facets, but fire is alone in the degree to which it resists our touch: In the presence of fire, we characteristically *draw back*. The only vehicles specifically designed to move through fire are spaceships that are designed to withstand combustion upon leaving and entering Earth's atmosphere.

We cannot, therefore, structure this chapter as we have the ones that have come before. We cannot make an inventory of fire vehicles and coincident modes of travel and thought. There are few meaningful "travelogues" in this chapter (though each of us has distinctive memories of fires we have witnessed and survived). Instead, we have to consider movement, thinking, and fire in a more abstract relation of interconnection. Our developmental account ends with the earth, and now we embark on a less linear story. In truth, it was never linear to begin with, and fire reminds us that nothing proceeds in one direction alone or according to a master plan. Life and its environs are more complex than that. Fire fans out. Fire scrambles categories. Fire is tied in human cultures to the end of life—to cremation and ashes and smoldering fields. But fire is also tied to the urgency of life—to passion, energy, and heat. Johnny Cash sang of falling "into a burning ring of fire," and his image is apt. You don't choose fire, as you might water, air, or earth. Fire *chooses you* by coming for you unexpectedly, for better or for worse.

Thinking about fire, we confront an element that has two utterly distinctive faces, as we have to keep acknowledging. In one guise, fire lights, warms, and soothes. On the side of a mountain in the darkness, campers build a fire and huddle around the flames—telling stories, singing songs. From a distance, the flickering light alerts someone far away that people are gathered. As Bachelard says, "fire is more a *social reality* than a *natural reality*"—we first learn about fire through the social interactions that it facilitates, the warnings about its dangers, and the "Prometheus complex" that arises in young children who steal matches and make secret fires.[1]

One's relationship to fire is culturally and individually specific, as is true for all the elements. Perhaps, like Ed, you were born far from the sea or never learned to swim, and water is, therefore, frightening and not a site of beckoning adventure. Perhaps when you think of air, you think of humidity sitting on your body on a hot night where nothing moves. Perhaps the earth is tied to desert sand. With fire, the relation depends in part upon historical uses of fire within your own community—whether in rituals, celebrations, open-fire cooking, bonfires, campfires, or something else. For some, fire is tied to the sense of gathering, heat, and the smells of food, while for others it might represent danger, destruction, or a warning signal.

James Baldwin emphasized the warning dimension of fire in his haunting title *The Fire Next Time*. The 1963 text, composed of two essays, borrows a couplet from an African American spiritual, "Mary Don't You Weep": "God gave Noah the rainbow sign / No more water, the fire next time!" The rainbow, God's sign of the "covenant" between himself and "all living creatures of every kind," marked the end of the deluge, but in the book of Genesis, God only promises that "never again will the waters become a flood to destroy all life." He makes no vow about the other elements: air, earth, fire. The spiritual therefore urges vigilance for the next calamity, even as it repeats the refrain: "Mary don't you weep, don't you mourn."

What is the "fire next time?" Baldwin invokes "fire and excitement that sometimes—without warning—fill a church," "fire of human cruelty," "fires of hell," and "fire and temptation."[2] In the first essay, "My Dungeon Shook," a letter to his young nephew, he writes, "Try to imagine how you would feel if you woke up one morning to find the sun shining and all the stars aflame. You would be frightened because it is out of the order of nature. Any upheaval in the universe is terrifying because it so profoundly attacks one's sense of one's own reality. Well, the black man has functioned in the white man's world as a fixed star."[3]

Baldwin entreats his nephew to break free from the identity white America has predetermined for him—to burn brightly in his own way. The fire Baldwin invokes in his title and throughout the text testifies to the multiple meanings of fire. It refers, in part, to a coming African American uprising (perhaps the closest to Baldwin's explicit intention) but also to religious passion, stamina, creativity, rebirth, contagion, love, torture, fear, and the fires of Hell—the final punishment awaiting those whose lives were less than virtuous. In the U.S. civil rights movement of the 1950s and 1960s, fire was also used by white supremacists to disrupt and destroy sites of Black congregation and resistance (as in the firebombing of the Sixteenth Street Baptist Church in Birmingham, Alabama, on September 15, 1963, or in the use of burning crosses by the KKK to terrorize people at their homes and workplaces). Even into the 1990s, there was an average of almost two hundred fires set intentionally at churches each year, with Black churches disproportionately targeted.[4] Historically, fire has been employed in warfare and efforts of violent control: Greek fire, a chemical weapon used by the Eastern Roman Empire; the German blitzkrieg in the United Kingdom; napalm used by American forces in Vietnam; bombs, explosives, and firearms used the world over. In our own time, it is hard to think about fire without recalling histories of violent oppression alongside the wildfires spreading because of climate change, whether in California, Canada, Greece, or (just as we are drafting this chapter in August 2023) in Maui.[5] "The fire next time" seems to be coming upon us as a species, ineluctably.

As an element, fire is fast, ruthless, and all-consuming. Fire does not follow from heat alone, but a rapidly warming planet produces the dry conditions in which combustion is more likely, with plentiful fuel in the form of parched plant life (and little resistance from diminishing water sources that might slow or extinguish the fire). The complex chemical reaction that produces a flame requires oxygen, friction, and fuel. Some external trigger (heat, light, a spark) must be present to mix with a combustible substance and activate an ignition temperature. Once reached, the surrounding layer of gases ignites, in turn igniting more combustible material and adjacent gases, layer by layer, in an intensifying cycle that continues until the fire is extinguished by an external force (water, loss of oxygen) or it runs out of combustible material. In his riveting, terrifying book about twenty-first-century forest fires, John Vaillant explains, "Just as a compelling scent draws a bloodhound through the woods, so volatile gases draw fire. In this sense, fire is *pulled* through space.... This phenomenon—pyrolysis—is the key to understanding the motives and behavior of fire."[6] Fires are gluttonous. The destructiveness of fire derives, in large part, from its rapid and self-generating intensification. A tiny spark from a faulty electrical line, for example, roiled into the 2018 Camp Fire in California, the deadliest fire (at that time) in America since 1918.[7]

On the other hand, fire is not always destructive. We need heat to survive. Fire enables the cooking of food; fire supplies warmth and light. Before electricity, most humans in colder climates began the day by lighting a fire in a fireplace and ended the day by raking the coals. There are also the metaphorical fires of romantic passion and of the hearth—the symbol of a warmly hospitable or receptive home life. Lovers often build fires before which they can draw close, inspired by the heat rising in their bodies as they embrace each other. Short of such passion, the warmth felt by family members who have gathered in a single place is akin to a low-level fire. Fire in this gentler guise not only symbolizes intimacy but draws creatures together in a circle of heat and light.

It is nothing short of extraordinary that fire can embody and/or symbolize two such different directions—destructive/violent as well as amatory/life sustaining. How can this be? The transformative, elusive, and polyvalent nature of fire seems built into its very nature, as we realize in the *lambency* of fire—its gleaming, lustrous aspect—as well as its *transiency*: It does not last for long on earth even if the sun retains its fiery core over many millennia. On Earth fire comes and goes—sometimes not going out soon enough. Its translucency can be taken to symbolize its unique combination of being something elemental yet ongoing—and sooner or later dying out. It's striking that we commonly talk about a "slow burn" to indicate a steady, relaxed pace while also invoking "wildfire" to describe something fast moving and out of control. Early settlers in the United States were at first puzzled but ultimately impressed by Native American practices of controlled fires that were essential in clearing fields. As Stephen J. Pyne cautions, in the present historical moment, "We have too many bad fires—fires that kill people, burn towns, and trash valued landscapes. We have too few good ones—fires that enhance ecological integrity and hold fires within their historic ranges. At the same time, with the incessant burning of fossil fuels, we have too much combustion on the planet overall."[8] Fire seems to live at extremes. It can be slow or fast, peaceful or violent, lifesaving or life taking. In Jack London's short story "To Build a Fire," the man feels invincible near his crackling fire on the first night outside in fifty-degrees-below-zero temperatures. Later, when he can't get a fire to start, things rapidly change.

In a gentler guise, candlelight embodies both transiency and translucency, and it is tied to yet a third quality of fire, namely, its mind-soothing flicker. Candles have long been associated with meditative and spiritual rituals, creating a calm and holy ambiance. Candlelight is the perfect intermediary between the extremities of fire. It is bright enough to read with—recall the young Abraham Lincoln reading by candlelight—but not so light as to dazzle those in its proximity.[9] In *The Psychoanalysis of Fire*, Bachelard described "this slightly hypnotized condition, that is surprisingly constant in all fire watchers," noting the mesmerizing power of fires and the calm stupor into which a candle can draw a person.[10] In the winter, white candles line windows of northeastern American houses, blue candles flicker in a menorah, and in the U.S. Southwest, tea lights burn inside sand-filled paper bags (luminaria) along walkways—beacons of welcome and safety.

The passing out of ordinary usage of the practice of reading by candlelight with the advent of electricity has meant a major loss of an easy-to-use resource that had been of special value for many previous centuries for those who preferred to read (or had no choice but to read) in nocturnal circumstances. Candles not only facilitated such reading but also graced evening meals with their controlled presence. Gathering around candlelight provides a congenial ambience to family reunions or on major holidays—the glow of candles atop a birthday cake. The warmth of the light conduces to conviviality. In Vincent van Gogh's painting *The Potato Eaters*, women gather around a platter of steaming potato wedges and hot cups of tea under the light of an oil lamp hanging from the ceiling. The little orange flame seems to crackle and spark, bathing them all in a yellow glow. Lamps and candles not only provide light but measure time as oil burns or wax melts and the flame dims before dying out. Reading or writing by candlelight has a built-in time span, which we lose in the era of electricity and open-ended, nonstop illumination.

From the candle, it is not far to the fire burning in a stove or a pit, which provides a central gathering location for eating and warmth. Here we find the commixture of fire with the sensory memory of the smell and taste of particular foods, the heat of a warm cup in hand, or the bustling sounds of kitchen pots and wooden spoons. Across the world, human beings gather around fires to prepare their meals. Richard Wrangham even ties fire and the advent of cooking to the transition from Australopithecines to the genus *Homo*.[11] Fire contributes to distinctive patterns of human experience, which can include painstaking preparations of foods warmed, grilled, broiled, seared, steamed, charred, or baked. Through cooking, we learn to use the fire at different intensities, to boil water or to simmer a soup. We learn about the different effects of heat on different bodies, learning techniques to intensify flavors and others to differentiate states of being, like the moment sugar caramelizes just before it burns. While thinking beside a single candle is usually meditative and slow, thinking in the kitchen is often fast and furious. Pots boiling over, mouths to feed, the kitchen cook (often an unpaid or underpaid woman) works with a focus and intensity comparable to the heat of the fire.

In addition to candles and cooking fires, controlled, "domesticated" fires take numerous forms. A fireplace offers a place to cluster cozily, above all for many on special occasions and holidays. Bonfires burn seasonal brush and might coincide with outdoor gatherings of friends or neighbors to mark the end of a harvest. Fires in metal trash cans warm the hands of homeless people in cities, while roadside, residential, and municipal trash burning in India and other parts of the world emits noxious fumes. Beyond the connection with homes, shelters, warmth, and food, Native Americans employed controlled fires to burn off unnecessary or unwanted plants, to open travel routes, to manage wildlife, to clear areas for crops, and for many other reasons. Indigenous fire practices promoted ecological diversity and reduced the risk of catastrophic wildfires. According to Frank Kanawha Lake, a wildfire fighter of Karuk descent, "Cultural burning links back to the tribal philosophy of fire as medicine. When you prescribe it, you're getting the right dose to maintain the abundance of productivity of all ecosystem services to support the ecology in your culture."[12] Today, the indigenous practices of "cultural burning" are at last being considered again in North America after decades of land-management policies based in fire suppression. Deb Haaland, the first indigenous U.S secretary of the interior, has promoted indigenous fire knowledge as a crucial part of climate awareness and land management. Firefighters are beginning to incorporate native practices, setting fires in certain stretches of land so long as they are under close supervision. Such a cultivated use of fire is in the interest of preventing fires that rage out of control; the burned-out portions of land are strategically placed so as to inhibit or at least slow down major fires. Fire against fire.

As an element, fire seems to sit at an intersection between control (candlelight, fireplaces, campfires, domesticated fires) and loss of control—which can happen in the blink of an eye. One moment the fire is calm and contained, and the next it is raging. Perhaps the inherent danger of fire is a part of its allure. "Don't play with matches," we tell young children—even though we know they are excited by the spark and the heat, by the sheer magic of rubbing flint against a rock, and by the thrill of burning things (books, photographs, report cards). Playing with fire seems like an intensified and one-sided version of the early childhood game Freud called "*Fort/Da*."[13] Setting things on fire accomplishes the "*fort*" or "gone" (over there) side of the equation, with no recourse to making things reappear here (*da*). Fire, however, can encourage a form of playing with reality: setting things aglow, experimenting with transubstantiation, seeing how far or how fast things can go. Within measure, a fascination with fire is a natural part of human development. Unchecked, it can develop into the dangerous obsession of an arsonist, whose crimes are against all living things enveloped in the wake of the fire they set.

In some sense, to control a fire is to control fate. Humans have long lorded fire over other creatures as an emblem of power, setting fires to ward off predators, to roast meat, and to alter landscapes (although the Salish creation myth *Beaver Steals Fire* tells the story of animals on earth stealing fire from the sky in order to make the earth more inhabitable for the humans, who have not yet arrived).[14] Some have used fire to conceal their crimes. Others have used fire to forge tools. In *The Iliad*, Hephaestus, the god of fire (the child of Zeus and Hera, banished from Olympus for his disabled body), battles the river Scamander in an effort to save Achilles from being drowned. In an image grimly prescient of our rapidly warming planet, he casts "inhuman fire" over fields of corpses and along the banks of the river until the waters are boiling and fish are jumping to escape the deadly heat. Scamander pleads for mercy: "The mighty river himself was on fire, and he shouted, 'Hephaestus, none of the gods can withstand your fury. It is useless for me to fight these devouring flames.'"[15]

Fire can do away with things, ashes to ashes, dust to dust. For this very reason, it is also associated with rebirth and new beginnings—a phoenix rising from the ashes, a trial by fire, nineteen-year-old Joan of Arc burned at the stake, reborn as the patron saint of France. As Michael Marder demonstrates in *The Phoenix Complex*, human beings have devised many versions of the phoenix figure: from the Egyptian *Book of the Dead*, where we read, "I am that great phoenix, which is in Heliopolis, the supervisor of what exists," to Schelling, who writes that "every combustion process is a sacrifice of individuality . . . which revives from the ashes by the power of its indwelling individuality and binds itself in a relation to the sun anew."[16] Marder argues that "the transformation of the phoenix in fire, or with the help of the fire released by the sun or by lightning, is the passage from a threadbare life through death to a fresh life."[17] Since ancient times, fire has been conjoined with the possibility of dramatic, cleansing reincarnation.

Given its polyvalent nature, any attempt at a single, stable account of fire will go up in flames: It will *burn up* and disintegrate before our eyes. Writing about fire, Bachelard warned that the "initial charm of the object is so strong that it still has the power to warp the minds of the clearest thinkers."[18] Of course, there are scientific definitions of fire that give to it a formal identity. But fire *as experienced* is something else. It ranges from a welcome and pleasant presence to something destructively raging. The only fires we can tolerate are those we can confidently control—that can be *put to our own uses*. Otherwise, a fire is inherently something dangerous, something to be feared as proceeding at its own pace and with its own intensity. Increasingly, the rising temperatures across the globe are being experienced as threatening and potentially or actually fatal. In *The Uninhabitable Earth*, David Wallace-Wells emphasizes the dangers for human beings in a rapidly heating environment, writing: "Humans, like all mammals, are heat engines; surviving means having to continually cool off, as panting dogs do. For that, the temperature needs to be low enough for the air to act as a kind of refrigerant, drawing heat off the skin so the engine can keep pumping."[19]

Wildfires spring up as if from nowhere and quickly destroy thousands of acres of plant and tree life, many resident animals, and virtually anything constructed by human beings, as with the wildfires recently in Canada (summer of 2023) that covered the entire Northeast of the United States with dense smoke or those in Greece that threaten buildings constructed by the same ancient peoples who identified fire as one of the four basic elements. Such all-consuming fires are about as close to Armageddon as humans ever get, only rivaled by nuclear bombs, which can bring massive fires in their immediate wake.

John Vaillant compares contemporary wildfires to massive "competition-killing" corporations like Standard Oil, Walmart, Amazon, and others insofar as both "follow similar growth patterns in that, once they reach a certain size, they are able to dictate their own terms across a landscape—even if it destroys the very ecosystem that enabled them to grow so powerful in the first place."[20] Vaillant links the intensifying cycle of CO_2 output across the globe to human mastery of fire and "exploitation of fossil fuels in all their varied forms," warning that "we are, right now, witnessing the early stages of a self-perpetuating and self-amplifying feedback loop."[21]

Regarding the *ferocity of fire*, we can say these several things:

1. It proceeds at its own pace and rhythm: sizzling, sputtering, flickering, flaring. It has a "mind of its own" and a rapidly expanding or expiring body.
2. It spreads so quickly that it easily gets out of control if there is anything combustible in its path.

3. It is no respecter of persons: Fire does not distinguish between one combustible thing and another. All is fodder for its voracious appetite.
4. There is no possible appeal to fire itself; it goes its own way.
5. Fire is one element that only rarely provides a form of transit whereby one can think things through. On the contrary, fire, or its imminent presence, limits or threatens thinking in transit. It is too dangerous to afford the leisure in which such thinking prospers. It is short on the kind of sheltering that ferries, airplanes, and automobiles provide, not to mention porches. Apart from its constructive role in combustion engines, it is more likely to be found in the kind of place where danger or destruction predominates. Such a place is inimical to reflective thinking. Rather than inducing the leisure that conduces to reflective thinking, it is more likely to precipitate the wish for evacuation as soon as possible, or at least keeping at a safe distance.

Apart from their own ambivalent character, destructive fires can lead directly to something constructive that would not have happened otherwise. Take, for one example, the 1911 Triangle Shirtwaist Factory Fire in Lower Manhattan, which trapped many female workers inside the clothing factory where they worked. In his poem "Shirt," Robert Pinsky describes an eyewitness watching a young man lift girls onto a window ledge of the burning building, "As if he were helping them up / To enter a streetcar, and not eternity."[22] As horrific as this was, the fire brought much-needed attention to working conditions of the time and led to important reforms. Beyond its deadly presence, fire here served as an alert, a call for the safety standards of workplaces to be materially improved.[23]

Perhaps, however, we have been too drawn into the extremes of fire, seduced into dichotomous thinking. Indigenous fire practices remind us that fire resists the stark either/or—a Western philosophical construction that goes back to what Richard J. Bernstein called a "Cartesian anxiety" that infects and pervades centuries of thinking.[24] We have made of fire a god or a demon when in fact fire is ambivalent and ambiguous. Controlled fires can have long-lasting positive environmental effects. But overzealous efforts to suppress fire in the United States have led to landscapes overgrown and ill-prepared to withstand natural cycles of burn. Logging and building practices have cleared lands of vegetation that would otherwise have provided protection and a buffer for more vulnerable sites. A part of the challenge in our contemporary moment is to learn from diverse cultures and various ways of life about living with fire creatively. This will have to include changing land-management and building practices that have created the conditions for catastrophic wildfires and submitting to the reality that fires are ongoing, crucial parts of the many intertwined life cycles on our planet. Despite their dangers, we cannot do without them.

Travelogue: Ed Remembering Fires in California

While I can sit on my porch and contemplate the interaction of air and earth in the plant life arrayed in my garden, I cannot so calmly and collectedly think of fire, given how alarming it can be. Two years ago, a raging fire descended from the mountains just above Santa Barbara, coming within several blocks of the house where I live. Only the breadth of Highway 101 kept it from reaching closer. Further north, the Paradise Fire destroyed an entire city, including the art studio of Daniel Ralston, a childhood friend. Earlier and closer to home, my young stepdaughter inadvertently allowed a defective lamp in her closet to burst into flames, starting a fire that soon consumed the entire part of the house where she and her sisters were living. Knowing that such fires, in one form or another, are ever possible in the otherwise safe territory where I live most of the year, I cannot be fully at ease while seated on the porch, outside the very part of the house that earlier burned. If another fire were to spring up nearby, I could no longer sit calmly on my Adirondack chair as if nothing were happening. I would have to get out of a fire's path as quickly as possible as well as alert others who might be exposed to the same danger.

Travelogue: Megan Remembering Fires in Goshen and in New York

It is relatively easy to think about fire from a distance but virtually impossible to think at all in the proximity of an uncontained fire. When I was in second or third grade, I was roused in the night by banging on my bedroom door. I had locked the door from the inside because of my older sister's habit of coming into my room in the night to sleep beside me (she was in a phase of reading Steven King novels at bedtime). The knocking persisted, and I finally woke to the frantic cries of my parents as they gathered the three of us (my sister, my brother, me) and our two cats and ushered us out of the house and into the yard (where the dog was already waiting). It was autumn in northwestern Connecticut, and I remember the cold feeling of the ground on my bare feet.

Only later would I learn that our wood stove, the sole source of heat in the wooden, saltbox house my dad was in the process of building, had ignited a piece of fabric, which set the whole laundry room ablaze. My dad tried to tame the flames with a fire extinguisher, but the smoke and fire were too much. The fire department arrived in a blur of flashing lights, pulling hoses into the house. The damp smell of smoke hung on everything for months, even years. From then on, I watched my dad build a fire in the stove with a mixture of awe and trepidation.

Years later, in New York City on September 11, 2001, I stood at the base of the World Trade Center at 8:48 in the morning, seeing the gash where a plane had just flown into the North Tower and watching the instantaneous flames blazing against the pale blue sky. Flames licking the building and everything they touched; flames flying through the air and toward the ground. The smoke trailed upward in a gray column. As fire worked its way through the metal over the next hour or so, the buildings buckled and then—in an image I will never forget for as long as I live—everything solid turned to dust.[25]

THE LANGUAGE OF FIRE

Perhaps we can resist overly simplistic, dichotomous thinking by looking at the ways in which fire has figured in human language. Fire works its way into many everyday expressions in English (and doubtless in other languages as well); among them are "fiery," "a firebrand," "fireball," "all fired up," "fire bomber." The common denominator is the factor of high or concerted energy that transforms what might have been a lethargic person or situation into one that is active—and often hyperactive. "Fire it up!" is a command to start an engine or get something going. "You're on fire!" complements a person's remarkable energy or prowess. "Fire!" is also the directive to shoot a cannon or a gun; a firing squad assembles a whole group of shooters.

Our everyday language seems to intensify the positive connotations of fire—celebrating its wild unpredictability and its ability to burn through almost anything it encounters. Transferred to a person, these characteristics describe someone who is just wild enough to be unabashed and unafraid (without becoming violent), someone with incredible drive and focus, and someone who lives at a higher intensity (or is hotter/sexier) than most. All of this suggests that fire itself occupies a position of esteem in our collective mentality, the mixture of awe and fear that Kant originally ascribed to the feeling of the sublime.[26] As with a sublime spectacle and with actual fire, one needs to be at the right distance to admire someone who is metaphorically "on fire"—distant enough to not be in danger of getting burned. A fiery person is like a force of nature—and their concern is often all-consuming and singular rather than collective. A "firebrand" is someone who is passionate about a particular cause, usually inciting change and motivating radical action: think of Susan B. Anthony or Malcolm X. The term is also used to describe individuals who are unpredictable and apt to thwart norms: think of Representative Marjorie Taylor Greene or the Baptist minister Jerry Falwell.

For our purposes, it is striking that "fire" is not often associated with qualities of thinking. It seems to be more associated with physical than with mental exertion. It's easy to imagine saying "You're on fire!" to an athlete in the midst of a race, but it's difficult to imagine saying the same thing to a philosopher writing an article (though perhaps it would help!). We do associate new ideas with turning on a light bulb (a highly modern, discrete, and controlled image of illumination). We might also talk about "sparks flying" in a lively conversation or even in a particularly energetic bout of thinking—though more often the expression refers to the advent of romantic love. Synapses themselves are said to *fire* as electrical currents move throughout the brain. But the popular image of a person deep in thought (Rodin's *Thinker* for example) is of sedentary, if tensed, repose—quite the opposite of the leaping, bright orange, thrill-seeking flame. Fire burns paper, the material substrate of externalized thought as it is written down or typed—almost as if fire and thinking repel each other. Could thinking ever become more akin to flame? Would it be more wild, colorful, audacious, and dangerous—ferocious, in short?

If we resist this last suggestion, it signals the fact that we consider thinking to be a largely *reflective* undertaking—one that flourishes in quiet and contemplative settings, while we are at leisure as regards our bodily positionality.[27] Even so, thinking can still be—and often *should be*—very challenging and demanding. But the places where we assume we think best are often some form of *retreat:* We say, "I need to find a quiet place to think this over." Such a place is typically far removed from anything that threatens or alarms us—as would an active and unanticipated fire. Between these extremes are the places of transit on which we have focused in this book, places where creative thinking is most likely to occur.

THINKING IN PROXIMITY

What might it mean, then, to travel through fire? We have discussed traveling through and upon water, air, and earth, each with a set of distinctive movements, vehicles, and modes of thought. But it makes no sense to travel in or on fire, unless perhaps one is a firefighter trained to rush headlong into the flames. We could argue that walking on hot coals is one form of traveling over fire. Perhaps certain excursions in the desert or through extreme heat also qualify as fire travel. In any case, these would not be forms of travel conducive to reflective rumination or writing anything down. "Keep your mind in hell and do not despair" is what the Lord told Saint Silouan the Athonite, as if to suggest that it is a *duty* to face the heat (the world's evils) and to think in the midst of fire. Such thinking is dangerous, daunting, and often impossible. But it is also noble and heroic to be a person who can proceed (not cower or flee) in the face of extremity, "taking the heat," so to speak. As for vehicles, one needs special equipment to move through fire without getting hurt, including oxygen tanks, masks, and various protective coverings. In addition to burning anything it touches, fire destroys the air—making it impossible for earthbound creatures to breathe. Many fire deaths result from smoke inhalation or the inhalation of toxic chemicals released into the air as things burn. For all these reasons, fire is the most uninhabitable element and the one least connected to conventional modes of human development or to a smooth transition between places.

More metaphorically, we might consider travel through fire in relation to experiences of endurance. Symbolically, moving through fire indicates an extreme trial or ordeal. Intense fevers can feel like fire. Soaked in sweat and shivering under covers, the feverish patient can barely speak or think until the body's temperature comes down. Fevers remind us of the narrow parameters of healthy human life, the fine calibration of temperature within which we can function as living beings. Under certain kinds of physical stress (running, climbing, lifting heavy weight), muscles can feel like they are on fire. Athletes know how to push past those feelings toward higher planes of achievement, chasing the edge where a fired-up body and fiery determination motivate speed and strength while trying to avoid injury and burnout. As with the other elements we have considered, the *mean* is crucial relative to fire, if more of a knife's edge than what we encounter with water, air, or earth. We need enough spark and heat to live, to move, and to feel alive—but only (as Aristotle would insist) the right amount at the right time and in the right conditions.

Each of the elements becomes dangerous and life threatening if taken to an extreme. Fire, however, is unique in the intensity of its alternatives. Light a candle, and you might be drawn into a meditative state, the flickering flame a part of the rhythm of thinking. But a mere candle tipped over can cause another kind of fire, and you might be fleeing for your life, caught in an emergency in which survival obliterates every other thought. If there is any middle ground, it might be in the form of bonfires that burn just at the edge of human control. Many human beings have regarded fire as connected to a distinctive feature of what it means to be human—equating the mastery of fire with a level of independence from and power over other living creatures and the rest of the natural world. Fire is the original medium of synthesis and dissociation, forging clay into bricks, sand into glass, or reducing solid matter to ash and dust.

Fire, more than any other element, poses the question of taking the right distance. The sun, the hottest thing in our solar system, is located conveniently distant from Earth (though current speculation has it that the sun will eventually draw in all the planets, including ours, and burn them up). Perhaps it is just because of the ravages of fire that humans, conversely, seek out the gentle heat of candles and fireplaces not only for the warmth they provide but because they are usually experienced at safe distances, "contained." Hence the specialness of being close to a congenial fire: In this case, the distance that we must take from dangerous fires is suspended, and we can draw close, though being careful not to situate ourselves *too* close. The awe occasioned by the emotion of the sublime, as mentioned earlier, is a case where we keep a certain distance from the very thing that, experienced too close, might overwhelm us.

Threatening as fire is in its uncontained state, a sheer lack of light can be quite disturbing, as during prolonged nights when we are lost, sick, or find ourselves with unwelcome or even threatening company. In any of these circumstances, human beings often find themselves overwhelmed by dark and depressed thoughts that they cannot completely control. These thoughts may be occasioned by despair at ever finding a safe, well-lit place or by a decided hopelessness that nighttime in such places may bring with it. Indeed, any of us may awaken with disturbing thoughts we cannot control: What if my test results show me to have an advanced cancer, or what will happen when the forecast deluge inundates my house? Something about the sheer lack of light, even if only the embers of a waning fire, precipitates such difficult thoughts—thoughts we are less likely to entertain on a bright day that embodies hope and a sense of agency that nighttime circumstances render remote and out of reach. Perhaps worst of all is solitary confinement in prison, when perpetual artificial light becomes its own form of darkness by dismantling the rhythm of night and day, exacerbating the aloneness and helplessness of a prisoner who is forcibly sequestered in a cell.[28]

Candles and lamps are rarely lit during the day. It is at night or in the darkest seasons when the sun crouches below the horizon early or barely rises at all that we tend to light fires and gather beside them for warmth, light, and the company of a dancing flame. All of this suggests that fire occasions what we might call "thinking in proximity." This occurs in situations where productive reflecting happens at the periphery of fire or its equivalent—where we are inspired to think by a fiery spectacle yet realize that we must keep the spectacle at a certain distance, moved to think something through yet not coming so close to the fire as to be consumed by it. We experience this in the early stages of a project that we know might lead to burnout if we dedicate ourselves altogether to it. So we seek a place that allows us to anticipate what a commitment to that project might bring, to survey the likely outcome without being consumed by it—to consider its likely consequences without throwing ourselves like Empedocles into the volcano. This can be considered *thinking from the edge*, itself a variant of thinking in proximity.[29]

Fire is usually associated with *speed*: a rapidly moving, transformative power. But insofar as it can occasion thought, it is also connected to a special sense of distance. Thinking-in-proximity denotes a form of thinking that remains attentive to how near or far one draws oneself toward or away from things. Perhaps fire teaches us about forms of proximity that we might otherwise fail to notice. A child draws back her hand abruptly from the hot stove, learning from a parent's stern and worried response that heat can burn. In the process, she learns that she can be close without touching, developing a sensitivity to the various proximities she should assume to better interact with her world. Later, this might manifest in a subtle social-emotional knowledge about how close to sit next to a friend, how much space to give her sister when she is swinging a bat, when and how to hug, how close to stand next to a stranger on the subway, or how much time and space to give a person who is upset. Fire educates us in these elemental lessons in temporal and spatial proximity, where proximity itself (what it means and how much is appropriate) always depends upon one's ability to discern the heat of the moment.

Fire turns out to be an immensely ambivalent element. It is essential to life on Earth: The evolution of plant and animal species would never have happened without the sunlight that is the effect of the sun's fires and the recurring, spontaneous fires that have been a feature of life on Earth since the advent of plants, crucial to the life and health of living landscapes. It is something we are drawn to in its milder and safer avatars, while being the cause of widespread fear and devastation when it goes out of control. It can be too intense to look at directly for more than a few seconds—as with the sun—but it can also be attractive in certain settings. In short, we can be drawn to or repelled by fire, depending on the exact context.

As for its effect on thinking in transit, we detect a comparable ambivalence. When under control, it can provide a welcome ambience where unhurried and inspired thinking is precipitated as if by a supportive medium. The nonrepeating flicker of flame and the occasional spark or crackle of embers contribute to slow-burning thoughts, while the smell of a wood fire might draw you back to early experiences of smoke and heat. Sitting close to a fire, you can feel your cheeks reddening and the descent, like a blanket, of a drowsy, hot stupor. But when a fire is threatening to us—as when a wildfire is known to be approaching a vulnerable building in which we reside—our thinking verges on desperation, given that we must think about how to escape injury and get to safe ground. This latter circumstance encourages thinking that is both rushed and pragmatic—hardly the context for creative and fresh thoughts. In such a situation, we are *driven to think* rather than thinking on our own initiative, when the thinking of genuinely new thoughts becomes more likely.[30] Thinking under duress tends to limit itself to what is most efficient or instrumental to do: locating the nearest exit in case fire might entrap us and others.

FIRE EXITS

Just as it was difficult to find a way into the element of fire, it is hard to find the way out. In our buildings, fire exits are typically clearly marked with bright letters, sometimes illuminated in the dark. In writing about fire, we don't have the clarity of any well-marked entrances or exits. Fire stories abound, and it is the nature of fire to draw us together in a ready position to hear and to tell stories in the fading light of the day. Heat rises, and sparks fly upward into the dark sky. These are reminders of ancient and mysterious connections between fire and the heavens, the soul, and language.

We have mentioned how fire invites a form of thinking-in-proximity that is sensitized to the importance of distance. Fire might teach social-emotional intelligence about how best to approach things: whether to touch or not to touch. But fire could also be tied to an all-consuming mentality that is experienced as unregulated and out of control. It is the nature of fire to intensify and expand as it burns, making it an ideal metaphor for a form of thinking, or even for a material work of some kind, that feeds upon itself in a frenzy, gaining strength in destruction. This is not far from how we experience manic or compulsive aspects of thought—episodes of obsessive fixation or cycles of uncontrollable desire. We are fire thinkers when we are set off by something relatively minimal or insubstantial but within moments find our brains consumed with the fast-moving flames set into action. We might lose ourselves in the fire of our own minds—becoming someone else than we usually are or acting in ways that are suddenly unpredictable even to ourselves. We are fire thinkers when we are enraged or impassioned to such a degree that we feel as if we cannot think at all—burning with anger, burning with love.[31]

Fire, often used in ceremonial rites of transformation, tests and tries whatever it touches. Clay pots fired in a kiln emerge glossy and waterproof, strengthened by the intensity of the heat that bakes them. American culture is rife with stories of heroes fired into formidable and forceful shape by experiences that might have crushed them. It's a common saw that "what doesn't kill you makes you stronger," but this also reflects an American infatuation with power and trauma, as well as a contorted sense that human beings are involved in a linear, progressive strengthening hewed to reality. (Freud abandoned such a view after talking with veterans returning from the First World War, which forced him to revise the predominance of the pleasure principle in his theory.) Perhaps the link between fire and strength is fueled by a reading of fire as a cleansing, fortifying agent of change, the analogue of a fierce deconstruction of ideas that leads one to think more clearly. One would like to convert fire—even in its most terrifying manifestations—into something good: Here we again encounter the Phoenix complex. But perhaps fire is more ambiguous and polymorphous than we have collectively allowed ourselves to imagine.

You're playing with fire. A word of caution. It could become something for which you are unprepared. Control, out of control. We tend to think of thinking itself as self-possessed, meditative, and deliberate. A thoughtful person is attentive. She seems reliable. But our images of thought remain mired in normative pictures of individuals (usually seated, male, white, in a suit) calmly *working things out*. Thinking is tied to accounts of rationality, speech, and contemplative reflection, which have predetermined who or what counts as rational. "Get a hold of yourself." "You're not thinking clearly." "Sit down." These are the kinds of things one might say to a person who appears overheated. Yet how many have been silenced, imprisoned, institutionalized, and marginalized in the name of a monoculture of *cool* level-headedness?

Fire remains to be reclaimed outside the pernicious dualities of good versus evil, punishment versus reward, destruction versus salvation. The only thing most of us can do is to think alongside fire in its multivalent manifestations, trying to find the right distance. A finger too close to the flame recoils from the heat. Thought close to fire does a similar thing. Infatuation and fright. An instinctive withdrawal. It won't help to creep up on it or to entice it into some gentler form. How far we have come from the flat waters and the ferry boat's smooth passage, which invited a woman wedged in a plastic booth to smooth her yellow legal pad over a Formica table. Or from the snug interior of a car, speeding along an illuminated highway, where a man pressed a red button on his tape recorder and began his monologue. Fire leaves us with barely a trace of what came before (only bones, bits of metal, and ash). It was alarming to Antoine-Laurent Lavoisier in 1772 to find that the ashes of sulfur weighed more than the original substance—leading him to hypothesize that oxygen itself must combine with the burning material and impart to it additional weight. It is almost as if fire contributes gravity to the things it touches, as if the transformation is not only physical but metaphysical. Of course, most things diminish in physical weight when they are burned. But the alchemy of fire remains mysterious. What burns can vanish completely yet nonetheless remain in the lingering scent of smoke and the space of memory. The weight of ashes cannot, therefore, be measured on a metrically determinate scale, as anyone knows who has scattered them out to sea, strewn them in a field, or held them in a box.

Fire is the element most tied to radical transformation. Water can erode and submerge things, wind can carry them away, earth can bury. But fire alone changes things at a molecular level all at once and forevermore. Of all the elements, it seems the most verbal, the least nominal. Our own planet hangs in careful balance between hot and cold, while other planets burn or freeze. Yet it's amazing to think that fire cannot burn by itself in outer space—where there is no heat, no air, no matter to transform. The stars and distant planets burn brightly, but in the dark in between lies the smoothest, most uninhabitable space of all. Human beings (and probably other creatures as well) live in fear of fires that rage out of control, but perhaps the scariest thought is a place so smooth, so free of friction, that one could never light a fire there. No spark, no warmth, no blaze, no inspiration, no comfort, and no exit.

Given the realities of our own warming planet, there is an urgency to thinking about and with, and even in the midst of, fire. We will have to seek out models and resources for knowing what this should look like, drawing on texts like Baldwin's *The Fire Next Time*, C. Eric Lincoln's *Coming Through Fire*, and others written from the crucible of experience. We are burning through material on Earth at an unprecedented rate. It is easy for wealthy and insulated communities to overlook how much burning transpires all around us, having moved from the open flames that fueled and illuminated human dwellings to largely invisible forms of combustion as we burn gas, oil, and coal. The lights go on with the flip of a switch, and it's much easier to forget to turn them off than it was to forget to blow out a candle or tamp down redhot coals hissing in a fireplace. It is also less dangerous—as we can leave the lights on all night, leave the shimmering lights on a Christmas tree plugged into the wall—and suffer no immediate calamity as a result. Except that the calamity is nearing us anyhow, coming from a planetary burnout for which we are all collectively responsible.

Perhaps we should close with a return to the candle. The flame dancing above the wick, the wax slowly pooling and dripping onto a table. Descartes wrote by candlelight in front of his fire. Wearing his nightdress, he must have smeared his white cotton sleeves as he dipped his quill into a pot of ink and wrote furiously through the night. It was, after all, a piece of wax that undid him. A bit of broken candle he had gripped in his hot hand until it became soft. He held it out next to his fire and saw it rapidly transform from solid to liquid. Amazed, aghast, he pulled it back from the heat and suddenly realized the transience of all things, the way that bodies age and decay, the insubstantiality of the material world.

Fire can occasion such thinking of transience. Nothing lasts. Or, as Flannery O'Connor wrote, "everything that rises must converge."[32] It happens suddenly or slowly—one never knows. We light candles to ward off the darkness, to issue prayers, to make a wish, and to remind ourselves that illumination is something precious and worthy of protection. Kant famously saw the "starry heavens above me and the moral law within me" as analogues of the same inspirational fire—sources of hope and orientation. Actual fires have done that as well, sending smoke signals across vast distances, giving an alert, providing a guide. We can't live without fire—we can hardly live with it. The temptation to valorize or demonize almost never reaches such a pitch as it does when we turn our minds to fire. A god, a demon. Neither, both. Fire forces us into subtler modes of thinking and reminds us of how precarious it is to be a body among bodies calibrated to survive within a narrow band of heat and light, utterly dependent on a distant blazing star, entirely at the mercy of things we can barely name.

Thus we bring to a close our shortest chapter—its limited length reflecting fire's capacity to burn quickly through that with which it comes into direct contact.

POSTFACE

Here we are. At the end of our travel through the four elements, as if arriving at the edge of a cliff. Who knew how bizarre and unwieldy things might become? Who knew how much we would learn about ourselves and each other? The ease with which Megan (a Pisces) thought about water—almost like a native habitat—compared to the trepidation Ed, despite being a Pisces, feels with respect to any aqueous body. The heady summits of thinking about the air—so tempting to connect to the high-flying thinking of so many philosophers. Our disparate relations to the earth, the walks and runs, and cars and canes, that have helped us move and think while grounded. The harrowing thought of fire, the memory of illness, the premonition of death. Everything opened onto something else while we were working, our memories triggering new avenues, our writing spreading out like watercolors efflorescing across a damp page.

Heidegger began *Was Heisst Denken?* (*What Is Called Thinking?*) with the following assertion: "We come to know what it means to think when we ourselves try to think." He goes on to warn us that "preoccupation with philosophy more than anything else may give us the stubborn illusion that we are thinking just because we are incessantly 'philosophizing.'"[1] Thinking, according to Heidegger, is something more focused and concerted than what we are normally engaged in. Meanwhile, philosophy lends itself to the illusion of *serious* thinking. Glasses, pipe, tweed coat, armchair, a heavy, leather-bound book on a table. The traditional trappings of philosophical thinking can be just that: traps.

While Heidegger was concerned with differentiating authentic from inauthentic modes of thinking, we are less worried about that. Thinking happens not in one mode or form but across endless variations, as our discussions have shown. The question is not *what* is thinking but *when*, and *how*? We have tried in these pages to inventory some of the scenes and modes of thinking, alert to the fact that understanding the nature of thinking is not just a matter of identifying and labeling a certain activity. How we talk about thinking says something significant about thinking itself, starting with the fact that in English we often prefer to speak of "thinking" as thinking of, thinking over, thinking about. Whenever we are talking about thinking, we are talking about an ongoing process. To talk about "thought," in contrast with "thinking," suggests that there *is* such a singular thing as *a thought* considered as a coherent unit of cognition. But it becomes progressively clear that thought is not one thing and that thinking is many things, each with its own characteristic mode of activity and location—sometimes overlapping in character and sometimes not, sometimes happening by and in bodily gestures and sometimes not, sometimes sheerly psychical and sometimes not, sometimes designatable in so many words and sometimes not, sometimes conscious and sometimes not. Thinking is *all over the place*: not just *in us* but also *around us*. It can be the center of our current lives, as when it is obsessive, but it can also take place at life's peripheries, as with fleeting thoughts that seem to pass us by like a whiff of smoke.

Where does thinking happen? We ask this question with some urgency as it is what most of this book is about. As philosophers, we have been trained in the practice of thinking according to rather strict directives and classical precedents: thinking in solitude in secluded locations, where lofty thoughts have time to develop. In contrast to such a tradition, we have identified various alternative and promising venues for thinking—especially for creative thinking—for thinking otherwise. We are questioning the long-established tendency to consider thinking (especially philosophical thinking) as occurring in a bare, quiet room sequestered from the rush of life. Innovative thinking occurs in many places, especially in those places we often consider in-between: in-between various places and in-between different activities we pursue in those places. In fact, thinking almost always transpires in such in-between places—and this is above all true of *thinking in transit*. This is thinking that has no proper or single location and that is not sealed off from the world. Such thinking proceeds differently from what is likely to happen in more staid settings. It is thinking that occurs on the way to somewhere and something else.

One of the surprising things about thinking in transit is that for both of us it was and continues to be an integral and necessary part of how we are able to think and to write. Our discipline (professional philosophy) seems mired in an image of philosophizing in some ideally cloistered setting, yet the discipline itself sends us on the road, commuting endlessly from work and home, from one conference or meeting to another. Few have the luxury of sitting quietly in place. As academic jobs have become scarcer, many adjunct and temporary teachers shuttle from institution to institution stitching together a living—frantically moving to and fro, thinking in between jobs until exhaustion sets in. In this respect, the two of us have been exceedingly lucky to benefit from continuous employment, regular research leave, and other amenities. However, living so much of our lives on the road, we have also had to rely on trial and error to devise strategies to think—to concentrate, to write, to imagine—while moving in between places. In the process, we've come to appreciate the possibilities afforded by letting thought transpire outside the narrow parameters of a supposedly *ideal* setting—a setting that turns out to be not only illusory but often all too constricting. Hence our emphasis on the variegated circumstances of thinking in the context of the four elements, which concretize and specify thinking considered as an ongoing process.

Travelogue: Ed on Thinking in Sequestered Spaces

I became quite accustomed to thinking in staid settings for a long stretch of my early life as a student. In a private high school I was required to go to a study hall every weekday evening from 7:00 to 10:00 pm. Rules of strict silence obtained while the students—each in an assigned seat—did their homework under the surveillance of a faculty member. I was reprimanded several times for "drifting": showing by my head motions that I was daydreaming rather than attending to my homework. At Yale as an undergraduate, by then habituated to such a routine, I imposed my own evening schedule, often staying riveted to a reading table in the university library until midnight: reading, making notes, etc. Sometimes I'd venture up into the stacks of the library, where there were small scholars' spaces. My favorite such secluded space was on the top floor of Sterling Library, looking down on a sizeable segment of the campus below and taking special pleasure from this overview.

Note how such spaces remove one from interpersonally lively circumstances such as playing sports or just talking with friends. I wrote my first book at a long table in Oxford's Bodleian Library, where people were not allowed to use typewriters because of the noise they made, much less converse with one another.

There was a pattern in all this: isolation in preassigned spaces, at first imposed on me and then increasingly chosen as the setting that

I thought fitting for thought. Only in Paris as a graduate student did I encounter a café culture in which reading and writing occurred outside, at randomly organized tables. But I still wasn't ready to take this step fully, given my history of thinking and writing in cloistered spaces. I say "cloistered" with intention, as my habitual spaces were reminiscent of what, in the training of monks, would be a way of mastering Holy Scripture by isolation and strict self-discipline.

Thinking itself was sheltered in such circumstances, and I now realize that it was throttled in many ways by being pursued mainly in preestablished places of study. My thinking—as shown in my writing—had a formal cast. There were few signs of new or nonstandard thinking—even though my main subject of study from sophomore year in college onward was philosophy, where fresh thinking is valorized and rewarded. (I recall reading Wittgenstein's later work at that time and finding its innovative and unconventional literary form striking to me yet something I could imagine doing myself.) My own writing in those years was in well-ordered paragraphs and pages laid out in predictable patterns. This held true for my college essays (including an honors thesis on Freud—who would doubtless have had something to say about this excess of superego) as well as in my first book, a phenomenological examination of imagining.[2] Ironically, at that time I could not imagine writing otherwise than in the well-ordered form that my early work took unhesitatingly.

In sum, my thinking and writing took place in privileged and highly sheltered locations for study. By long tradition, these are held to be ideal spaces for free thought and thus also for both mastery of form and experimental modes of writing. I did not realize to what extent these spaces might well be more inhibiting than releasing. Only later in my career—by my mid-thirties—did I gain a critical perspective on such established spaces. In fact, it was precisely while driving late at night and recording my spontaneous thoughts—as recounted earlier in chapter 3—that I began to become liberated from these all-too-scholastic spaces, finding that unconventional settings in open air and with others around me were in fact more conducive to free and creative thinking and writing.

Also contributing to my liberation from strictly sheltered places and forms of writing was my becoming active as a painter about this same time. My painting instructor in Connecticut, Dan Rice, advised me to "paint your unconscious." The result has been an adventure of freeform painting that has lasted for many years, in which I have found modes of free movement not yet attainable in my writing. It was not accidental that landscapes and seascapes became my favorite subjects of paintings: The open and smooth spaces they offered were the virtual converse of the secluded and striated spaces in which I had been confined (and confined myself) in earlier years. The action of painting and the open talk in Rice's art studio in Connecticut acted to liberate me from my earlier cloistered life. The practice of freely ideating into the tape recorder while driving followed soon after.

Travelogue: Megan on Thinking in Crowded Places

Unlike Ed, I never had the experience of reading and studying in quiet places. Or rather, when presented with the opportunity to inhabit such spaces (the library at my high school and, later, the grand Sterling Library at Yale University), I fled. At Yale the rows of long wooden tables lined with green-glass lamps, the high ceilings, and the gold-embossed volumes lining the shelves all converged to create what I experienced as a terribly foreign and oppressive climate. Everything seemed too precious. Too quiet. Instead, I stationed myself at the Daily Café, a small coffee shop on the corner of Broadway and York Streets, a dingy, smoke-filled place frequented by local skateboarders and grunge or metal musicians. There I would read Kant or Heidegger to the soundtrack of Nina Simone and the din of people talking with one another. My sense at that time was that being interrupted by the noise and commotion of ordinary life was crucial to my ability to study philosophy. Or perhaps, I felt that it kept me honest—tied back into the feeling of my public high school and reminders of the world as a place of multiple activities. I never felt at ease or at home at Yale, and I worried about the way that philosophy might pull me even further from people and places I had grown up with. The antidote seemed to be to philosophize, as much as possible, in a crowd.

I have no illusions about whether this made my work better. My work was a mess. It was impossible to maintain one train of thought, and often my texts were marked up with snippets of conversation from adjoining tables more than they were with notes that may have helped me navigate the texts. I doodled endlessly—drawing the people around me, the cups and rows of bottled syrups behind the counter— and I came home reeking of cigarettes (though never smoking them myself). But I pressed on and wrote the entirety of my senior thesis in cafes and on a few extravagant trips on Metro North. Once I had the taste for writing in public and in motion, there was no going back.

My habits continued in graduate school at the New School for Social Research, where, to my delight, the library was a dingy, pedestrian space located in the basement of the old department store we called our university. I loved the porous quality of that building at 65 Fifth Avenue in its intimate relation to New York City. There I didn't need to seek out crowds and commotion and common life, as I had in New Haven. I read and wrote anywhere I could in New York: on the subway, in coffee shops, in my shared apartment in Clinton Hill. The major development in those years was that I had gone to New York to be a painter, and I had started painting cityscapes because I couldn't think of what else to paint. I would set up my easel on the street, in a park, or (if I was lucky and resourceful enough) on a fire escape or rooftop. I painted the city in an effort to get to know it and to try to love it (it was not an easy transition). In the process, I learned so much about the architecture and feel of specific buildings, the intersections of rooflines, the texture of concrete and bricks. I painted in all kinds of weather and under all manner of conditions. This taught me stamina as well as more about how to focus in public, how to be open and closed at the same time, and how to establish concrete parameters for myself and my own work.

The entirety of my dissertation (on Levinas) was written at Woodland Coffee and Tea in New Haven, where I returned to live with my partner in 2003. Locals and regulars came to know me as a fixture in the same seat in the back corner, and I came to rely on them as sources of distraction and accountability. They all knew what I was doing, and they all expected me to finish. I continued to take the train for teaching jobs (north to Providence or south to New York), writing as I went. I continued to paint cityscapes as well as landscapes and seascapes. In all of my writing and painting in those years and since (including the years and years on the ferry between Bridgeport and Port Jefferson, Long Island), the faces and voices of particular people—mostly strangers—figured into my work. The rhythm of the train, the high-pitched whir of the boat, music playing on the radio, the clink of dishes, the shouts from the street. It all forms a part of the backdrop of whatever it is that I am thinking about or trying to make—a substructure of commotion on which to balance a form.

———

The contrasting examples just sketched—each with its own work ethic and characteristic practice—indicate that committed thinking can occur in highly diverse settings. They also point to the special virtues of being in transitory settings that put *thought in motion*, taking flight in words and images. Whether the motion is found in city streets of New York or the late-night open highway, creative thinking shows itself to be diversely modalized in and by the setting in which it emerges and from which it *takes off* rather than occurring restrictedly in a fixed place. It takes off into a space and time of its own where unbound thinking can occur.

We have said relatively little here about the basic nature of thinking, of thoughts, ideas, mentality, or the brain. We have steered clear of categorizing thinking itself as an activity, an effort, or of any certain type. Our text, like any piece of writing, performs thinking—in the special category of *thinking in writing*. Thinking in writing is different than forms of thinking in other mediums (thinking in painting, thinking in dancing, thinking in singing, in cooking, hammering, sewing, driving, and on and on . . .). Thinking in writing entails thinking with a degree of concerted effort at verbalization. We have tried to think about thinking itself, about its environments, its emotional tenor, its material manifestations, and its interconnection with many varieties of movement and elemental specificity. We have tried to put these thoughts into more or less complete sentences, arranging the sentences into paragraphs. Writing, no matter how freeform, seems highly structured compared to the free-floating nature of ordinary thought (despite Woolf's, Joyce's, or Faulkner's best efforts, there is no escaping the stubborn linearity of words on a page). In writing, we pin things in place. We work them over. We look for the right wording, punctuation, and rhythm to try to capture the momentum of thought.

Pulling all of our ideas together has led us to create a text realized in several forms of writing (and punctuated by a few paintings and one photograph). It could have, of course, been a *more* experimental or inventive text than it is—one verging on what Julia Kristeva has called the "semiotic," the expression of meaning without precise signification as conveyed by silence, hesitation, "displacement, condensation, alliterations, vocal and gestural rhythms."[3] Such a "text" would not be legible in the traditional sense of the term. One would have to invent a new form of reading to hear its strange message—just as Kristeva describes the psychoanalyst engaging in a new form of listening to hear the speech of depressed patients. Instead, we have aimed for a middle ground. We have largely kept to the structure and order of symbolic-syntactical language, hoping to write a text that is coherent while keeping it open at the edges. To this end, we have employed an ancient, mythic structure—following the four elements as our cardinal points of orientation, even as we know that no element lives in isolation and that no thinking or writing can exhaust their enmeshed meanings.

Thinking not only accompanies various activities but is realized in and by these activities. This is what Erin Manning and Brian Massumi call "thinking-in-the-act" and "thinking in action," and they make it the subject of various ingenious experimental procedures to explore whether we can "enact thought" instead of talking about it or engaging in other indirect modalities. Their aim is to "make felt the intensity of thought in practice," where "practice" means engaging in activities such as dancing, constructing various physical objects, discussing things in small groups, and so forth.[4] It is a matter of "the passing of the threshold into the event," where "threshold" signifies the emergence of that which we are about-to-say and "event" the bringing-forth of unexpected and often unprecedented thoughts.[5] When bodily action, accompanied by affect, induces such a threshold, it becomes the primary place where emergent thinking is articulated and expressed. This happens all the time in everyday life, when we find that what we were just thinking about consolidates in concrete actions of gesturing and speaking as well as in mute bodily movements that express our thought. Consider when your facial configuration makes clear the disgust you have been feeling toward a certain line of thought on the part of your interlocutor. As Manning and Massumi put it: "Every practice is a mode of thought, already in the act. To paint: a thinking through color. To perceive in the everyday: a thinking of the world's varied ways of affording itself."[6]

Our thesis—simple and complex at once—has been that thinking emerges in very different circumstances and that it takes multiple forms depending on the concrete context in which it occurs. One of these forms is the kind of thinking that being in transit brings with it. In this book we have explored basic settings in which such thinking emerges. We have also indicated that such thinking itself can take very different forms depending on the circumstances. Sometimes it is experimental, as when we set out on a journey whose outcome we cannot fully foresee. At other times, it occasions reflective thinking (as in Ed's feeling trapped on a moving plane). In still others, it represents new thinking, as when in cycling we follow a route we've never before tried out, forcing us to rethink how we should travel safely over a road whose exact character may not yet be known by us. Here thinking and traveling converge.

Thinking in transit offers a new route when it comes to considering the full range of thinking of which we are capable. It takes us away from the comforts of thinking in fully familiar ways and starts us on a journey into previously unknown territory. Except for brief glimmerings—for example, in Rousseau, Thoreau, James, and in our own day Gary Snyder and Rebecca Solnit—it has not received full recognition, much less adequate examination. We trust that our book offers significant inroads into this basic dimension of human existence while leaving much else to be explored further. For it is while moving from one place to another in a comparatively carefree way—alleviated by the mode of transportation we are on—that some of our most creative thinking occurs. It is in such transitions that there is likely to occur a "releasing of the tension of the mind on the problem at hand [thereby freeing] a space where new ideas can arise."[7]

A space where new ideas can arise: this is just the kind of space from which the inspiration for this book first arose. Megan had the practice of writing papers and preparing for classes while she was deep in the hull of the Bridgeport–Port Jefferson ferry: Down there, on a plastic tabletop, she found she could pursue new directions in her writing—directions that continually surprised her as she wrote them out longhand. Ed found freedom in thinking while driving on freeways between Long Island and Connecticut, recording thoughts as they made their way to his moving lips. Where Megan's movements were largely in her hands as she wrote, Ed's were in his voice as words tumbled out into a recorder. In the two cases, there were variant modalities by which our bodies transcribed our thoughts in a medium that preserved them and made their eventual retrieval possible, whether on paper or on tape.

Beyond bodily movements and transcriptive media—different as these are—these two practices shared one other parameter: *thinking in transit*. It was on voyages, one on water and the other on land, that these two paradigmatic practices took place. Each had a determinate starting point and an equally determinate ending point. In between, and on two very different carriers (ferry and car), acts of thinking arose on the voyages from one place to another: at once enabled and enhanced by the levitation provided by these voyages. And inspired by them as well, as if the thoughts generated on these trips came not only from below (water, land, active bodies) but from some indeterminate place: outside the body, beyond the head, as if emerging from the air, the soil, the steering wheel, the ferry's blasting horn. Bodies transported find themselves uprooted from habitual patterns and enmeshed in new relations. Thinking, caught up in the web, takes on a different quality, pace, and scope. If "to think is to voyage," as stated in *A Thousand Plateaus*, it is in thinking while voyaging that human beings generate some of their most creative and remarkable thoughts, whether in philosophy or any other domain of human experience.[8]

Perhaps, in sum, we can say that thinking, in the way we have carried it out on these pages, can be something of an adventure.

Describing an "adventure," Gadamer writes, "An adventure is by no means just an episode.... An adventure interrupts the customary course of events, but is positively and significantly related to the context which it interrupts. Thus an adventure lets life itself be felt as a whole, in its breadth and in its strength."[9] Thinking together, much more than thinking or writing alone, has felt adventurous. It has taken us to places we could never have anticipated. It has returned us to times and scenes of our own lives that seemed remote and even buried. In this sense, thinking itself is an extraordinary vehicle of transit. It carries us forward into the unknown and backward into the past. It carries us sideways toward each other and up and down and all around—into the air, over the water, across the earth, and toward (and away from) the fire. When thinking transpires together with someone else, as it has over the course of this book, it is almost as if the ship of one's own mind merges with the ship of another's, and the combined vehicle is something categorically different and grander. What before could only sail alone on a calm sea develops wings to take flight, or wheels, or some other form of mobility. Of course, two minds are better than one. We all know that. But we have discovered that two minds are *different* than one. When we put our minds together, drawing on the diverging trajectories our different bodies have taken through the world, thinking itself changes.

William James saw thought as a river moving in a continuous stream. Arrest any part of it, and you abstract from the essence of what it means to be conscious, like reeling in a silvery fish who now lies thrashing on the dock. Thinking goes on as a mixed medley, only rarely settling down or into decisive or definitive forms. When it does, as sometimes happens in a conversation, in meditation, in paintings, poems, songs, novels, buildings, laws, and so on—the thinking staring back at you can seem strangely autonomous, as if it had dropped from the sky or sprung like Athena full-grown from the head of some god. There is the inevitable transformation of *thinking*, with its open, gerundive quality, into *thought*, with its decisive nominalism. Writers resist this transmutation in various ways, hoping to keep the words on the page alive enough to move on their own. Hoping to catch the fish with just enough water to let it breathe.

We had not intended to write a book about writing, but it turns out that our thinking in transit is connected to writing in transit—writing back and forth between the two of us, writing while moving between places, and writing as a form of travel between thinking and thought, act and content. Thinking is a vehicle that takes us far and wide, no matter how stationary or inert we might seem to be. Writing is another vehicle of travel, the text and the pages becoming papery airplanes that shuttle us off to distant shores and leave a network of trails between us. In writing, we pack our words onto the page as if carefully choosing the right shoes and coat, the *essentials*, for a long trip. We unpack and try again, weighing the suitcase, lifting it up. At some point, we have decided enough is enough—it's time to go, and the bag is zipped shut and heaved out the door.

Writing has its own pace and speed. Sentences roll out like perfectly smooth blacktop or rumble about like dirt roads strewn with rocks. Writing helps you think in longer lines than is possible while just thinking casually. Suddenly the thinking, which before seemed light and full of air, feels heavy and gelatinous. Sticky prose. Gooey thoughts. How to inject a bit of levity and pick up the pace? We have our own routines of trying to combat the isolation and gravity of writing: Ed looking out over the vista of New York City shimmering in the distance far below and Megan scribbling on yellow legal pads on the ferry, in the car, on the train. Our writing carries the traces of those places where we have turned thinking into prose. We have carried our pages around with us, and they have absorbed the hues of our various environments. Thinking gets knocked about in any writing process. If it survives, it is a monument of resiliency.

Transit—the word at the center of our conjunctive thinking—is such an odd and mechanical term. It makes us think about "transit systems," like New York City's subways or bus routes defined by colorful maps and elaborate keys. It comes from the Latin *transire*, "to go across." Words go across a page. Ferries go across the water. When Megan's younger daughter was learning to talk, she heard that her mother was "taking the ferry" to Long Island and pictured her with a tiny, winged creature—a fairy—in her pocket. We carry things in all kinds of ways. We are carried—not just by our bodies but by the elemental matrices through which we move. All of our thinking in these pages revolves around various modes of going across and crossing over, crossing out, crisscrossing. "Transit" may not lend itself to poetry, but it is a sturdy word for expressing the open-ended ways in which we carry and cross. Life is lived in transit, in transition. Some days the roads are clear and the travel easy. Other days storms bear down upon us, and it is all one can do to sit up in bed. We have leaned on each other in writing a book that carries us further than either of us could have gone alone. Transit includes all of those chapters in which we have been carried (by our mothers, by our families, by our friends, by a line of poetry or a picture on the wall, by the grace of some unknown power). We have tried to elaborate some of the modes and means of human transportation that carry us into new places, relations, and forms of life. We have also tried to write ourselves into new places and forms of thinking, hoping you will travel along.

ACKNOWLEDGMENTS

We are grateful to the New School for Social Research, the site of our first meeting, and Stony Brook University for bringing us together as colleagues in the Philosophy Department. Many thanks to our first readers, Ralph W. Franklin and Caleb Ward, who offered invaluable insights, corrections, and ideas for further study. We are particularly grateful to Caleb for pointing us to sources we would otherwise have missed. Thank you to our editor, Wendy Lochner, at Columbia University Press, whose enthusiasm and dedication propelled the text into a book. We are grateful for generous comments and suggestions from Cynthia Willet and Kelly Oliver. Ed thanks highway I-95 for providing the space to think through certain philosophical issues as well as Mary Watkins for her inspiration and receptivity. Megan wishes to acknowledge the Bridgeport and Port Jefferson Ferry and MetroNorth for carrying her (on time) for so many years and, above all, her family: Nick, Cora and Violet, to whom she always returns.

NOTES

PREFACE

1. Megan Craig and Edward S. Casey, "Thinking in Transit," in *Philosophy, Travel, and Place: Being in Transit*, ed. Ron Scapp and Brian Seitz (Palgrave Macmillan, 2018), 51–68.
2. In an interview with Ezra Klein about his 2024 book, *The Work of Art: How Something Comes of Nothing*, Adam Moss said, "Over and over again, people describe being most creative when they're in motion. So whether they put themselves in motion when they're running or swimming or something like that or biking or even just on a train or an airplane, just moving, the body physically in space moving seems to unleash something in them." *The Ezra Klein Show* (podcast), April 23, 2023, https://www.nytimes.com/2024/04/23/podcasts/transcript-ezra-klein-interviews-adam-moss.html.
3. Gilles Deleuze and Félix Guattari, *A Thousand Plateaus*, trans. Brian Massumi (Continuum, 2004), 3.
4. For an elaboration of the Presocratic and classical Greek origins of the four elements, see David Macauley: "We are, in effect, increasingly sheltered from rather than brought into closer contact with the elements, which, in turn, have retreated from the forefront of daily thought and experience." David Macauley, *Elemental Philosophy: Earth, Air, Fire, and Water as Environmental Ideals* (State University of New York Press, 2010), 1.

1. WATER

1. A pivotal 1987 study by Paul Hickey and Kanwaljeet Anand argued against the then prevalent view that infants don't feel pain by showing the mechanisms by which infants and newborns experience pain, concluding that "current knowledge suggests that humane considerations should apply as forcefully to the care of neonates and young, nonverbal infants as they do to children and adults in similar painful and stressful situations." K. J. S. Anand and P. R. Hickey, "Pain and Its Effects in the Human Neonate and Fetus," *New England Journal of Medicine* 317, no. 21 (1987).
2. William James, *The Principles of Psychology* (Harvard University Press, 1981), 1:496.
3. Many but not all. Some of the claims we are making about water and thought relate to work Megan has done with those in the autism community, specifically in her 2016 multimedia interactive installation *The Way Things Felt*. Autistic individuals often deviate at a young age from standardized motor and speech "milestones." Nonverbal autistic individuals may never acquire speech, which does not mean that they are without thought, feeling, empathy, affection, or anything else. Steve Silberman explains that "children with autism were particularly vulnerable to institutionalized prejudice because psychologists believed they were incapable even of rote learning. This theory was debunked in the 1970s, but subtler forms of discrimination persist." Steve Silberman, *Neurotribes: The Legacy of Autism and the Future of Neurodiversity* (Avery, 2015), 51.
4. Deleuze and Guattari write, "The desert, sky, or sea, the Ocean, the Unlimited, first plays the role of an encompassing element, and tends to become a horizon." Gilles Deleuze and Félix Guattari, *A Thousand Plateaus*, trans. Brian Massumi (Continuum, 2004), 546.
5. In *Black Sun*, Julia Kristeva describes the semiotic as "preverbal semiology—gestural, motor, vocal, olfactory, tactile, auditory." She goes on to stress "the power of semiotic rhythms, which convey an intense presence of meaning in a presubject still incapable of signification." Julia Kristeva, *Black Sun: Depression and Melancholia,* trans. Leon S. Roudiez (Columbia University Press, 1989), 62. Compare this with Levinas's description of "the Saying" (*le dire*), which he describes as "pre-reflective iteration" at the origin of language: "The Saying is . . . not a communication of something Said. . . . To Say is thus to exhaust oneself in exposing oneself, to make a sign of that of which

one makes a sign, without resting in its form as a sign." Emmanuel Levinas, "Sincerity of the Saying," in *God, Death, and Time*, trans. Bettina Bergo (Stanford University Press, 2000), 191–92.

6. This is not to diminish or ignore the experiences of people who lose their speech because of illness or injury. It is possible to lose and regain language. It is not possible to regain the alinguistic experience of infancy.
7. Note different religious and cultural rituals of water and rebirth, baptism, cleansing, and so on. See, for example, Malidoma Patric Somé, *Of Water and the Spirit* (Penguin, 1995); Celeste Ray, ed., *Sacred Waters* (Routledge, 2020); and Ta-Nehisi Coates, *The Water Dancer* (One World, 2020).
8. Michael Benedikt, "Water," *Poetry*, March 1969, 383.
9. Note the 2010 discovery of stone tools on the island of Crete, which suggests human navigation across open water and sophisticated abilities to conceive and assemble sturdy, seafaring vessels much further back than scientists thought possible, 130,000 to 190,000 years ago.
10. "The house we were born in is more than an embodiment of home, it is also an embodiment of dreams. Each one of its nooks and corners was a resting place for daydreaming." Gaston Bachelard, *The Poetics of Space*, trans. Maria Jolas (Beacon, 1969), 15.
11. Oliver Sacks, *On the Move: A Life* (Knopf, 2015), 232.
12. Sharpe continues: "Some of the ships made only one trip; others made multiple trips under the same and different names, under the same and different owners, and under the same and different flags, under the same and different insurers. The ships kept going and coming; over thirty-five thousand recorded voyages." Christina Sharpe, *In the Wake: On Blackness and Being* (Duke University Press, 2016), 102.
13. Audre Lorde, "A Trip on the Staten Island Ferry," in *The Collected Poems of Audre Lorde* (Norton, 1997), 119.
14. In his chapter "Intimate Immensity," Bachelard also references a ship: "Writing about the vastness of a ship, [Baudelaire] wrote, 'The poetic idea that emanates from this operation of movement inside the lines is the hypothesis of a vast, immense creature, complicated but also eurhythmic, an animal endowed with genius, suffering, and sighing every sigh and every human ambition.' Thus, the ship, beautiful volume resting on the waters, contains the infinite of the word *vast*." Bachelard, *The Poetics of Space*, 193.
15. Stanislavsky describes the difficulty of sustaining energy and intention in a given role for the length of a whole play, writing, "This calls for extremely

complicated creative work. It is carried on in part under the control of our consciousness, but a much more significant portion is subconscious and involuntary." Method acting includes various exercises that occupy the conscious mind (counting, sorting, etc.) in order to free the subconscious and allow for native, *unforced* inhabitation of the character. Constantin Stanislavsky, *An Actor Prepares*, trans. Elizabeth Reynolds Hapgood (Bloomsbury Academic, 2013), 12.

16. Shelbi Nahwilet Meissner describes the incommensurability between Indigenous languages and Indigenous worlds using the metaphor of two kinds of canoe voyages: "impassable incommensurability (*big water through a rock garden*)" and "incommensurably with technical passage (*heavy water through a rock garden*)." Reflecting on her own language community (Payómkawichum [Luiseño] and Kúupangaxwichem [Cupeño]), she writes, "It is not uncommon to hear that the land is in the language—that if one listens carefully, one can hear the land within each piece of the language." Such intimacy between land, elements, spirits, and human expression cannot be simply translated into English or gleaned from paddling a canoe. Shelbi Nahwilet Meissner, "'World'-Travelling in Tule Canoes: Indigenous Philosophies of Language and an Ethic of Incommensurability," *Hypatia* 38, no. 4, special issue (Fall 2023): 849–70.

17. Chronicling the 1865 trip that James took with Agassiz to Rio de Janeiro to collect and document native fish, Robert D. Richardson notes that James spent five months on the Amazon, covering five thousand miles, "but for two of those months and perhaps a thousand miles he went by small boats that used oars and by canoe." Robert D. Richardson, *William James: In the Maelstrom of American Modernism* (Houghton Mifflin, 2006), 68.

18. In *The Principles of Psychology*, James writes, "Consciousness . . . does not appear to itself chopped up into bits. Such words as 'chain' or 'train' do not describe it fitly as it presents itself in the first instance. It is nothing jointed; it flows. A 'river' or a 'stream' are the metaphors by which it is most naturally described." James, *The Principles of Psychology*, 1:241.

19. Annie Dillard cites a long passage from Peter Freuchen about a "kayak sickness" common to Greenland Inuits. Quoting Freuchen, she writes, "The Greenland fjords are peculiar for the spells of completely quiet weather; when there is not enough wind to blow out a match and the water is like a sheet of glass. The kayak hunter must sit in his boat without stirring a

finger so as not to scare the sly seals away.... The sun, low in the sky, sends a glare into his eyes, and the landscape around moves into the realm of the unreal. The reflex from the mirrorlike water hypnotizes him, he seems unable to move, and all of a sudden it is as if he were floating in a bottomless void, sinking, sinking, and sinking." Annie Dillard, *Pilgrim at Tinker Creek* (Harper Perennial, 2007), 24.

20. Shelbi Nahwilet Meissner, "'World'-Travelling in Tule Canoes," 865.
21. Iris Marion Young explains that female bodies are more often constricted than male bodies, and she asks: "How do girls and women constitute their experienced world through movement and orientation in place? What are some of the feelings of ambivalence, pleasure, power, shame, objectification, and solidarity that girls and women have about bodies, their shape, flows, and capacities?" Iris Marion Young, *On Female Body Experience: "Throwing Like a Girl" and Other Essays* (Oxford University Press, 2005), 9.
22. Deleuze and Guattari, *A Thousand Plateaus*, 380–87.
23. Ralph Waldo Emerson, *The Essay on Self-Reliance* (The Roycroft Shop, 1905), 31.
24. Thich Nhat Hanh, *You Are Here: Discovering the Magic of the Present Moment*, trans. Sherab Kohn (Shambhala, 2010), 7. See also Pico Iyer, *The Art of Stillness: Adventures in Going Nowhere* (Simon & Schuster, 2014).
25. Sullivan explains, "Whether literal or metaphorical, ontological expansiveness operates with an assumed right to enter and feel at ease in whatever space a person inhabits, and inhabiting a space in this way both shapes and is shaped by a person's individual habits." Shannon Sullivan, "Ontological Expansiveness," in *Fifty Concepts for a Critical Phenomenology*, ed. Gail Weiss, Ann V. Murphy, and Gayle Salamon (Northwestern University Press, 2020), 249.
26. Mariá Lugones, "Playfulness, 'World' Travelling, and Loving Perception," in *Pilgrimages/Peregrinajes: Theorizing Coalition Against Multiple Oppressions* (Roman & Littlefield, 2003), 77–100.
27. bell hooks, *Belonging: A Culture of Place* (Routledge, 2009), 24.
28. T. S. Eliot, *Four Quartets*, in *The Complete Poems and Plays: 1909–1950* (Harcourt, Brace, 1980), 120.
29. Naadi Todd Lee Ormiston describes a fifty-five-day canoe trip with his brother in Alaska, highlighting lessons learned along the way. Among those, he writes about experiences of intense presence and "serenity after days on

the river," explaining "the Canoe Journey teaches me that in the silence, there is memory, experience, and a place for bearing witness. The journey teaches me that in the silence is a spirit, recorded history, and, as human beings, we must prepare for accountable listening to hear the stories that silence offers." Naadi Todd Lee Ormiston, "Haa Shageingyaa: 'Point Your Canoe Downstream and Keep Your Head Up!,'" in *Indigenous and Decolonizing Studies in Education*, ed. Linda Tuhiwai Smith, Eve Tuck, and K. Wayne Yang (Routledge, 2019), 41.

30. Naoki Higashida explains why many in the autism community often cup their ears: "The problem is you don't understand how these noises affect us. It's not quite that the noises grate on our nerves. It's more to do with a fear that if we keep listening, we'll lose all sense of where we are. At times like these, it feels like the ground is shaking and the landscape around us starts coming to get us, and it's absolutely terrifying." Naoki Higashida, *The Reason I Jump*, trans. K. A. Yashida and David Mitchell (Random House, 2007), 51.
31. Virginia Woolf, *On Being Ill* (Paris Press, 2012), 8.
32. Clare describes the prevalent ideology of "cure" as "imagined time travel," warning that "this promise can also devalue our present day selves. . . . It can fuel hope grounded in nothing but the shadows of *natural* and *normal*." Eli Clare, *Brilliant Imperfection: Grappling with Cure* (Duke University Press, 2017), 57.
33. Megan Craig, "A Philosopher on Brain Rest," *New York Times*, June 25, 2019.
34. Woolf, *On Being Ill*, 21.
35. Havi Carel, *Illness* (Routledge, 2013), 35.
36. Hannah Arendt, *The Life of the Mind* (Harcourt, 1978), 200.

2. AIR

1. Miller uses "midworld" in a technical sense to indicate the totality of functioning objects that *"project the environment."* Though he was not talking about matter poised halfway between earth and sky, his term seems apt for expressing the narrow band in which human life is sustained. John William Miller, *The Midworld of Symbols and Functioning Objects* (Norton, 1982), 13.
2. Francis Bacon, "The History of Winds," in *The Works of Francis Bacon*, vol. 12, B2 (London: M. Jones Paternoster-Row, 1815).

3. Gaston Bachelard, *Air and Dreams: An Essay on the Imagination of Movement* (Dallas Institute Publications, 1988), 6.
4. Bachelard, *Air and Dreams*, 127.
5. Howard Moss, "Air," in *The Toy Fair: Poems* (University of Michigan Press, 1976), 25.
6. Thomas Mann, *Death in Venice* (Bantam, 1988), 57.
7. Mohawk Mountain is a 1,683-foot peak located in Cornwall, Connecticut, on indigenous land natively inhabited by the Tunxis and Paugussett tribes, who used the mountain to send smoke signals warning of the approach of the Mohawk from the north and the west. The mountaintop became part of a state preserve in the 1920s, and the ski area opened in 1947.
8. "Saharan Dust Blowing Across the Atlantic Could Reach South Florida," *New York Times*, July 9, 2023.
9. "Surviving the Dust Bowl," *American Experience*, PBS, August 31, 2022, http://www.pbs.org/wgbh/americanexperience/features/transcript/dustbowl-transcript/.
10. Toni Morrison, *Sula* (Vintage, 2004), 51.
11. Robert Louis Stevenson, "The Swing," in *The Poems of Robert Louis Stevenson* (New York: Thomas Y. Crowell & Co., 1900), 46.
12. Cynthia Willet recalls seeing a Minoan sculpture in Crete representing their god on a swing, "moving through the air with ease and grace, like a child lost in thought." So many depictions of aerial heights are tied to patriarchal imagery of gods towering or ascending in a vertical dimension. As Willet points out, the Minoans give us a different, nonpatriarchal reference for thinking about our relationship with the air, with flight, and with the divine.
13. Petit returned to New York to walk across the nave at the Cathedral of St. John the Divine in "The Ribbon Walk" in 2024. Describing his preparation, he said, "I am always like a kid . . . I am always so excited. Why? I grab the pole and I start gliding on the wire, finally life is beautiful, life is beautiful and life is safe, which will make people look up and say: 'Are you crazy? You are, you know, thousands of feet in the air. You call that safe?' But yes, it's safe, because I cannot have left a single technical detail to chance." "Philippe Petit Returns to the High Wire at Age 74," *New York Times*, January 25, 2024.
14. Marjolein Oele, *E-Co-Affectivity: Exploring Pathos at Life's Material Interfaces* (SUNY Press, 2020), 65.

192   2. AIR

15. Simone Weil, *Gravity and Grace*, trans. Emma Crawford and Mario von der Ruhr (Routledge, 2002), 99.
16. Emily Dickinson, "'Hope' is the thing with feathers," in *The Poems of Emily Dickinson, Valorium Edition*, ed. R. W. Franklin (Belknap, 1998), 333.
17. Charles Coulston Gillispie, *The Montgolfier Brothers and the Invention of Aviation, 1783–1784, with a Word on the Importance of Ballooning for the Science of Heat and the Art of Building Railroads* (Princeton University Press, 1983), 16.
18. Ed remembers being mesmerized by an enormous dirigible that would periodically fly over Topeka. It was emblazoned with a single word: GOODYEAR. Here a floating object high up in the air was advertising a brand of tires that are designed for travel on land, even if unintentionally referring to an auspicious time ahead.
19. About the film, Miyazaki said, "Our goal in completing this film is to send an expression of solidarity to young viewers who find themselves torn between dependence and independence. We too, after all, were once boys and girls, and Kiki's problems are also the problems of our younger staff members." Hayao Miyazaki, *Starting Point 1979–1996*, trans. Beth Cary and Frederik L. Schodt (Viz Media, 2009), 264.
20. Hayao Miyazaki, "Kiki—The Spirit and the Hopes of Contemporary Girls," in *Starting Point 1979–1996*, 263.
21. Mariá Lugones critiques the aerial view for its disengaged, hierarchical remove from the realities of everyday life—especially the lives of the oppressed. She celebrates "streetwalker" or "pedestrian" theorists who "cultivate the ability to sustain and create hangouts by hanging out." Such theorists do their work by loitering and embedding themselves in the common fray of daily existence, refusing to retreat to the closed world of academia or the abstraction of a distant overview. Streetwalker theory stays close to the ground. "Streetwalker theorizing, curdling, and tres-passing are all different and related forms of noticing oppression and its logic and moving against it." Mariá Lugones, *Pilgrimages/Peregrinajes: Theorizing Coalition Against Multiple Oppressions* (Roman & Littlefield, 2003), 221, 12. Adrienne Rich makes a similar plea for grounded thinking in her 1984 lecture "Notes Toward a Politics of Location," urging us to "pick up again the long struggle against lofty and privileged abstraction" and reminding us that "theory—the seeing of patterns, showing the forest as well as the trees—theory can be a dew that rises from the earth and collects in the rain cloud and returns to earth over

and over. But it doesn't smell of the earth, it isn't good for the earth." Adrienne Rich, "Notes Toward a Politics of Location," in *Blood, Bread, and Poetry: Selected Prose, 1979–1984* (Norton, 1994), 213–14.

22. "Disorder is simply the order we are not looking for. You cannot suppress one order, even by thought, without causing another to spring up. But when you expect one of these orders and you find the other, you say there is disorder.... All disorder thus includes two things: outside us, one order; within us, the representation of a different order which alone interests us." Henri Bergson, *The Creative Mind: An Introduction to Metaphysics*, trans. Mabelle L. Andison (Dover, 2007), 80.

23. For a discerning analysis of what being a passenger entails, see Michael Marder, *Philosophy for Passengers* (MIT Press, 2022).

24. Annie Dillard, *The Writing Life* (Harper Perennial, 2009), 215.

25. A similar thing could be said about deep-sea exploration, as was documented in the implosion of the submersible carrying five people to view the remains of the *Titanic* on June 23, 2023. At extremes of travel into the air, under the water, or into the earth, bodies are utterly dependent on the vessels which carry them.

26. "Life as a whole—animal life and plant life together—appears in essence to be an effort for accumulating energy and releasing that energy into flexible and deformable canals at the end of which it will accomplish an infinite variety of works. This is what the *élan vital*, passing through matter, wanted to obtain in a single stroke." Henri Bergson, *Creative Evolution* [1911], trans. Donald Landes (Routledge, 2023), 223.

27. On such rootedness, see Edward S. Casey and Michael Marder, *The Place of Plants: Toward a Phenomenology of the Vegetal* (Columbia University Press, 2024).

28. Floral decoration occurs when flowers are picked up and packed together in a "bouquet" that is meant to enliven and embellish various parts of human dwellings or special events—as if they were replanted in these artificial settings that are at a certain remove from the earth itself: on a table, on a blouse, on which they are propped up for a certain finite period of time.

29. Gilles Deleuze and Félix Guattari, *A Thousand Plateaus*, trans. Brian Massumi (Continuum, 2004), 532.

30. "A democratic meeting place capable of containing folks from various walks of life, the porch was free-floating space, anchored only by the porch swing,

and even that was a symbol of potential pleasure. The swing hinted at the underlying desire to move freely, to be transported. A symbol of play, it captured the continued longing for childhood, holding us back in time, entrancing us, hypnotizing us with its back-and-forth motion." bell hooks, *Belonging: A Culture of Place* (Routledge, 2009), 147.

31. "In our small-town segregated world, we lived in communities of resistance, where even the small everyday gesture of porch sitting was linked to humanization. Racist white folks often felt extreme ire when observing a group of black folks gathered on a porch. They used derogatory phrases like 'porch monkey' both to express contempt and to once again conjure up the racist iconography linking blackness to nature, to animals in the wild." hooks, *Belonging: A Culture of Place*, 148.

32. "Throughout our history, African-Americans have recognized the subversive value of homeplace, of having access to private space where we do not directly encounter white racist aggression." bell hooks, "Homeplace as a Site of Resistance," in *Yearning: Race, Gender, and Cultural Politics* (Routledge, 1990) 47.

33. "One of the problems associated with public sculpture is context, deciding what the function of sculpture is in society today. It's one of the most difficult things to settle. I feel more and more that gardens offer me a clue, a self-justifying kind of context, because gardens are by nature gratuitous places." Martin Puryear, "Conversation with Hugh M. Davies and Helene Posner (1984)," in *Theories and Documents of Contemporary Art*, ed. Kristine Stiles and Peter Selz (University of California Press, 1996), 631.

3. EARTH

1. Perhaps this is one of the root anxieties in our age of climate change. As the planet heats and tides rise, we are facing the eradication of traversable land, which has been a part of our sense of an inhabitable planet. Journeys are becoming more dangerous and complex—involving movement across greater distances and often, as is the case for many climate migrants, across desert, jungle, and water.

2. In the descriptions of various earth-places recounted in this chapter—the family yard in Topeka, the open space just outside town, and the Flint Hills—we single out three very different scenes in terms of their local

topographies. But if we view them historically as well as spatially, they are seen to share one basic trait: Each was seized outright from the Native Americans who lived in the Great Plains. They each represent cases of settler colonialism in the heartland of America. Even if it is not the focus of our descriptive and narrative efforts in this book, this dark history must be acknowledged. The precise measurements of the plot of the family home in Topeka contrasts with the unmarked boundaries of the area to which Ed had eager recourse in his early adolescence. It is as if these rough boundaries defied the exact shapes of building plots and the carefully determined city limits of the Midwestern city they enclosed—such plots and limits being forms of striated space in the vocabulary of *A Thousand Plateaus*. The same is true for the Flint Hills region, whose indeterminate outer boundaries reflect something of the originally open arena that was the homeland of the Kaw and other Native American tribes who had lived for many centuries in that same area. These various spatial-cum-historical dimensions cannot be denied even if our main concern in this book is with the elemental nature of moving through these places on foot or by automated means in the present era.

3. "Hillbilly folk chose to live above the law, believing in the right of each individual to determine the manner in which they would live their lives. . . . Away from the country, in the city, rules were made by unknown others and were imposed and enforced. In the hills of my girlhood, white and black folks often lived in a racially integrated environment, with boundaries determined more by chosen territory than race. The notion of 'private property' was an alien one; the hills belonged to everyone or so it seemed to me in my childhood. In those hills there was nowhere I felt I could not roam, nowhere I could not go." bell hooks, *Belonging: A Culture of Place* (Routledge, 2009), 8.

4. Our point is that creative thinking happens all the time in spaces that are not designed for thinking or creativity. Audre Lorde, describing the suitability of poetry to working-class life, writes, "Even the form our creativity takes is often a class issue. Of all the art forms, poetry is the most economical. It is the one which is the most secret, which requires the least physical labor, the least material, and the one which can be done between shifts, in the hospital pantry, on the subway, and on scraps of surplus paper." Audre Lorde, *Sister Outsider* (Penguin, 2019), 116. Thanks to Caleb Ward for pointing us to this quotation.

5. D. W. Winnicott, *Playing and Reality*, 2nd ed. (Routledge, 2005).
6. This coincides with the feminist insight that the lived body is never a universally consistent or stable essence but a multiple, shifting set of possibilities, experiences, and feelings that are affected by history, social realities, geography, and more. See, for one example, chapter 3, "Feminist Theories of the Body: The Material Subject," of Ann Cahill, *Rethinking Rape* (Cornell University Press, 2001), where she explores Rosi Braidotti's idea of the "nomad . . . a wandering yet embodied subject, whose specific characteristics are derived from the particular environment in which it is developing (the nomad is never complete but always in process)" (73).
7. "The noblest man living in a desert absorbs something of its harshnesss and sterility, while the nostalgia of the mountain-bred man when cut off from his surroundings is proof how deeply environment has become part of his being." John Dewey, *Art as Experience* (Perigee, 2005), 359.
8. Compare Robert Smithson's notion of artworks that are "non-sites." Smithson defines a non-site as "an abstraction that represents the site." Robert Smithson, *Collected Writings*, ed. Jack Flam (University of California Press, 1996), 178–79. See also "Non-site Sights: Interview with Anthony Robbin," 181.
9. This is the action of two young African American women on a farmstead in rural Mississippi, as depicted in Raven Jackson's lyrical 2023 film *All Dirt Roads Taste of Salt*.
10. Beyond the facilitation of movement, canes, walkers, and wheelchairs can offer entirely new possibilities for movement and momentum, altering and expanding the repertoire of creative motion and thinking available to a given body.
11. Ludwig Wittgenstein, *Philosophical Investigations*, trans. G. E. M. Anscombe (Macmillan, 1968), ¶2, 3e.
12. Gary Snyder, *The Practice of the Wild: Essays* (North Point, 1990), 18.
13. Ed, recently walking with a cane because of a failing knee, suddenly became painfully aware of looking old, reinforced by a young boy in Portugal who yelled out upon his approach: "old man!" He didn't *feel* old but, on the contrary, rejuvenated by his dexterous use of the cane, which gave him extra strength in walking and helped with balance. But the boy's exclamation reminded him of how using a cane is construed in Western culture.
14. Frédéric Gros, *A Philosophy of Walking* (Verso, 2003), 10.
15. Ferris Jabr, "Why Walking Helps Us Think," *New Yorker*, September 3, 2014.

16. Rebecca Solnit, *Wanderlust: A History of Walking* (Penguin, 2000), 4.
17. The experience of the body receding from consciousness does not hold when one is forced to be sedentary because of illness or injury—moments in which the body looms in pain. Those forced into confinement might also experience a sense of the loss of body, though discomfort and prolonged confinement in stifling space often dismantle the body and the mind in tandem.
18. Henry David Thoreau, *Walking* (Tilbury House, 2017), 31.
19. "Traveling is a fool's paradise. We owe to our first journeys the discovery that place is nothing. . . . The rage of traveling is itself only a symptom of a deeper unsoundness affecting the whole intellectual action." Ralph Waldo Emerson, "Self-Reliance," in *Essays, Lectures, and Orations* (London: William S. Orr & Co., 1851), 39.
20. Thoreau, *Walking*, 29.
21. Thoreau, *Walking*, 83. Adam Tuchinsky notes Thoreau's strange infatuation with westward conquest in his introduction to Thoreau's text, writing, "'Walking,' conceived in the aftermath of the Mexican-American War, oddly seems to embrace the cultural nationalism inherent in the idea of Manifest Destiny, according to which a divinely ordained continental destiny for the United States had been revealed in its imperial subjugation of the modern-day Southwest" (15). Zaida Verónica Olvera Granados connects Thoreau's concept of "wilderness" with a romanticized and Christian longing for paradise lost, stressing that such ideas figured in both Transcendentalism and American landscape painting and exacerbated the colonial, European "assumption that indigenous people lack social (economic and/or religious) links with their environment: an explicit form of epistemological racism." Zaida Verónica Olvera Granados, "A Critical Genealogy of the Concept 'Nature Reserve': Naturalistic Ontology, Landscape, and Space of Exception" in *The Political Dimension of Nature: An Intercultural Critique*, ed. Abbed Kannor and Niels Weidtmann (Metzler, forthcoming).
22. Haruki Murakami, *What I Talk About When I Talk About Running* (Vintage Canada, 2009), 7, 17.
23. Alan Sillitoe, *The Loneliness of the Long-Distance Runner* (Plume, 1992), 19.
24. The principle of "just getting around" is also depicted in a famous scene from *Butch Cassidy and the Sundance Kid*, in which Paul Newman as Butch Cassidy rides a bicycle to the tune of "Raindrops Keep Fallin' on My Head." George Roy Hill, dir., *Butch Cassidy and the Sundance Kid* (Twentieth Century Studios, 1969).

25. "Motorcycles," Sacks wrote, "seemed, even in stiff England, to bypass the barriers, to open a sort of social ease and good nature in everyone." In the 1970s, Sacks gave up motorcycles around the same time that he gave up drugs and a lifestyle that had spun out of control. Oliver Sacks, *On the Move: A Life* (Knopf, 2015), 73.
26. Sacks, *On the Move*, 97.
27. Susan B. Anthony said, "Let me tell you what I think of bicycling. I think it has done more to emancipate women than anything in the world.... It gives a woman a feeling of freedom and self-reliance . . . the moment she takes her seat, she knows she can't get into harm unless she gets off her bicycle." Lynn Sher, *Failure Is Impossible: Susan B. Anthony in Her Own Words* (Random House, 1995), 277.
28. Walt Whitman, quoted in William James, "On a Certain Blindness in Human Beings," in *Talks to Teachers on Psychology and to Students on Some of Life's Ideals* (Harvard University Press, 1983), 143.
29. Tens of thousands of people are currently living in their cars in America. Rukmini Callimachi, "In Many Cities the 'Mobile Homeless' Are Now the Majority of the Homeless Population," *New York Times*, October 17, 2023.
30. William James and Henry James, *Selected Letters*, ed. Ignas K. Skrupskelis and Elizabeth M. Berkeley (University Press of Virginia, 1997), 357.
31. Primo Levi, *Survival in Auschwitz* (Touchstone, 1996), 16–17.
32. Zaida Verónica Olvera Granados explores the connections between landscape painting and the emergence of public parks, gardens, and other "spaces of exception" where native inhabitants have been removed to fabricate purified sites of contemplation. "The birth of landscape painting is a crucial moment for understanding the emergence of this *space of exception*," which tends to "reproduce neocolonialism, epistemological racism, exclusion, and dispossession." Granados draws our attention to a tension at the heart of Romantic American landscape painting, which is mired in histories of dispossession, genocide, and belief in Manifest Destiny. Gardens, national parks, and other "wild" sites where landscape painters have historically set up their easels are also places that obscure the violence of earlier colonization. Olvera Granados, "A Critical Genealogy of the Concept 'Nature Reserve.'"
33. Maurice Merleau-Ponty, "Eye and Mind," in *The Merleau-Ponty Aesthetics Reader*, trans. Galen A. Johnson (Northwestern University Press, 1993), 147.
34. See Edmund Husserl, *Ideas I*, trans. Daniel O. Dahlstrom (Hackett, 2014), section 70.

35. "Firstness is the mode of being of that which is such as it is, positively and without reference to anything else. Secondness is the mode of being of that which is such as it is, with respect to a second but regardless of any third. Thirdness is the mode of being of that which is such as it is, in bringing a second and third into relation to each other." Elsewhere, Peirce connects these with three forms of consciousness: (1) feeling or "Primisense," (2) "Altersense (a sense of otherness), and (3) "Medisense" (a sense of association, abstraction, or suggestion). Of these possibilities, we are describing the painter as encountering the world in its raw Firstness with feeling or "Primisense." Charles Sanders Peirce, *Collected Papers of Charles Sanders Peirce*, ed. Arthur W. Burks (Harvard University Press, 1958), 221, 337.
36. Georg Wilhelm Friedrich Hegel, *Phenomenology of Spirit*, trans. A. V. Miller (Oxford University Press, 1977), 60.
37. Martin Heidegger, "The Origin of the Work of Art," in *Poetry, Language, Thought*, trans. Albert Hofstadter (HarperCollins, 1975), 35.

4. FIRE

1. Gaston Bachelard, *The Psychoanalysis of Fire*, trans. Alan C. M. Ross (Beacon, 1964), 10.
2. James Baldwin, *The Fire Next Time* (Modern Library, 2021), 22, 81, 14, 20.
3. Baldwin, *The Fire Next Time*, 7.
4. Aleksandra Sandstrom, "Half of All Church Fires in Past 20 Years Were Arsons," Pew Research Center, October 26, 2015, https://www.pewresearch.org/short-reads/2015/10/26/half-of-all-church-fires-in-past-20-years-were-arsons/.
5. "Fleeing Into Sea as Deadly Fires Overtake Maui," *New York Times*, August 10, 2023.
6. John Vaillant, *Fire Weather: On the Front Lines of a Burning World* (Vintage, 2024), 59.
7. Cal Fire, "Remembering the Camp Fire," https://www.fire.ca.gov/our-impact/remembering-the-camp-fire.
8. Stephen J. Pyne, "Our Burning Planet: Why We Must Learn to Live with Fire," *Yale Environment 360*, October 8, 2020, https://e360.yale.edu/features/our-burning-planet-why-we-must-learn-to-live-with-fire.
9. "On the circuit, after his return from Congress, Lincoln read widely, carrying books with him, among them Euclid's geometry, the Bible, Shakespeare,

and volumes of poetry by Burns, Poe, and others. After dinner he would often fetch a candle and read well into the night." Robert Burlingame, *Abraham Lincoln: A Life* (Johns Hopkins University Press, 2008), 333–34.

10. Bachelard, *The Psychoanalysis of Fire*, 3.
11. "Cooking increased the value of our food. It changed our bodies, our brains, our use of time, and our social lives. It made us into consumers of external energy and thereby created an organism with a new relationship to nature, dependent on fuel." Richard Wrangham, *Catching Fire: How Cooking Made Us Human* (Profile, 2009), 2.
12. Frank Kanawha Lake, quoted in "Indigenous Fire Practices Shape Our Land," National Park Service, https://www.nps.gov/subjects/fire/indigenous-fire-practices-shape-our-land.htm.
13. "The act of flinging away the object to make it 'gone' may be the gratification of an impulse on the child's part—which in the ordinary way of things remains suppressed—to take revenge on his mother from having gone away from him; and it may thus be a defiant statement meaning 'Alright! Go away! I don't need you. I'm sending you away myself.'" Sigmund Freud, *Beyond the Pleasure Principle* (International Psycho-Analytical Press, 1922), 13.
14. Confederated Salish and Kootenai tribes, *Beaver Steals Fire: A Salish Coyote Story* (Bison Books, 2008).
15. Homer, *The Iliad*, trans. Stephen Mitchell (Free Press, 2011), 345.
16. Michael Marder, *The Phoenix Complex: A Philosophy of Nature* (MIT Press, 2023), vii.
17. Marder, *The Phoenix Complex*, 16.
18. Bachelard, *The Psychoanalysis of Fire*, 2.
19. David Wallace-Wells, *The Uninhabitable Earth: Life After Warming* (Tim Duggan Books, 2020), 44.
20. Vaillant, *Fire Weather*, 32–33.
21. Vaillant, *Fire Weather*, 299, 298.
22. Robert Pinsky, "Shirt," in *The Want Bone* (Ecco, 1990).
23. See "Monument to the Times," *New York Times*, July 27, 2023.
24. "With a chilling clarity Descartes leads us with an apparent and ineluctable necessity to a grand and seductive *Either/Or. Either* there is some support for our being, a fixed foundation for our knowledge, or we cannot escape the forces of darkness that envelop us with madness, with intellectual and moral chaos." Richard J. Bernstein, *Beyond Objectivism and Relativism* (University of Pennsylvania Press, 1983), 18.

25. Megan Craig, "Blue Skies: Memories of a September Morning," *American Scholar*, September 9, 2021, https://theamericanscholar.org/blue-skies/.
26. "Thus in our mind we find a superiority to nature even in its immensity. And so also, the irresistibility of its might, while making us recognize our own [physical] impotence, considered as beings of nature, discloses to us a faculty of judging independently of, and a superiority over, nature; on which is based a kind of self-preservation, entirely different from that which can be attacked and brought into danger by external nature." Immanuel Kant, *The Critique of Judgment*, trans. J. H. Bernard (Dover, 2012), ¶28, 75.
27. "Images and ideas come to us not by set purpose but in flashes, and flashes are intense and illuminating, they set us on fire, only when we are free from special preoccupations." John Dewey, *Art as Experience* (Perigee, 2005), 287.
28. For an account of the rigors of solitary confinement—which includes being alone at night in a locked cell—see Lisa Guenther, *Solitary Confinement: Social Death and Its Afterlives* (University of Minnesota Press, 2013).
29. See Edward S. Casey, *The World on Edge* (Indiana University Press, 2017).
30. For further on this situation, see Elaine Scarry, *Thinking in an Emergency* (Norton, 2011).
31. Audre Lorde wrote about the usefulness of rage, and Myisha Cherry continues the exploration, writing, "Anger of the kind we have been calling 'Lordean rage' can fuel positive action directed toward ending racial injustice and creating an anti-racist world." Myisha Cherry, *The Case for Rage: Why Anger Is Essential to Anti-Racist Struggle* (Oxford University Press, 2021), 62.
32. Flannery O'Connor, *Everything That Rises Must Converge* (Farrar, Straus & Giroux, 1965).

POSTFACE

1. Martin Heidegger, *What Is Called Thinking?*, trans. J. Glenn Gray (Harper, 1956), 3, 5.
2. Edward S. Casey, *Imagining: A Phenomenological Study*, 2nd ed. (Indiana University Press, 2000).
3. Julia Kristeva, *Black Sun: Depression and Melancholia*, trans. Leon S. Roudiez (Columbia University Press, 1989), 65.
4. Erin Manning and Brian Massumi, *Thought in the Act: Passages in the Ecology of Experience* (University of Minnesota Press, 2014), 97–98.

5. Manning and Massumi, *Thought in the Act*, 98.
6. Manning and Massumi, *Thought in the Act*, preface.
7. Donata Schoeller and Vera Saller, eds., *Thinking Thinking: Practicing Radical Reflection* (Karl Alber, 2016), 33.
8. Gilles Deleuze and Félix Guattari, *A Thousand Plateaus*, trans. Brian Massumi (Continuum, 2004), 482.
9. Hans Georg Gadamer, *Truth and Method*, trans. Joel Weinsheimer and Donald G. Marshall (Continuum, 2000), 69.

BIBLIOGRAPHY

Arendt, Hannah. *The Life of the Mind*. Harcourt, 1978.
Bacon, Francis. "The History of Winds." In *The Works of Francis Bacon*, vol. 12, book 2. London: M. Jones Paternoster-Row, 1815.
Bachelard, Gaston. *Air and Dreams: An Essay on the Imagination of Movement*. Trans. Edith Farell and Frederick Farell. Dallas Institute Publications, 1988.
——. *The Poetics of Space*. Trans. Maria Jolas. Beacon, 1969.
——. *The Psychoanalysis of Fire*. Trans. Alan C. M. Ross. Beacon, 1964.
Baldwin, James. *The Fire Next Time*. Modern Library, 2021.
Benedikt, Michael. "Water." *Poetry*, March 1969.
Bergson, Henri. *Creative Evolution*. Trans. Donald Landes. Routledge, 2023.
——. *The Creative Mind: An Introduction to Metaphysics*. Trans. Mabelle L. Andison. Dover, 2007.
Bernstein, Richard J. *Beyond Objectivism and Relativism*. University of Pennsylvania Press, 1983.
Burlingame, Robert. *Abraham Lincoln: A Life*. Johns Hopkins University Press, 2008.
Cahill, Ann. *Rethinking Rape*. Cornell University Press, 2001.
Carel, Havi. *Illness*. Routledge, 2013.
Casey, Edward S. *Imagining: A Phenomenological Study*. 2nd ed. Indiana University Press, 2000.
——. *The World on Edge*. Indiana University Press, 2017.
Casey, Edward S., and Michael Marder. *The Place of Plants: Toward a Phenomenology of the Vegetal*. Columbia University Press, 2024.

Cherry, Myisha. *The Case for Rage: Why Anger Is Essential to Anti-Racist Struggle*. Oxford University Press, 2021.

Clare, Eli. *Brilliant Imperfection: Grappling with Cure*. Duke University Press, 2017.

Coates, Ta-Nehisi. *The Water Dancer*. New York: One World, 2020.

Craig, Megan. "Blue Skies: Memories of a September Morning." *American Scholar*, September 9, 2021.

———. "A Philosopher on Brain Rest." *New York Times*, June 25, 2019.

Craig, Megan, and Edward S. Casey. "Thinking in Transit." In *Philosophy, Travel, and Place: Being in Transit*, ed. Ron Scapp and Brian Seitz. Palgrave Macmillan, 2018.

Deleuze, Gilles, and Félix Guattari. *A Thousand Plateaus*. Trans. Brian Massumi. Continuum, 2004.

Dewey, John. *Art as Experience*. Perigee, 2005.

Dickinson, Emily. "'Hope' is the thing with feathers." In *The Poems of Emily Dickinson Valorium Edition*, ed. R. W. Franklin. Belknap, 1998.

Dillard, Annie. *Pilgrim at Tinker Creek*. Harper Perennial, 2007.

———. *The Writing Life*. Harper Perennial, 2009.

Eliot, T. S. *Four Quartets*. In *The Complete Poems and Plays: 1909–1950*. Harcourt, Brace, 1980.

Emerson, Ralph Waldo. *The Essay on Self-Reliance*. The Roycroft Shop, 1905.

———. *Essays, Lectures, and Orations*. London: William S. Orr & Co., 1851.

Freud, Sigmund. *Beyond the Pleasure Principle*. Trans. James Strachey. International Psycho-Analytical Press, 1922.

Gadamer, Hans Georg. *Truth and Method*. Trans. Joel Weinsheimer and Donald G. Marshall. Continuum, 2000.

Gillispie, Charles Coulston. *The Montgolfier Brothers and the Invention of Aviation, 1783–1784, with a Word on the Importance of Ballooning for the Science of Heat and the Art of Building Railroads*. Princeton University Press, 1983.

Granados, Zaida Verónica Olvera. "A Critical Genealogy of the Concept 'Nature Reserve': Naturalistic Ontology, Landscape, and Space of Exception." In *The Political Dimension of Nature: An Intercultural Critique*, ed. Abbed Kannor and Niels Weidtmann. Metzler Publishing House, forthcoming.

Gros, Frédéric. *A Philosophy of Walking*. Verso, 2003.

Hanh, Thich Nhat. *You Are Here: Discovering the Magic of the Present Moment*. Trans. Sherab Kohn. Shambhala, 2010.

Hegel, Georg Wilhelm Friedrich. *Phenomenology of Spirit*. Trans. A. V. Miller. Oxford University Press, 1977.

Heidegger, Martin. *Poetry, Language, Thought*. Trans. Albert Hofstadter. HarperCollins, 1975.

———. *What Is Called Thinking?* Trans. J. Glenn Gray. Harper, 1956.

Higashida, Naoki. *The Reason I Jump*. Trans. K. A. Yashida and David Mitchell. Random House, 2007.

Homer. *The Iliad*. Trans. Stephen Mitchell. Free Press, 2011.

hooks, bell. *Belonging: A Culture of Place*. Routledge, 2009.

———. *Yearning: Race, Gender, and Cultural Politics*. Routledge, 1990.

Husserl, Edmund. *Ideas I*. Trans. Daniel O. Dahlstrom. Hackett, 2014.

Iyer, Pico. *The Art of Stillness: Adventures in Going Nowhere*. Simon & Schuster, 2014.

Jabr, Ferris. "Why Walking Helps Us Think." *New Yorker*, September 3, 2014.

James, William. *The Principles of Psychology*. Vol. 1. Harvard University Press, 1981.

———. *Talks to Teachers on Psychology and to Students on Some of Life's Ideals*. Harvard University Press, 1983.

Kant, Immanuel. *The Critique of Judgment*. Trans. Werner S. Pluhar. Hackett, 1987.

Kristeva, Julia. *Black Sun: Depression and Melancholia*. Trans. Leon S. Roudiez. Columbia University Press, 1989.

Levi, Primo. *Survival in Auschwitz*. Touchstone, 1996.

Levinas, Emmanuel. "Sincerity of the Saying." In *God, Death, and Time*, trans. Bettina Bergo. Stanford University Press, 2000.

Lorde, Audre. *Sister Outsider*. Penguin, 2019.

———. "A Trip on the Staten Island Ferry." In *The Collected Poems of Audre Lorde*. Norton, 1997.

Lugones, Mariá. "Playfulness, 'World' Travelling and Loving Perception." In *Pilgrimages/Peregrinajes: Theorizing Coalition Against Multiple Oppressions*. Rowman & Littlefield, 2013.

Macauley, David. *Elemental Philosophy: Earth, Air, Fire, and Water as Environmental Ideals*. State University of New York Press, 2010.

Mann, Thomas. *Death in Venice*. Bantam, 1988.

Manning, Erin, and Brian Massumi. *Thought in the Act: Passages in the Ecology of Experience*. University of Minnesota Press, 2014.

Marder, Michael. *Philosophy for Passengers*. MIT Press, 2022.

———. *The Phoenix Complex: A Philosophy of Nature*. MIT Press, 2023.

Meissner, Shelbi Nahwilet. "'World'-Travelling in Tule Canoes: Indigenous Philosophies of Language and an Ethic of Incommensurability." *Hypatia* 38, no. 4, special issue (Fall 2023): 849–70.

Merleau-Ponty, Maurice. *The Merleau-Ponty Aesthetics Reader*. Trans. Galen A. Johnson. Northwestern University Press, 1993.

Miller, John William. *The Midworld of Symbols and Functioning Objects*. Norton, 1982.

Miyazaki, Hayao. *Starting Point 1979–1996*. Trans. Beth Cary and Frederik L. Schodt. Viz Media, 2009.

Morrison, Toni. *Sula*. Vintage, 2004.

Moss, Howard. "Air." In *The Toy Fair: Poems*. University of Michigan Press, 1976.

Murakami, Haruki. *What I Talk About When I Talk About Running*. Vintage Canada, 2009.

O'Connor, Flannery. *Everything That Rises Must Converge*. Farrar, Straus & Giroux, 1965.

Oele, Marjolein. *E-Co-Affectivity: Exploring* Pathos *at Life's Material Interfaces*. SUNY Press, 2020.

Ormiston, Naadi Todd Lee. "Haa Shageingyaa: 'Point Your Canoe Downstream and Keep Your Head Up!'" In *Indigenous and Decolonizing Studies in Education*, ed. Linda Tuhiwai Smith, Eve Tuck, and K. Wayne Yang. Routledge, 2019.

Peirce, Charles Sanders. *Collected Papers of Charles Sanders Peirce*. Ed. Arthur W. Burks. Harvard University Press, 1958.

Pinsky, Robert. "Shirt." In *The Want Bone*. Ecco, 1990.

Puryear, Martin. "Conversation with Hugh M. Davies and Helene Posner (1984)." In *Theories and Documents of Contemporary Art*, ed. Kristine Stiles and Peter Selz. University of California Press, 1996.

Ray, Celeste, ed. *Sacred Waters*. Routledge, 2020.

Rich, Adrienne. "Notes Toward a Politics of Location." In *Blood, Bread, and Poetry: Selected Prose, 1979–1984*. Norton, 1994.

Richardson, Robert D. *William James: In the Maelstrom of American Modernism*. Houghton Mifflin, 2006.

Sacks, Oliver. *On the Move: A Life*. Knopf, 2015.

Scarry, Elaine. *Thinking in an Emergency*. Norton, 2011.

Schoeller, Donata, and Vera Saller, eds. *Thinking Thinking: Practicing Radical Reflection*. Karl Alber, 2016.

Sharpe, Christina. *In the Wake: On Blackness and Being*. Duke University Press, 2016.

Sher, Lynn. *Failure Is Impossible: Susan B. Anthony in Her Own Words*. Random House, 1995.

Silberman, Steve. *Neurotribes: The Legacy of Autism and the Future of Neurodiversity*. Avery, 2015.
Sillitoe, Alan. *The Loneliness of the Long-Distance Runner*. Plume, 1992.
Skrupskelis, Ignas K., and Elizabeth M. Berkeley, eds. *William and Henry James: Selected Letters*. University Press of Virginia, 1997.
Smithson, Robert. *Collected Writings*. Ed. Jack Flam. University of California Press, 1996.
Snyder, Gary. *The Practice of the Wild: Essays*. North Point, 1990.
Solnit, Rebecca. *Wanderlust: A History of Walking*. Penguin, 2000.
Somé, Malidoma Patric. *Of Water and the Spirit*. Penguin, 1995.
Stanislavsky, Constantin. *An Actor Prepares*. Trans. Elizabeth Reynolds Hapgood. Bloomsbury Academic, 2013.
Stevenson, Robert Louis. "The Swing." In *The Poems of Robert Louis Stevenson*. Thomas Y. Crowell & Co., 1900.
Sullivan, Shannon. "Ontological Expansiveness." In *Fifty Concepts for a Critical Phenomenology*, ed. Gail Weiss, Ann V. Murphy, and Gayle Salamon. Northwestern University Press, 2020.
Thoreau, Henry David. *Walking*. Tilbury House, 2017.
Vaillant, John. *Fire Weather: On the Front Lines of a Burning World*. Vintage, 2024.
Wallace-Wells, David. *The Uninhabitable Earth: Life After Warming*. Tim Duggan Books, 2020.
Weil, Simone. *Gravity and Grace*. Trans. Emma Crawford and Mario von der Ruhr. Routledge, 2002.
Winnicott, D. W. *Playing and Reality*. Routledge, 2005.
Wittgenstein, Ludwig. *Philosophical Investigations*. Trans. G. E. M. Anscombe. Macmillan, 1968.
Woolf, Virginia. *On Being Ill*. Paris Press, 2012.
Wrangham, Richard. *Catching Fire: How Cooking Made Us Human*. Profile, 2009.
Young, Iris Marion. *On Female Body Experience: "Throwing Like a Girl" and Other Essays*. Oxford University Press, 2005.

INDEX

academic thinking, 18, 63, 169–70, 192–93n21; in sequestered spaces, 170–72. *See also* philosophy
adolescent thinking, 56–57
adventure, 178–79
aerial gymnastics, 57–58, 191n13
Afghanistan, 62
Agassiz, Louis, 19, 188n17
air: accessories for suspension in, 46; aerial gymnastics/tightrope walking, 57–58, 191n13; "aerial psyche," 44–45; "airhead," 44; balloons, 58–61, 192n18; breathing, 43; breathing of plants, 73; Canadian wildfires, 49–50, 151; circumambience, 45, 77; dangers of travel, 57–59; dust storms, 50–51; earth viewed from, 63–64; and emotion, 46; falling though, 52–54; "head in the clouds," 44; hurricanes, 48, 49; as invisible mixture of gases, 45; mechanical travel through, 51–52; "midworld," 43–44, 190n1; as most cosmopolitan element, 70; as most protean element, 45; and painting, 134; patriarchal imagery tied to, 191n12; planes, 61–65; pollution, 50; pressure, 62; privileged access to, 50; rockets, 67–70; scarcity of leading to panic, 46; as second element experienced by humans, 43; swings, 54–56; tornadoes, 47–49; unpredictability of, 49; vacuous and profound forms of thinking associated with, 44; vision and hearing in, 45; weight of, 46, 47; wings, 56–58. *See also* gardens
Anaximenes, 51
animals: beaver, 22; bird cries, 76; birds' wings, 58, 59; carrying by, 82
Anthony, Susan B., 198n27
aqueous thinking, 15, 19, 25, 77; in infants, 2–4
Arendt, Hannah, 42

Aristotle, 45, 46–47; peripatetic school, 98
autonomy/liberation, 17, 61, 71; and bicycling, 111–14; and cars, 116; and fire, 158–59; and running, 103–4; on uncultivated land, 83–85

Bachelard, Gaston, 6, 14, 44–45, 141, 142, 150, 187n10
Bacon, Francis, 44
Baldwin, James, 143–44, 165
balloons, 58–61, 192n18
Baudelaire, Charles, 28, 187n14
Beaver Steals Fire (Salish creation myth), 149
Beckett, Samuel, 81
Bedknobs and Broomsticks (film), 78
Belonging: A Culture of Place (hooks), 78
Bergson, Henri, 30, 63, 193nn22, 26
Bernstein, Richard J., 153, 200n24
bicycles, 111–15, 198n27
bird cries, 76
birds' wings, 58, 59
Black diaspora, 11
Black Sun (Kristeva), 4, 186n5
Blue Note jazz album, 113
boats: feeling of being carried, 14, 16; ferries, 10–15; minimal separation from water, 11, 17; pregnant quality of, 14; removed from pace of ordinary life, 12; ships, 11, 187nn12, 14; survival thinking, 16. *See also* canoe; kayak
Bodleian Library (Oxford), 170
body: embodiment, 32–33; as extension of tool, 17; heavy, transformed in water, 8, 20; "lived," 35–37; "objective," 35; occupied in background, 18; "ontological expansiveness" of privileged, 30–31, 189n25; and pain, 196n17; as set of possibilities, 196n6; suspended between earth and air, 44; swimming as first movement, 5–6; as terrestrial, 83; transported out of usual form of embodied movement, 25; as vehicle, 75–76, 78–79; weight of, 8, 69–70, 108
Braille, 136
brain rest, 39–40
breath, 29, 43; soul associated with, 43, 51; and vegetation, 71, 73
Breughel, Pieter the Elder, 24
Bridgeport–Port Jefferson Ferry, 12–14
Burnt Cove (Casey), *127*, 127–28, 133, 134

California, 66, 70–71, 88–89; wildfires, 145, 153–54
candlelight, 146–47, 165–66
canes, walkers, and wheelchairs, 99, 196nn10, 13
canoe, 16–19, 189–90n29; agency required for, 16–17; Indigenous languages and worlds, 19–20, 188n16
Carel, Havi, 41
carrying, 14, 16, 33, 82, 96, 98
cars, 115–20; and homelessness, 116–17, 198n29; as private spaces, 119–20; as recording studio, 117–19, 171; "rides," "giving rides," 116

Cartesian thinking, 29
Cash, Johnny, 142
Challenger space shuttle, 67–68
Cherry, Myisha, 201n31
children: bikes and independence, 113–14; daydreaming in childhood home, 6, 187n10; development, 1–6, 160–61; dreams of flight, 61; first steps, 93, 97
civil disobedience, walking as, 100
Clare, Eli, 38, 190n32
claustrophobia, 62
climate change, xv–xvi, 194n1; dangers of heat, 150–51; and earth, 81–82; melting glaciers and ice, 25–26; migration due to, xv, xvi, 51, 82, 194n1; wildfires, 49–50, 144–45, 153–54
colonialist/capitalist expansiveness, 30–31
Coming Through the Fire (Lincoln), 165
com-presence, 126
Connecticut: Goshen, 93–94; tornadoes in, 48–49
consciousness, 9, 41, 45, 188n18; Firstness, Secondness, and Thirdness, 134–35, 199n35
cooking, 147–48, 200n11
COVID, 41, 50, 64–65, 101–2
Crete, 18/119, 191n12
curtailment, 40–41

Dahl, Roald, 34
Daily Café (New Haven), 172–73
daydreaming, 6, 13, 44, 98, 170, 187n10
death: associated with breath, 43; earth as final resting place, 88, 96; fire-related, 157–58; response to prospect of, 41
"Death in Venice" (Mann), 46
deep-sea exploration, 193n25
de Kooning, Willem, 18, 116, 121
Deleuze, Gilles, xiv–xv, 3, 27, 75, 81, 100, 178
depression, 39, 40, 70–71
Derrida, Jacques, 30
Descartes, René, 29, 30, 98, 200n24
desk or table, thinking stunted at, 18
determinate presence, 29–30
Dewey, John, 91, 93, 196n7, 201n27
Dickinson, Emily, 58
digital technologies, 36
Dillard, Annie, 69, 188–89n19
disabilities, 8–9; autism, 36, 186n3, 190n30; canes, walkers, and wheelchairs, use of, 99, 196nn10, 13; chronic illness, 40; "cure" as "imagined time travel," 190n32; mental illness, 39–40, 70–71. *See also* physical illness
disorder, 63, 193n22
Diving Bell and the Butterfly, The (Schnabel), 78–79
doing, thinking as, 29
dualism, 99
Dune Shack (Atlantic Ocean) (Craig), 128–29, *129*, 134

earth: being, 138; bicycles, 111–15, 198n27; cars, 115–20; and climate change, 81–82; diversity of, 71, 86, 95; "earthlings," 83; as final resting place, 88, 96; and grounded forms of thinking, 96; high-rise

earth (*continued*)
    apartments, 88–90; humility as *humus*, ground, 97; inhabitable terrain, 95–96; landlocked areas, 9–10; and linguistic striation, 4; livable land mass, 82; as most vulnerable to change, 82; and painting, 126–28, *127*, 133; perimeter provided by, 133; running, 103–8; in seascapes, 126–28, *127*; as sedentary, 81; skis and sleds, 108–11; as striatable, 81; texture of, 86–87; uncultivated fields, 83–85; walking on, 87, 96, 97–103; writing at level of, 90–91. *See also* gardens
E-Co-Affectivity: Exploring Pathos and Life's Material Interfaces (Oele), 58
ecocommunity, 71
Egyptian *Book of the Dead*, 150
élan vital, 193n26
elemental knowing, 134–35
elements, xv, 81, 125–26, 185n4; at atomic level, 138; culturally and individually specific relation to, 142–43; modalities of thinking keyed to, 77; pondering, 137; trifecta of water, land, and air, 130. *See also* air; earth; fire; water
Eliot, T. S., 35
Emerson, Ralph Waldo, 29, 100, 197n19
Empedocles, 81, 160
engagement, 135
Erdeboden, 63
exception, spaces of, 198n32
exercising, thinking during, 18

falling, 52–54; "free fall," 53
Faraday, Michael, 59
ferry, 10–15, 116; feeling of being carried, 14; grounded aspects of, 13–14; nested aspect of, 14; pitch and heave of stormy weather, 14–15; sounds of, 12–13; time pressure of trip, 12; visual palette of, 13
fire: being chosen by, 142; candlelight, 146–47, 165–66; chemical process of, 144–45, 164–65; church arson, 144; and cooking, 147–48, 200n11; culturally and individually specific relation to, 142–43; death caused by, 157–58; destructive use of, 144; electricity, 147; and exploitation of resources, 151; ferocity of, 151–52; fire exits, 162; flash of images and ideas, 201n27; and hot air balloons, 59; and independence, 158–59; Indigenous controlled fire practices, 146, 148, 152–53; at intersection between control and loss of control, 149, 152–53; and lack of light, 159–60; lambency and transiency of, 145–46; language of, 155–57; mean as crucial to, 158; as metaphor, 143–44, 145, 162–64; as most uninhabitable element, 158; pyrolysis, 145; and rebirth, 150; as social reality, 142; spaceships designed to withstand, 141–42; and speed, 160; and speed of thinking, 147–48; strength associated with, 162; sun, 145, 159, 161; of sun, 134, 141; and survival, 141, 145; thinking in proximity to, 157–62, 164;

unpredictability of, 155–56; and
U.S. civil rights movement,
144; wildfires, 49–50, 144–45,
151, 153–54
Fire Next Time, The (Baldwin),
143–44, 165
firmament, 73
Firstness, Secondness, and Thirdness,
134–35, 199n35
Flint Hills, Kansas, 85–86
floating, 6
flow, 87
Freuchen, Peter, 188–89n19
Freud, Sigmund, 149, 162, 171,
200n13

Gadamer, Hans-Georg, 179
gardens, 70–80, *74*, 92, 193n28, 198n32;
biaxiality of floral spectacle, 73–75;
flora as *fil conducteur*, 73; as
"gratuitous places," 79; upward-
moving scenario, 76–77. *See also*
earth
Godfrey-Smith, Peter, 1
Goethe, Johann Wolfgang von, 27
Goodyear (dirigible), 192n18
Gordon, Dexter, 113
Granados, Zaida Verónica Olvera,
198n32
gravity: and air, 52, 55, 58, 61, 69;
defied by vegetation, 72; and earth,
125; and fire, 164; and illness,
38–39; in water, 8
Gravity and Grace (Weil), 58
Greek mythology: Daedalus, 56–57;
Hephaestus, 149–50; Icarus, 56–57,
58, 59; Odysseus, 32; Penelope, 32

Gros, Frédéric, 99
Guattari, Félix, xiv–xv, 4, 27, 75, 81,
100, 178

Haaland, Deb, 148
hearing, 45
Hegel, G. W. F., 30, 135–36
Heidegger, Martin, 30, 45, 138–39, 167
Higashida, Naoki, 190n30
hillbilly culture, 85, 195n3
Hindenburg (dirigible), 60
Holocaust, 123–24
home, 29; carried with us, 33; hidden
nooks for daydreaming, 6, 187n10;
homeplace, 78, 194n31
homelessness, 116–17, 198n29
hooks, bell, 32–33, 78, 85, 193–94n30,
194nn3, 31, 32, 195n3
hope, 58
hopelessness, 38–39
horizon, 12, 186n4
horse-drawn stagecoach, 115–16
Housatonic River Race, 16
humanization, porch-sitting linked to,
78, 194n31
humility, as *humus*, ground, 97
hurricanes, 48, 49
Husserl, Edmund, 45, 63, 131

ice, 22–26; becoming rare, 25–26; as
brutal, 24; as halfway between
fluid and solid, 22; pejorative sense
of, 26; process of water turning to,
26; and traversability, 24, 27
ice-skating, 22–25, 108; changed
posture, 25; commute by, 24
Iliad, The (Homer), 149–50

imagery, 131–32
imagination, 36; imaginifying, 135; "open," 44–45; and swinging, 55–56
immigrant laborers, 120. *See also* migration, forced
incomprehensibility, 40
Indigenous peoples, 19–20, 188n16; controlled fire practices, 146, 148, 152–53; and early American pioneers, 83; Inuit and Aleut, 20; Kaw people, 84; land extracted from, 194–95n2; Shawnee tornado wisdom, 47–48
infancy: aqueous thinking in, 2–4, 25; assumptions about pain in, 2, 186n1; origin in water, 1–2; smooth thought, 3–4; swimming as first movement of fetus, 5–6; thinking as "bloom of confusion," 2, 3
interplaciality and intraplaciality, 33

Jabr, Ferris, 99
James, William, 2, 3, 19, 91, 102, 179, 188nn17, 18; train travel, 120–21
journeys to nowhere (traveling in place), 27–38, 93, 100; "inner journey" versus "outer journey," 30–31; just here as place of, 27, 28, 31; linguistic voyage, 75–76; meditation and mindfulness, 29, 31–32; and painting, 138–39; paradox of im-motion, 34; during physical illness, 36–38; and prospect of death, 41; psychedelic drugs, 29; psychical and physical at same time, 33–35; psychic travel, 29, 32; staying in place, model of, 27–29; and witnessing, 28, 35; "'world'-traveling," 32. *See also* water

"just getting around," 113, 197n24

Kansas: Flint Hills, 85–86; Topeka, 47–48, 83–85
Kant, Immanuel, 30, 156, 166, 201n26
kayak, 19–21, 188–89n19
Keats, Ezra Jack, 26
Kentucky, 32–33
Kierkegaard, Søren, 39
Kiki's Delivery Service (Miyazaki), 60–61
King Lear (Shakespeare), 43
Kleist, Heinrich von, 27
knowledge: elemental knowing, 134–35; immersive knowing, 51, 136; knowledge-in rather than knowledge-about, 135–36
Kristeva, Julia, 4, 175–76, 186n5

Lake, Frank Kanawha, 148
language, 168; of fire, 155–57; Indigenous languages and worlds, 19–20, 188n16; linguistic striation, 4
Lavoisier, Antoine-Laurent, 164
"*le dire*" (saying), 4, 186–87n5
Le petit prince (de Saint-Exupéry), 69
Levi, Primo, 124
Levinas, Emmanuel, 4, 186–87n5
levitation, 68
Life of the Mind, The (Arendt), 42
Lincoln, Abraham, 146, 199–200n9

Lincoln, C. Eric, 165
linguistic voyage, 75–76
Little House on the Prairie (TV show), 93–94
"lived body," 35–37
London, Jack, 146
"Loneliness of the Long-Distance Runner, The" (Sillitoe), 105
Lorde, Audre, 195n4, 201n31
Lugones, María, 28, 32, 33, 192n21

Macauley, David, 185n4
Manifest Destiny, 101, 197n21, 198n32
Mann, Thomas, 46
Manning, Erin, 176–77
Marder, Michael, 65, 150
Mary Poppins (film), 47
Massumi, Brian, 176–77
material contributions to thinking, 19, 93
Matilda (Dahl), 34
McAuliffe, Christa, 67–68
mean, ethical, 46–47
mechanical travel, 30, 51–52, 111, 115
meditation, 29, 31–32; walking, 99
Meissner, Shelbi Nahwilet, 21, 188n16
memory, 27, 33; and brain injury, 39–41; of health, 38, 39
mental illness, 39–40, 70–71
Merleau-Ponty, Maurice, 34–35, 129
method acting, 17, 187–88n15
middle-class values, 83–86, 92
middle plane between earth and sky, 72–73
"midworld," 43–44, 190n1

migration, forced: due to climate change, xv, xvi, 51, 82, 194n1; walking, 102–3; by water, 11
Miller, John William, 43–44, 190n1
mindfulness, 29, 31–32
Minoans, 191n12
Miyazaki, Hayao, 60, 192n19
Mohawk Mountain (Cornwall, Connecticut), 48–49, 191n7
moment, differentiated from minute, 34
momentum, 174–75; back-and-forth movement required for thinking, 63–64; created by sounds of ferry engines, 12–13; immobility, 65–66, 72; and journey to nowhere, 35–36; paradox of im-motion, 34, 65–66; required for thinking, 18, 185n2; TPM (thoughts per moment), 34; and walking, 98–99
Morrison, Toni, 55
Moss, Adam, 185n2
Moss, Howard, 45
motorcycles, 113, 198n25
Murakami, Haruki, 104

New School for Social Research, 173
New York City: high-rise apartments, 88–90; September 11, 2001, 155
Nhat Hanh, Thich, 29, 31–32
Nietzsche, Friedrich, 45, 101
nomad, 27, 196n6

"objective body," 35
O'Connor, Flannery, 166
Odyssey (Homer), 33

Oele, Marjolein, 58
On the Move (Sacks), 8
ontological expansiveness, 30–31, 189n25
On Walking (Thoreau), 29
opaqueness, 40
"open mind," 106
Ormiston, Naadi Todd Lee, 189–90n29

painting, 84, 123, 198n32; and air, 134; cityscapes, 173–74; and earth, 126–28, *127*, 133; freeform, 172; "free variations," 131; imagery in, 131–32; interplay of elements in, 131; land and water as co-requisite factors in, 127, 128, 138; sense of being-there, 132; swimming compared with, 129; thinking in, 125–39; as thinking in transit, 138–39; as transit, 132–33; transit of artist to site, 132; viewer, transit of, 133, 138–39; and water, 126–29, *127*, 133–34; writing about, 135–37
passengers: of balloon, 59–60; on ferry, 16–17; on plane, 65–66
Peirce, Charles Sanders, 134–35, 199n35
Petit, Philippe, 57, 191n13
Phaedrus (Plato), 61
Phenomenology of Spirit (Hegel), 135–36
philosophy, 44, 167–68, 171. *See also* academic thinking
Phoenix complex, 150, 163
Phoenix Complex, The (Marder), 150

physical illness, 36–3; cancer, 37; curtailment, sense of, 40–41; and heat, 158; "locked-in syndrome," 78–79; pneumonia, 38–39. *See also* disabilities
Pinsky, Robert, 152
place, 95; in painting, 132; place-proclivity, 93; transitional, 91–92. *See also* space
planes, 61–67; being bound in place on, 62, 65–67; creative thinking on, 62; as submarines of the sky, 62
Plato, 30, 61, 87
"Playfulness, 'World'-Traveling, and Loving Perception" (Lugones), 28
poetic thinking, 18, 116
poetry, 195n4
pondering, 137
porch, 78, 193–94n30, 194n31
position, 91
Potato Eaters, The (van Gogh), 147
prelinguistic self, 2–4
pre-presence, 134
presence, 36
Presocratic thought, 125
Principles of Psychology (James), 121
privacy, 119–20
progress, sense of, 21
"Prometheus complex," 142
psychedelic drugs, 29
psychic traveling, 29, 32
Psychoanalysis of Fire, The (Bachelard), 146
pure mind (*res cogitans*), 29
Puryear, Martin, 79, 194n33
Pyne, Stephen J., 146

Rahm, Dave, 69
Ralston, Daniel, 153
rationality, 163–64
Red Balloon, The (Le ballon rouge) (film), 58–59
retreat, 157
Reveries of the Solitary Walker (Rousseau), 102
Rice, Dan, 172
Rich, Adrienne, 192–93n21
river, thought as, 19, 179, 188n18
rockets, 67–70
Rodin, Auguste, 156
Rousseau, Jean-Jacques, 101
running, 103–8; for commute, 104; long-distance, 105; transubstantiation of into flight, 108

Sacks, Oliver, 8–9, 20, 113, 198n25
Saharan dust, 50
Saji, Alia Al-, 8
Schelling, Friedrich Wilhelm Joseph, 150
Schnabel, Julian, 78
seascapes, 126–28, *127*
seasons, 22, 47, 80, 148, 160
sedentary posture, 98–100, 156
self, 36; and global changes of illness, 41
semiotic, the, 4, 175–76, 186n5
"sense-certainty," 135–36
September 11, 2001, 155
sequestered spaces, 170–72
settler colonialism, 30, 70, 194–95n2, 198n32; early American pioneers, 83; Manifest Destiny, 101, 197n21, 198n32
Sharpe, Christina, 11, 187n12
"Shawnee Mound," 47–48
"Shirt" (Pinsky), 152
Silberman, Steve, 186n3
silence, 60, 64, 76, 170, 189–90n29
Sillitoe, Alan, 105
Silouan the Athonite, Saint, 157
skis and sleds, 108–11
sky, 70–73
slave trade, 11, 187n12
sledding, 109–11
Smithson, Robert, 196n8
smoothness, 3, 15, 81, 86, 172
Snowy Day, The (Keats), 26
Snyder, Gary, 97
solitary confinement, 42, 159–60
Solnit, Rebecca, 99
soul, 43, 51, 61
sound, 45
space: of exception, 198n32; interplaciality and intraplaciality, 33; for new ideas, 177–78; place, 91; "smooth" vs. "striated," 3, 15, 81, 86, 172. *See also* place; smoothness; striation
space, outer, 51, 70, 165
speech, 2–3, 187n6
speed and acceleration, 31; fire associated with, 160; immobility during, 65–66; and planes, 64
spoken recording, 117–19, 171
Stanislavsky, Konstantin, 17, 187–88n15
staying in place, model of, 27–29

Sterling Library (Yale University), 170, 172
Stevenson, Robert Louis, 55
"stream of thought," 121
"streetwalker" or "pedestrian" theorists, 192n21
striation, 3–4, 15, 81, 86, 172
sublime, 156, 159
Sula (Morrison), 55
Sullivan, Shannon, 30–31, 189n25
Sunset at Barbados (Casey), *130*, 134, 137–38
survival, 7; in boats, 16; of brain injury, 40; and fire, 141, 145; and forced walking, 103; and heat dangers, 150–51; ice-skating, 23–24; kayak, 19–20; and tornadoes, 49
swimming, 5–9; as form of thinking, 8; in open water, 8; painting compared with, 129; training for competition, 7–8
swings, 54–56, 114
sympathy, immersive, 9

Tenth Mountain Division Ski Troops, 108–9
Tereshkova, Valentina, 67–68
Thales of Miletus, 44
Thinker (Rodin), 156
thinking: as active doing, 29; adolescent, 56–57; as adventure, 178–79; aqueous, 2–4, 15, 19, 25, 77; back-and-forth movement required for, 63–64; breathless, 111; in canoe, 17–18; contribution of vehicles and tools to, 5; in crowded places, 172–74; crystallization of thought, 26–27; discovery, sense of, 85, 87; while driving, 117–20; under duress, 161–62; elemental, 18; and exercise, 18; fire metaphors for, 162–64; forms of, 29–30; as gift, 107; grounded forms of, 96; icy, 26–27; location of, 168–69; material contributions to, 19, 93; meandering, in canoe, 18; meditative, meandering, and open, 18; mimetic with landscape, 87; modalities keyed to environmental givens, 77; momentum required for, 18, 185n2; optimal pace for, 106; in painting, 125–39; in place, 27–38; poetic, 18, 116; prelinguistic, 18; as reflective undertaking, 156–57, 160; and repetition, 17; while running, 105–8; in sequestered spaces, 170–72; while skiing, 109; spoken recording, 117–19, 171; swimming as form of, 8; syncopation inherent in, 26; "thinking-in-the-act" and "thinking in action," 176–77; thought versus, 179–80; top-down, 63–64; on trains, 120–25; as voyage, 75–76, 178; while walking, 97–98; Western academic mode, 18, 63; work of, 14
thinking-feeling-sensing-breathing, 29
thinking in transit, 169; in cars, 117–19, 171; on ferries, 12–14; fire as limit on, 152, 156; painting as, 138–39; swimming as early form of, 8
thinking in writing, 175

thinking otherwise, 92, 126, 169
third things, 111
Thoreau, Henry David, 29, 100–101, 197n21
Thousand Plateaus, A (Deleuze and Guattari), xiv–xv, 3, 27, 178
"Throwing Like a Girl" (Young), 22, 189n21
tightrope walking, 57–58, 191n13
time: bending of in air, 64; on ferry, experience of, 12, 15; "railroad time," 121; "smooth" and "striated," 3, 15; synchronic, 34–35
"To Build a Fire" (London), 146
tools, 5, 17, 187n9
top-down thinking, 63–64
Topeka, Kansas, 47–48, 83–85
tornadoes, 47–49
TPM (thoughts per moment), 34
trains, 120–25; and Holocaust, 123–24; MetroNorth train line, 121–23; visual images, 122–23
Transcontinental Railroad, 120
transience, 23, 145–46, 166
transit, as term, 180–81. *See also* thinking in transit
transition, 61, 86, 91–92
transitional objects, 91
traversability, 24, 27, 194n1
Triangle Shirtwaist Factory Fire (1911), 152
"trip," 29
True Travelers, The (Baudelaire), 28

The Uninhabitable Earth (Wallace-Wells), 150–51
Up (film), 69

Vaillant, John, 145, 151
van Gogh, Vincent, 147
verbalizing, 135
vessels, 4–5; bodies dependent on, 193n25; expedited vehicles, 31. *See also specific vessels*
Viet Nam, 48
virtue, pursuit of, 46–47
vision, 45, 133

walking, 87, 97–103, 197n21; and forced migration, 102–3; precariousness of, 97; psychophysical benefits of, 99; sauntering, 100–101; striding, 101; using canes, crutches, or wheelchairs, 96, 99, 196nn10, 13; wheeling, 98–99
"Walking" (Thoreau), 100–101, 197n21
WalkingStick, Kay, 1
Wallace-Wells, David, 150–51
Was Heisst Denken? (What Is Called Thinking?) (Heidegger), 167
water: accessories for suspension in, 46; aversion to, 9–10; canoeing, 16–19; deep-sea exploration, 193n25; as first environment for humans, 1–2; floating in, 6; hardened form, 25; ice-skating, 22–26; international classification for canoes and kayaks, 20–21; kayaking, 19–21; mechanical travel through, 51–52; as outward-going and downward-coming, 129, 133–34; and painting, 126–29, *127*, 133–34; as protean, 5; sea, materiality of, 15; in seascapes, 126–28, *127*; smell of, 17;

water (*continued*)
  smoothness and striation in, 3;
  solubility of painting media, 127;
  swimming, 5–9; thinking while
  being in or near, 4–5. *See also*
  journeys to nowhere; vessels
weather: and canoeing, 17; and ferry,
  14; storms during plane flight, 66;
  tornadoes, 47–49
Weil, Simone, 58
Whitman, Walt, 115–16
Wilder, Laura Ingalls, 93–94
Willet, Cynthia, 191n12
wind, 44
wings, 56–58
Winnicott, D. W., 91
witnessing, and journey to nowhere,
  28, 35

Wittgenstein, Ludwig, 45, 96, 171
Wizard of Oz, The (film), 47
Woodland Coffee and Tea (New
  Haven), 174
Woolf, Virginia, 37, 40–41
World Trade Center (New York City),
  57, 155, 191n13
"'world'-traveling," 32
Wrangham, Richard, 147
writing, 180; about fire, 162; about
  painting, 135–37; at earth level,
  90–91; on ferry, 12, 90; in planes,
  62; public and private places, 91;
  supportive surfaces for, 93; thinking
  in, 175; on trains, 121–23; twenty
  stories above ground, 89–90

Young, Iris Marion, 22, 189n21

GPSR Authorized Representative: Easy Access System Europe, Mustamäe tee 50, 10621 Tallinn, Estonia, gpsr.requests@easproject.com

www.ingramcontent.com/pod-product-compliance
Lightning Source LLC
Jackson TN
JSHW020424140825
89344JS00008B/271

"*Thinking in Transit* speaks to the heart of our transitory existence. The authors bring us on a wondrous journey, showing that some of our best thoughts are mobile, itinerant, searching—odysseys of both mind and body. This is a brilliant and timely book."
—RICHARD KEARNEY,
CHARLES SEELIG PROFESSOR IN PHILOSOPHY, BOSTON COLLEGE

"Craig and Casey share a singularly original project, interweaving personal recollections with insightful philosophical ruminations. They challenge the assumption that thinking must be solitary and sedentary, bringing thought back into the motion and emotion of everyday life."
—DAVID MICHAEL KLEINBERG-LEVIN, PROFESSOR EMERITUS,
DEPARTMENT OF PHILOSOPHY, NORTHWESTERN UNIVERSITY

"From their form to their moving details, these essays slide between authors, across elemental fields, and in and out of vessels, from boats to swings to sleds. And along the way, we find ourselves invigorated by a transformed feel for where we've always been: on the move."
—JOHN LYSAKER, WILLIAM R. KENAN UNIVERSITY PROFESSOR AND
DIRECTOR OF THE CENTER FOR ETHICS, EMORY UNIVERSITY

"A deeply meditative book. Craig's and Casey's voices—sometimes blended, sometimes separate—eloquently evoke the wonder and significance of everyday movements: swimming, falling, skating, and flying, just to name a few. I'll never think of taking the ferry the same way again!"
—SHANNON SULLIVAN, PROFESSOR OF PHILOSOPHY AND HEALTH
PSYCHOLOGY, UNIVERSITY OF NORTH CAROLINA AT CHARLOTTE

"Captivating reflections from two thinkers and visual artists on the nature of water, air, earth, fire—the elements of existence. As the authors travel via trains, planes, and cars or even just inhabit gardens beyond the cloistered walls of academia, they develop a singular style of painterly thinking."
—CYNTHIA WILLETT, SAMUEL CANDLER DOBBS PROFESSOR
OF PHILOSOPHY, EMORY UNIVERSITY

MEGAN CRAIG is associate professor of philosophy at the State University of New York at Stony Brook as well as an artist and essayist.

EDWARD S. CASEY is distinguished professor emeritus of philosophy at the State University of New York at Stony Brook and past president of the American Philosophical Association.

Cover design: Milenda Nan Ok Lee   Cover photo: Megan Craig

Columbia University Press | New York
CUP.COLUMBIA.EDU